SOCIAL EFFECTS
OF
MASS MEDIA IN INDIA

Sarbajana

SOCIAL EFFECTS OF MASS MEDIA IN INDIA

N. Bhaskara Rao
G.N.S. Raghavan

GYAN PUBLISHING HOUSE
New Delhi-110002

Social Effects of Mass Media in India
(Mass Communication, Information and Broadcasting, Journalism, Advertising, Culture)

ISBN: 978-81-212-0521-4

Price: ₹ 780

Reprinted 2014 in India by
Gyan Publishing House
23, Main Ansari Road, Daryaganj,
New Delhi - 110002
Phones : 23282060, 23261060
Fax : (011) 23285914
E-mail : books@gyanbooks.com
website: gyanbooks.com

Printed at: G. Print Process, Delhi

PREFACE

India has entered the space age in communication technology. This has increased manifold the social impact, for good or ill, of the media of mass communication. It is the need, as seen by us, to promote critical awareness among policy makers and managers as well as the audience of the media that has impelled us to undertake this work.

Both of us have known, from inside, the working of the Press and of the official agencies of communication. We have also been analysing their performance, one as a researcher of media reach and content, and the other as a practitioner and teacher of development communication. We have a shared anxiety about the trend in the media in recent years towards profit maximisation regardless of the social consequences, immediate and long-term, of the means employed.

In the first part of the book we survey the origin and the initial role, as well as the post-independence growth, of each of the mass media as part of the country's developing political economy. Our discussion of negative features in the functioning of the media is unsparing. However, it is not in a spirit of captious criticism but in the hope of stirring the social conscience of communicators, as well as citizens, at a time when it is in danger of getting benumbed by a deluge of hedonism through consumerist advertising and mindless or meretricious entertainment.

In the second part of the book we present the findings of the first-ever countrywide study, in depth, of the social effects of the mass media. The exercise was conducted by the Centre for Media Studies, employing a pioneering combination of methods. One was a multi-State, questionnaire-based sample survey, which remains the primary tool for quantitative research, with its reliability depending on the rigour of sample selection rather than size of sample. The second method was a series of focus group discussions, conducted in various parts of the country, with students, parents, teachers and housewives. Then, four colloquial at national level, in Delhi, with participation by persons prominent in public life, legal luminaries, social scientists, media practitioners and social activists including those engaged in work among women and children. And, finally, round-table discussions at regional level in six centres across the country in the north, east, south and west. These encounters yielded diagnoses from different perspectives and backgrounds of experience, of the maladies of the media as well as a range of suggested remedies.

An action plan for reform is outlined by us in the third part of the book. It covers not only the mass media but formal education, which continues to be the largest stream of organised communication. While our schools and colleges stuff more and more information into the young, they impart no values to live by and to strive for. This is largely because of certain provisions in the Constitution which prohibit religious instruction in State-run educational institutions—attended by the great majority of Indian students—while permitting it in schools and colleges run by religious minorities even if they receive State aid.

With the driving out of the ethical values associated with religion from most centres of learning, the vacuum is being filled by the Mammon of consumerism and the Satyr of eroticism—the new deities propagated by the mass media of non-formal education or miseducation. The prime culprit is television—Doordarshan, with its wide reach, no less than foreign satellite channels available through cable. These are seducing the young, degrading public taste, and deadening the social conscience through alluring advertisements and lewd or vacuous entertainment. Commercial films and market-driven television have dragged sexual intimacy out of the private domain—including fantasy—where it properly belongs, into public view for titillation. Viewers, young and old, are thus turned into voyeurs, and every TV-endowed drawing room into a cabaret hall, by Doordarshan and cable TV.

However, it would be wrong to regard cable TV as inherently bad. There have been instances of cable operators functioning as socially conscious managers of local television. A cable operator at Vijayawada got blood donors to line up within a matter of an hour to help victims of a major road accident in town. In Ahmedabad, cable TV helped to prevent the spread of wild rumours at a time of communal conflict. At another place, cable TV assisted school students in preparing for their final examination. Thus, cable can be utilised—like television in the broadcast mode—either for good or for aggrandisement at the cost of social health. The tragedy is that television in both the modes has been employed, mainly, to maximise profit rather than public good.

But we see hope. It is provided by such reactions to media vulgarity as the decision by a sizeable section of the nursing sisterhood to substitute the skirt uniform—introduced during British rule and now besmirched by indecent depiction in a televised film—by sari or by salwar-kameez, which are at once both more dignified and Indian; the strong condemnation of the depiction of sex and crime in the media by at least three Supreme Court judges in recent months; and the protest demonstrations led by teachers and social activists in a groundswell of public revulsion against the peddling of sexism and sadism for profit.

The present work, we hope, will help policy makers, media managers and media practitioners to resist the lure of audience rating—an amoral criterion which is no yardstick of either quality or social relevance but is useful only to the advertiser and the advertising agency seeking maximisation of sale and profit. In order to drive home this central point of the need for the mass media to be relevant and morally responsible to society, we have included in some chapters, articles by competent analysts; they supplement and underscore our own presentation with additional information and insights.

We trust that managers and practitioners in the arena of the Press, which is the prime non-official medium, do not take amiss our criticism of recent trends towards sensationalism in pursuit of circulation—and eventually profit maximisation—to the neglect of the primary problems of mass poverty and mass illiteracy in our society. As the freest of the mass media, the Press has a special responsibility. If the salt should lose its savour, wherewith shall it be salted ?

At the other—receiving—end of the spectrum of the mass media, we trust that the book will help to promote among consumers of the media, specially TV viewers, a realisation that responsible parenthood today calls not only for limiting the number of children. Responsible parenthood requires also that the quality of life of the children be paid attention. A large number of those who spoke in the colloquia in Delhi and in regional centres, and who participated in the focus group discussions, were at one in pointing out that parents who lack self-control in their own TV viewing cannot obviously regulate the exposure of their children to TV.

New Delhi

N. BHASKARA RAO
G.N.S. RAGHAVAN

CONTENTS

Part—I
Growth and Changing Role

Part—2

Social Audit of the Media

Part—3
Agenda for renewal

Part-I

Growth and Changing Role

1 AS DEVELOPMENT, SO COMMUNICATION

In a modern democracy the personality and values of the head of the government have a significant influence on, though they do not wholly determine, public policies including those related to economic development and mass communication. Attempted here is a rapid survey of the course of free India'a development, and the fortunes of the media, during the tenures of successive Prime Ministers.

From idealism to consumerism

During the first seventeen years, free India was led by one who had already, during the struggle for independence, acquired a charisma to which the office of Prime Minister did not add much; he therefore stood in little need of image building. What was Nehru's attitude to development and to mass communication ?

Taking first the earliest of the modern mass media, freedom of the Press was an article of faith for leaders of the independence movement. They needed to disseminate their messages through the Press to a larger audience than could be addressed in person at any single public meeting. Many national leaders, Nehru included, doubled as journalists.

Nehru was a democratic socialist, both the adjective and noun being vital. He believed in extensive state ownership of industries and regulation of what remained in the private sector. He was distrustful of the ownership of newspapers by industrialists and business men, but not to the point of wanting to nationalise or regulate the Press. A journalist protege of Nehru's, M. Chalapathi Rau, was a member of the First Press Commission (1952-54) and wielded an influence quite out of proportion to the small circulation of the National Herald of which Rau was editor. The Commission, though it included many moderates and liberals, recommended government intervention in newspaper economics to the extent of determining the number of pages which could be offered at a given price, and the proportion of newspaper space that could be applied to advertisements. This recommendation was sought to be enforced through the Newspaper (Price and Page) Act of 1956. When an Order issued in 1960 in terms of that Act was struck down by the Supreme Court in the Sakal Newspapers case, in 1962, as being violative of the Fundamental Right to freedom of expression guaranteed in Article 19 of the Constitution, Jawaharlal Nehru with his liberal instincts left the matter at that.

In contrast, his daughter Indira Gandhi (Prime Minister for a total of nearly 16 years in two terms from 1966 to 1976 and from 1980 to 1984) adopted a confrontationist attitude when verdicts of the higher judiciary did not suit her purpose, as in the case of bank nationalisation and abolition of the privy purses of princes. This was in 1969 when, following a split in the party, she emerged as leader of the majority faction of the Congress but lost her majority in the Lok Sabha. Since many influential newspapers were critical of Indira Gandhi's populist plank, she was allergic to the Press too. Continuing in office with the support of the Communists, who were no great friends either of Press freedom or of independence of the judiciary, the Congress (Indira) won a two-thirds majority in the 1971 elections though with only 43.5 per cent of the popular vote, thanks to the electoral system of first-past-the-post. During the internal emergency which Indira Gandhi got President Fakhrudin Ali Ahmed to proclaim in mid-1975, and which lasted a year and a half, the Fundamental Rights stood suspended, Press freedom was abrogated through rigorous censorship, and the Constitution was stood on its head through a series of sweeping amendments which were annulled after the Congress lost power in the 1977 elections.

Indira Gandhi returned to power early in 1980, and there was a revival of various proposals mooted during her first term for laws to regulate the ownership of newspapers and the economics of newspaper publishing. Following her assassination in October 1984, her son Rajiv Gandhi, an airlines pilot with no experience of public life, was pitchforked into prime ministership by sycophants of the Nehru family. After making what seemed a promising start, the youthful Prime Minister ran into heavy weather following disclosures and allegations in the Press about kick-backs received by or on behalf of Rajiv Gandhi and/or the Congress (I) from Nobel Industries of Sweden in a contract for the purchase of the Bofors gun for the Indian Army. A defamation Bill was introduced by the government in August 1988. It placed the onus on the person accused of having made a defamatory statement to prove the truth of the statement, and to establish also that the statement was made for the public good. Section 13 created a new class of offence called criminal imputation, which the Minister piloting the Bill described as "an aggravated form of defamation calling for aggravated punishment". In a remarkable display of unity, newspaper employees as well as employers demonstrated all over the country against the Bill as an attack on Press freedom. It was dropped.

Following Rajiv Gandhi's assassination in June 1991, P. V. Narasimha Rao became Prime Minister. He himself as well as members of his Cabinet and of his family have been targets of allegations, widely reported in the Press, of bribe taking and financial irregularities. But newspapers have not been penalised for carrying such reports. The decades since the coming into force of India's republican Constitution have thus witnessed a swing of the pendulum between the spirit and the letter of Article 19 which guarantees freedom of expression subject to certain limitations.

While the best service that Jawaharlal Nehru did to the Indian Press was to leave it alone—as governments in mature democracies do—he did not do equally well in leaving All India Radio untouched.

The broadcasting system was owned and run by the government prior to India's independence. It provided entertainment to the middle and upper classes who could afford to buy a radio receiver in the pre-transistor age, and purveyed such information as was not adverse to the interests of the British authorities. Soon after the transfer of power, Jawaharlal Nehru said on 15th March 1948, while replying to a debate on external publicity in the Constituent Assembly which functioned as the provisional parliament of India : "My own view of the set-up for broadcasting is that we should approximate, as far as possible , to the British model, the British Broadcasting Corporation : that is to say, it would be better if we had a semi-autonomous corporation under the government, of course, with the policy controlled by the government, otherwise being not conducted as a government department but as a semi-autonomous corporation". Nehru's impulses were liberal but he did not always act on them. The continuance of A. I. R. as a government department during all the 17 years of Nehru's prime ministership was one of many instances in which a shadow fell between his perceptior and his practice.

A great difference would have been made to radio's role in free India had he remembered and acted on the recommendations of a sub-committee on communication of the National Planning Committee formed by the Congress in 1937 with Nehru as chairman. The sub-committee's report laid great emphasis on the potentiality of radio as the only literacy-free medium of mass communication then available. Sharing the socialist inclination of Nehru, and convinced that development had to be powered and guided by the state, the sub-committee used the expression 'State propaganda' for what is now connoted by the term 'development communication'. "The principal functions of broadcasting," the report said, "are : (a) dissemination of news and useful information; (b) adult education and fighting rural ignorance; (c) propaganda by the State; (d) entertainment."

The sub-committee's report called for an innovative approach to broadcasting hardware, stating that "many problems of communication engineering are peculiar to the country and their solution can only be obtained by carrying out investigations in the country itself." Broadcasting was envisaged as the most effective link between "the vast majority of the population who are still illiterate and a large section of the women who do not go out into the public, on the one hand, and the progressive part of India on the other." Radio, the report said, should provide "an easy channel for bringing to the masses useful information on agriculture, animal husbandry, current political thought, etc." The planning for broadcasting had to serve the objective of "providing populous regions of the country with first-grade service, and installing community receivers on a wide scale in the rural areas."

The approach was thus oriented to rural development, and there was lively awareness of the need not only to put out broadcasts of relevance to the village population but to provide access to radio to the rural poor through the facility of community listening.

The role of communication in development as envisaged in the document on the First Five Year Plan was in line with the approach of the National Planning Committee's sub-committee. The Plan document, published in December 1952, had in Chapter VIII a section on 'Reaching the people' which said : "A widespread understanding of the Plan is an essential stage in its fulfilment. An understanding of the priorities which govern the Plan will enable each person to relate his or her role to the larger purposes of the nation as a whole. The Plan has, therefore, to be carried into every home in the language and symbols of the people, and expressed in terms of their common needs and problems...with the assistance of creative writers and artists, which has to be specially enlisted. All available methods of communication have to be developed and the people approached through the written and the spoken word no less than through radio, film, song and drama. Above all, steps have to be taken to provide literature and information for the people in simple language on a scale equal to the needs of the country."

This early document is remarkable also for its recognition of the need for candid feedback and for decentralisation of development planning : "It is only in terms of local programmes that local leadership and enthusiasm can play their part...If obstacles are encountered and things go wrong anywhere, it would be helpful in every sense if information is imparted candidly and the people are acquainted with the steps being taken to set things right. It is an error to belittle the capacity of the common man to find out and accept what is good for him."

Post-independence reality turned out to be very different from this vision of decentralised communication which would be bottom-upward as well as top-down, and supportive of progress towards an egalitarian social and economic order. Radio continued to serve with entertainment and information the middle and upper classes. The transistor revolution did not alter the role of radio. Instead of serving the new mass audience with information relevant to improvement of their living conditions, A. I. R. regaled them with tinsel film music and brought them commercial messages such as this one from Modern Bread, a unit of the Central public sector which was meant to control the 'commanding heights' of the economy : 'Mummy, mummy, Modern Bread'. Children in the majority of Indian families neither eat packaged and branded bread, nor do they mummy their mothers. The failure to utilise the advent of the transistor to turn radio into an instrument for democratising communication and conveying to the rural and urban poor locally relevant and useful information reflected the elitist orientation of free India's economic growth.

The course of planned development began to take an elitist turn even in Jawaharlal Nehru's days. This was perhaps because of the time and energy that, as Prime Minister, he devoted to international affairs as his own Foreign Minister (and it is tragic that he failed in this field of his own choosing in the handling of Kashmir and of India's relations with China). He tried to replicate in India both the Soviet model of heavy industrial development and the Chinese Communist model of cooperative joint farming, without the instrumentality of a totalitarian system in which a single party stifles the expression of dissent and liquidates dissenters. The regime of government controls, permits and licences introduced by the bureaucracy in the name of socialism was taken advantage of by unscrupulous politicians, businessmen and civil servants for self-aggrandisement.

Nehru's own vision, even if dimmed over the years, remained basically egalitarian. In the course of a letter to Chief Ministers on 7th June 1961, Nehru said : "We should think in terms of concentrating on production of goods that a person or family with an income of Rs. 500 per month or so might require. From this point of view, a bicycle is far more important in India today than a motor car, even if a small one." Considering the then value of the rupee, Nehru obviously had in mind the middle class rather than the poor. Subsequently, towards the close of his life, he noted with anguish that the Five Year Plans had made little difference to the living conditions of the masses. While replying to a debate on planning in the Lok Sabha in December 1963, Nehru said : "One thing that distresses me very greatly is that there are a good number of people in India who have not profited by planning, and whose poverty is abysmal and most painful...I begin to think more and more of Mahatma Gandhi's approach."

It took that long for Nehru, though he had been a close lieutenant of the Mahatma, to realise that only the Gandhian approach of decentralised, labour-intensive production, and of compassion and sharing, would enable India with her vast under-employed manpower to achieve self-reliant economic growth. Not surprisingly, Nehru's successors were unable to act in accordance with Gandhi's talisman : "Recall the face of the poorest and the weakest man whom you may have seen, and ask yourself if the step you contemplate is going to be of any use to him."

In contrast to Gandhi's distrust of big government and of economic controls, Indira Gandhi retained and tightened Central regulation of the economy. She was not unaware that controls bred corruption. Abdul Rehman Antulay (now a member of the Narasimha Rao Cabinet at the Centre) as Chief Minister of Maharashtra collected large donations for a trust in honour of Indira Gandhi in return for the issue of permits to buy cement at the controlled price which was uneconomically low. He had to step down because of the cement scandal. When the commodity was decontrolled, its blackmarket price crashed, though the post-decontrol market price was—as it had to be in order to recover the cost and yield a return—higher than the former controlled rate.

Indira Gandhi said in the course of her address to a conference of vigilance officers in New Delhi on 23rd March 1981 : "The constant emphasis of the media on material goods, the vision of the comforts enjoyed in advanced societies, proliferation of regulations, the pressure of inflation, the breakdown of religious and ethical constraints, a general rise in permissiveness, all these contribute to corruption." Yet she not only persisted with a regulated economy but promoted advertising with its emphasis on material goods. Having sanctioned commercials on All India Radio in November 1967, she went on to make Doordarshan a carrier of commercial messages, promotive of a self-centred and hedonistic culture of consumerism from 1st January 1976.

There was as little of the Mahatma's influence on Rajiv Gandhi (Prime Minister for five years from the close of 1984) as on his mother, though the spelling of their surname misleadingly suggested a relationship. (Feroze Gandhy was how Indira's husband used to spell his surname, in Parsi fashion, till March 1942 when he married Nehru's daughter.) Westernised to his fingertips, Rajiv Gandhi frequently spoke of taking India into the 21st century. He continued the policy of what was called a mixed economy. In this dispensation,politicians and bureaucrats benefited from the public sector which offered chairmanships equivalent to ministership and managing directorships equal to senior official positions, with lavish perquisites and powers of patronage. Many captains of trade and industry in the private sector, for their part, were happy with a situation in which, in return for favours to politicians in power, they could enjoy a non-competitive domestic market through restrictions on imports, and could influence pricing and distribution policies.

Meanwhile the over-staffed, inefficient, often corrupt and loss-incurring public sector, on the one hand, and on the other hand prodigal government spending on populist schemes in pursuit of votes led to the growth of public debt, domestic and foreign, to a staggering level. National indebtedness means a burden not only on the present but on future generations.

If fell to P. V. Narasimha Rao, the first Prime Minister with a normal five-year tenure drawn from outside the Nehru family, to halt and reverse in 1991 the ruinous policy of stifling private investment, enterprise and competition in the name of socialism. Prime Minister Rao will be remembered for his courage in launching through his Finance Minister Manmohan Singh a New Economic Policy (NEP) even if, in respect of other matters, the criticism of him be true that he believes in masterly inactivity in accordance with the dictum that a problem will solve itself if it is left alone sufficiently long. But Narasimha Rao's NEP did not mark a return to the Gandhian approach. On the contrary, it marked the acceptance of the World Bank philosophy of a global market in which the financially powerful, within a country as well as transnationally, pursue maximum profit while the weak fall by the wayside. It has made the Indian public sector slightly more cost-conscious and competitive than it used to be, but it has brought no relief to the poorest.

India has the dismal distinction, a half-century and four substantive Prime Ministers after freedom, of carrying the largest numbers of the world's illiterate and the poor. If the Maruti car has been a symbol of India's dual society since the 1980's, the latest symbols are the American soft drinks and mod apparel that have become ubiquitous in urban

India. Government-run Doordarshan advertises luxury goods and services for the delectation of the well-to-do, while the Prime Minister, with both eyes on the next elections to the Lok Sabha, promises yet more doles for the poor. The increasing remoteness of Indian advertising from social reality is in direct proportion to the decline from the idealism of the pre-independence era to economism and consumerism.

Menace of Advertising

There has been a sea-change in the attitude of the country's leaders to commercial advertising.

Mahatma Gandhi excluded advertisements altogether from his journals. He was against the multiplication of wants (as distinct from needs), and expressed the wish in the course of an article in '*Young Indias*' in October 1919 that "there were, for each province, only one advertising medium—not a newspaper—containing innocent, unvarnished notices of things useful for the public." Annie Besant, after she acquired the 'Madras Standard' and ran it as the daily *'New India'* from 1914, wrote to a friend that the first thing she did was to "clear off all the coarse advertisements".

In *The Discovery of India,* written in 1944, Jawaharlal Nehru said : "The advertiser is one of the symbols of our age with his continuous and raucous attempts to delude us and dull our powers of perception and induce us to buy unnecessary and even harmful products." In an address to the All India Newspaper Editors' Conference at Allahabad on 16th February 1946, he said : "The quality of advertisements appearing in some newspapers sometimes pains me. I appeal to the editors that they should exercise a strict censorship over advertisements so that undesirable advertisements are not accepted." Referring to commercial advertisements carried by Radio Ceylon and other foreign broadcasting systems, Nehru said in 1963 : "Personally I react strongly if an advertisement comes through radio. My reaction is never to encourage that advertiser. What does he mean by interfering with my peace of mind ? It angers me when it suddenly comes in; it upsets me."

In order to counter the pull of Radio Ceylon which was broadcasting Indian film songs, the Vividh Bharati channel was introduced in Nehru's time, on 3rd October 1957. But it did not adversely affect popular taste because film music at that time was not the organised noise that much of it is today but had a lyrical quality and aesthetic appeal. Though radio listenership went up with the introduction of the Vividh Bharati service by more and more stations, creating an audience of tempting size for the commercial advertiser, it was out of the question for A. I. R. to go commercial as long as Nehru was Prime Minister.

After commercials were introduced on 1st November 1967, during Indira Gandhi's prime ministership, the standard of Vividh Bharati began to decline, along with the quality of film music which began to be dominated by love songs ranging from the inane to the lewd. Vividh Bharati also began to carry commercial advertisements promoting the sale of consumption goods of interest to the growing urban middle class and to the affluent, but of no relevance to the urban poor and the majority of India's rural population. To the extent that these latter have exposure at all to television, advertisements on TV have a disorienting effect and serve to provoke envy, frustration and crime.

On the destabilising effects of the consumerist culture associated with industrialism, Jawaharlal Nehru said in the course of the Maulana Azad Memorial Lecture delivered by him in November 1959 : "We see the effects of rapid technological changes more especially in young men and women today. There is a tendency to criminality, alcoholism, destructiveness, eroticism, in addition to a cynical and negative attitude towards life and work. In a world of constant change, and without any assurance of certainty, the hedonistic principles of life have a strong appeal. These tendencies are present more in the developed societies than in India or other under-developed countries. But it is important to note them because similar forces are likely to affect our life too." The words have proved prophetic.

Indira Gandhi, who succeeded her father as Prime Minister after Lal Bahadur Shastri's brief tenure, was also aware of the danger of the pursuit of more and more wants to the detriment of moral integrity. In the course of the Raul Prebisch Lecture at Belgrade on 8th June 1983, she spoke of the continuance of colonial educational systems perpetuating the psychology of imitation. "Educated and articulate persons", she said, "view progress and development in terms of the level of goods and services they can command, and not the inherent self-reliant strength generated in the economy. Transnational advertising arouses new desires which distort economic priorities, and lure people into artificial consumption patterns." It is, of course, not only transnational advertising that arouses new desires but, equally, advertising by wholly 'national' producers of luxury goods and by fully Indian-owned advertising agencies. Secondly, there was an obvious mismatch between Prime Minister Indira Gandhi's wise words and her practice because it was she herself who had permitted commercial advertising on the Doordarshan screen from as far back as 1st January 1976.

Unmindful of the contradiction between precept and action, she went on to say in an address to the United Nations General Assembly in New York on 28th September 1983 : "In this age of instant globe-encircling information technology, the media dazzle eyes and fill ears with images and reports of affluence. Even the modest expectations of our people are far beyond our present means."

Why did the government-owned electronic media go in for commercial advertising, despite the warnings of Mahatma Gandhi and Jawaharlal Nehru ? The reason lies in the need felt by those who have led the country after Nehru for the building of their image at the personal level as well as for propaganda in favour of the policies and performance of the governments headed by them at the Centre. This could be done day after day through the news and current affairs programmes of All India Radio and Doordarshan, since both are run as government departments.

It was necessary for the same reason to maximise the size of the audience for the rulers' messages. One way to achieve this was to establish community listening and viewing facilities on the largest scale so as to cover rural India where only a small percentage of the population could afford their own radio and television sets. But this would have entailed problems of organisation beyond the capacity of an apathetic bureaucracy whose primary concern has been to secure improvement, from Pay Commission to Pay Commission, of its salaries and perquisites. Secondly, the Congress party which has been in power most of the time at the Centre was more secure in its rural basis than in the urban. Abolition, in the early years of independence, of Zamindari and allied forms of intermediaries between the cultivator and the State had created, and ensured for the Congress the support of, a vote-controlling class of landed proprietors and cultivating tenants with security of tenure. In urban centres, on the other hand, literacy and political consciousness were higher and they generated an attitude of critical appraisal of government performance which found expression in the Press. Disenchantment with the Congress, the party that won freedom though it could not avert partition, set in soonest in the major cities of India which had been centres of modern English education and of national awakening. The results of the first three general elections to the Lok Sabha bring out the urban-rural difference in the pattern of voting.

The four metropolitan cities—Calcutta, Bombay, Madras and Delhi—are the centres of publication of many of India's oldest and largest circulated daily newspapers. Several of them were critical of some of the Central Government's policies even in Jawaharlal Nehru's time, and more so of the populist policies of Indira Gandhi during and after the Congress split of 1969. The electronic media operated by the Central Government came to be regarded by the ruling party as weapons with which to counter the Press which was privately owned. Soon there grew a division of labour under which the citizen received from radio and television only good news, favourable to the Government, and it was left to the Press to report what was going wrong.

There was an additional reason for the Central Government concentrating its energies on addressing the urban audience. The middle classes and the affluent who form the bulk of the population in cities and towns could afford to buy their own receiving sets. There was no need to organise community access to the electronic media. All that the Government had to do was to make the audio and visual fare popular enough to attract a large clientele. This it proceeded to do with total disregard for the aesthetic standards and moral health of society. Cheap film music became the main pulling power of radio. Feature films, far too many of them laden with sex and violence, and song-and-dance sequences compiled therefrom became the chief attraction of Doordarshan. The new mass audience, mainly urban and with increasing purchasing power in its hands, attracted the commercial advertiser in a big way. This brought in, specially in the case of Doordarshan, commercial revenue to supplement budgetary provisions for expanding the reach of the electronic media through additional stations and relay transmitters.

An impetus was given to the sale of radio receivers when, in August 1980, the requirement of paying a licence fee was abolished in respect of one-band and two-band receivers. The number of licensed radio receivers in the country at that time was 17.9 million besides a large number manufactured in small-scale industrial units and not reported to the authorities. The latest estimate of radio receivers in the country, by the audience research directorate of All India Radio, is of the order of 105 million. The commercial revenue of A. I. R. has gone up correspondingly :

A. I. R.'s Income from Commercials

Year	*Rs. million*
1980-81	122
1985-86	198
1990-91	390
1991-92	530
1992-93	590
1993-94	640
1994-95	650

The growth of television in terms of receiving sets as well as of commercial revenue earned by Doordarshan has been even more spectacular. The number of licensed TV sets was 2,060,727 as on 31st December 1982—a meagre figure considering that Delhi Kendra (established in 1959 as an experimental station to put out educational programmes exclusively, for the rural population and for school students) had begun to run a service of entertainment and information for general viewers from 1965 and that six more Kendras had come up : Bombay (1972), Srinagar (1973), Amritsar (1973), Calcutta (1975), Madras (1975) and Lucknow (1975).

There was a big spurt in the number of television receiving sets following the introduction of colour transmission on 15th August 1982 in preparation for the telecast, from November 1982, of the Ninth Asian Games in Delhi. Twenty low-power transmitters were specially imported for live telecast of the Games in far corners of the country. With the subsequent multiplication of television stations as well as relay transmitters, the number of TV homes in the country was, as of December 1994, 45,683,000—29,972,000 urban and 15,711,000 rural. Doordarshan's commercial revenue has gone up by leaps and bounds since the introduction of commercials on 1st January 1976 :

Doordarshan's Income from Commercials

Year	*Rs. million*
1976-77	7.7
1977-78	20.7
1978-79	49.7
1979-80	61.6
1980-81	80.8
1981-82	112.7
1982-83	158.9
1983-84	179.9

Year	*Rs. million*
1984-85	314.3
1985-86	602.0
1986-87	933.1
1987-88	1363.0
1988-89	1612.6
1989-90	2101.3
1990-91	2538.5
1991-92	3006.1
1992-93	3602.3
1993-94	3729.5
1994-95	3980.0

The social cost of the burgeoning commercial revenue is incalculable. The tie-up between two categories of persons with a stake in securing a mass audience—the political ruler wanting dissemination of image-building propaganda, and the advertiser wanting to maximise the sale of his product or service—has proved to be a deadly combination in terms of its effect on popular taste, social order and the moral health of the nation.

The Working Group on Doordarshan Software recalled the criticism by the Second Press Commission, in its report of April 1982, of certain types of advertisements in newspapers which promoted sexism and a consumerist culture; the Group pointed out that government-run Doordarshan should be even more conscious of its social responsibility than the privately owned Press. The Press Commission had said : "It was recognised that classified advertisements relating to employment, matrimony, housing and the like serve a useful function, but a considerable part of display advertising was prodigal and had to be curtailed. The glossy magazines and the glossiest of advertisements in the Press—of jeans and soft drinks, cigarettes and cosmetics, air travel or entertainment in five-star hotels—are directed at the newly affluent and their children. We are of the view that the Press must address itself to the question of what contribution it is making to the strengthening of the moral fabric of society and discouraging the trend towards conspicuous and excessive consumption which a developing country can ill afford.... There has been an increasing tendency to exploit sex appeal. The exploitation of the female form in commercial advertising promotes the notion of women as sex objects and runs contrary to the news items and articles which many newspapers carry in support of treating women as equals and respecting their personality as individuals endowed with as much human worth as males."

The Software Group also recalled the momentous decision made by the Indonesian President in 1981 to discontinue commercial advertising on Indonesian television because of its socially destabilising effect through the generation of wants not matched by the means of satisfying them. The decision was taken despite the fact that, according to 'Asian Advertising, 1980', 28 per cent (the highest share) of all advertising in Indonesia was being incurred through the television medium as of 1979.

Considering all this, some members of the Software Group were of the view that Doordarshan should altogether discontinue commercial advertising, and the only 'messages' in advertising style on Doordarshan henceforth should be public service messages such as for the promotion of savings, family planning, health practices, girls' education, blood donation, environment, traffic safety, and the like. According to these members of the Software Group, it was absurd for the Government with one hand to stoke the fires of consumerism through its media and with the other hand to try and contain the consequences in terms of crime and corruption.

"While appreciating and respecting the concerns felt by these colleagues", the report said, "the majority of us in the Working Group are of the view that advertising is inseparable from a modern industrial economy in which production is not organised locally to meet locally felt needs but is based on a national and an international market. However, we are emphatically of the view that advertising should not promote male chauvinism and sexism."

Noting that the time most sought after by commercial advertisers is during and around the telecast of feature films and film-based programmes, the report said : "Our recommendation, in the chapter on Entertainment, of a reduction in the time devoted to such programmes may possibly, but not necessarily, lead to a drop in earnings from commercials. Since the advertiser is interested in audience rating and not in the nature of the programme that attracts high viewing, it is up to Doordarshan to offer attractive programmes of excellent content during part of the time now being applied to films and film-based programmes, much of them in poor taste and socially harmful. If indeed there should be a drop in commercial revenue, it should be accepted as the price for correcting Doordarshan's wrong practice hitherto in the selection of commercial films and in the compilation of song-and-dance sequences therefrom. Doordarshan is not in the business of television for raking in the maximum revenue from commercials; advertisements are incidental to its essentially educative role as a publicly owned mass medium."

Sex and Violence : Rousing the Beast

The Software Group made it clear that its condemnation of sexist programmes on Doordarshan did not proceed from prudery : "The objection is to vulgarity, and not to so-called permissiveness which has always existed, in every society, and entails relationships not sanctioned by a society's mores, specially the mores of the middle class which tend to be more prudish and hypocritical compared to working people or the very rich."

Needless to say, every person so inclined should have the freedom to view films portraying sex in the raw, or sadistic violence, on his own video equipment or in X-rated theatres, even as he should be free to read pornographic literature in privacy. But, surely, no organisation whether publicly or privately owned should be allowed to broadcast such material, via transmitter or cable, for reception inside homes. In violation of this principle, and of the objectives underlying legislation such as the Cinematograph Act and the Indecent Representation of Women (Prohibition) Act, Doordarshan has been telecasting, and the Government has permitted cable operators to disseminate foreign channel telecasts of, programmes that are grossly offensive to decency and good taste.

How vulgar Doordarshan had become in its pursuit of ever larger viewership was summed up by the Software Group in these words : "Even worse than the third-rate feature films screened in full are the compilations from such films, many of which are a concentrated offering of love duets accompanied by obscene gestures and scenes of imbecile hero chasing imbecile heroine round bushes or down a city street, teasing and harassing and finally winning her. The compilers of Chitrahaar and similar song-and-dance sequences appear to think that it promotes national integration if they show, from different regions of India, a man and woman rolling over each other down a grassy slope, or allegedly 'folk' dancers from different parts of the country swinging hip and bosom.

"Unlike a pornographic book or journal read in privacy by an individual, or a lewd or sadistic film viewed by a person in the anonymity of the crowd in a darkened cinema hall, a film screened on television is often viewed by three generations of a family. To watch these lewd scenes in a family group is highly embarrassing. It is unfortunate that most of the feature films and song-and-dance sequences telecast by Doordarshan reduce to repulsive public exhibition so private and precious an experience as the man-woman relationship."

Similar views were expressed at a seminar on 'Films for Television' organised by the Indian Institute of Mass Communication in January 1983. At this seminar Adoor Gopalakrishnan regretted that with the expansion of the TV network in the country, the Chitrahaar type of vulgarity would be more widely disseminated. Basu Bhattacharya, another renowned film-maker, spoke of the need to learn from the experience of other countries where the depiction of unbridled violence and sex on TV had promoted crime.

Nothing daunted, and without waiting for the Software Group's views, the Ministry of I & B decided in March 1983 to offer the TV viewer more of the same. Two Hindi feature films instead of one began to be screened by the Delhi Kendra each week and relayed by the low power transmitters. A content analysis of 14 days of Delhi Doordarshan's offerings, from 25th March 1983 to 7th April 1983 showed that feature films and film related programmes occupied the largest single chunk of telecast time : 21.1 per cent. Even a decade later, according to 'Doordarshan 1995' brought out by the Audience Research Unit of Doordarshan, film-based programmes occupied 21.4 per cent of the National Network telecast time during December 1994. Though the increase percentage-wise is marginal, the actual amount of time devoted to feature films and film-based entertainment is now much more, since total telecast time has gone up steeply since 1983.

Views on Doordarshan's sexist entertainment similar to those expressed by the Software Group were voiced by several—but not all—participants in a seminar organised by Centre for Media Studies on 22nd September 1994 in New Delhi on 'Violence and vulgarity in the media'. In a seminar paper titled 'Beyond lewdness and vacuity, Swadeshi or Videshi', G. N. S. Raghavan said that the upper crust of Indian society may well be described, in cultural terms, as Resident Non-Indians devoted to Samantha Fox, Michael Johnson and their ilk, on disc or on the TV screen or in person. They are also among the audience "hooked to Doordarshan's Chitrahaar and similar compilations of lewd cinema songs and dances, and to the Metro channel which includes clips of cartoon strips and girlie shows from the very same foreign TV programmes which we are told are un-Indian."

On the other hand, a woman participant in the CMS seminar disagreed with those who criticised the depiction of bedroom scenes in films, including those screened by Doordarshan. Ms. Vijayalakshmi Bose, from Jamia Millia's Mass Communication Centre, said : "There is no immaculate conception in India." True enough. It is equally true that Indians, men and women, are not free of the need to urinate and defecate. Would that make it necessary or desirable for the film or TV camera to linger long and lovingly on men and women relieving themselves ?

Worth poindering are the remarks of some wise men and women, Indian and foreign, on the difference between two modes of the man-woman relationship : vulgar, lustful and aggressive; or tender and mutually enriching. Gerald Heard in 'The Third Morality' (1937) says : "There will probably be no trouble with lust if tenderness is allowed its natural full play. The rule of the Third Morality about sex expression must run : always and only with tenderness. In the deepest sense of the word, all sexual expression can be and should be religious. Sex is the possibility of a real communion with life. In that expression, each touches something profounder than his lover. The lover is kissed, but the lover embraces and is embraced by the underlying life of both and all."

Khasa Subba Rau, founding editor of *Swatantra*, wrote in the 9th July 1949 issue of the Madras weekly : "The sex-body is remarkably independent and its demands often exceed and at times even contradict the demands of love...No direct relation can be predicated between sexual tendencies and gifts of mind and character. The great Goethe of giant intellect was throughout his life the victim of uncontrollable sensual passions, and at seventy he was convulsed with violent desire for the youthful Ulrikạ." Do we, as individuals and as parents, want ourselves and our children to be influenced by Goethe the thinker and poet, or the sex-body ? There lurks in us a beast that needs little stimulus to be roused. Doordarshan and foreign TV channels between them keep providing the stimulus round the clock.

Aldous Huxley wrote that we are all much of a muchness between the navel and the knee. Do we wish to stay there, between the navel and the knee, as MTV and ATN invite us to do all the time and as Doordarshan does much of the time ?

Sai Paranjpe, a gifted film-maker who was a member of

the Working Group on Doordarshan Software, has written : "We have to remember that entertainment is like fire. To be of service to men, it has to be utilised with care and judiciousness. Otherwise it can devour and destroy. Commercial formula films have become a fixture on Doordarshan. There is no way one can soft-pedal the fact that great harm in being done by nurturing this kind of film culture. By feeding the hungry giant of TV regularly with third-rate films, we are taking a short cut to popularity. But at what cost ?"

Kapila Vatsyayan, who heads the Indira Gandhi National Centre for the Arts, said at the CMS seminar that India had, through the ages, a coherent society which was held together by an application of norms of conduct from within. The body, mind and soul of a man or woman were seen as one organic whole. "But the mass media in our country", she said, "are now imitating the popular culture of the West which glorifies the body dissociated from the rest of human personality. Viewing of the erotic sculpture in the temples of Khajuraho does nothing to the villagers, men and women, who visit the temples; but the same sculpture excites the prurient interest of educated urban Indians. An integral culture or yoga of the body, mind and soul which has endured for three thousand years is now being disrupted, and that too in the name of 'development' and 'progress'."

She noted that some participants had referred to pelvic thrust and gyrations in the course of folk and tribal dances, and said : "These movements of the body are entirely natural in their normal setting and context, not focussed on by the camera long and lasciviously. They coarsen our sensibility only when they are exploited as material to titillate the viewer." Obscene sound in the name of music, Kapila Vatsyayan added, was even more vulgar : it was polluting, disturbing and violent.

On the subject of freedom of sexual expression in public, worth pondering are the following observations in the report of the Committee on the Future of Broadcasting (in England) headed by Lord Annon : "There is a school of thought which maintains that the greater the freedom of sexual expression in public, the more enlightened, honest and candid the society. That argument cannot be sustained. All societies have a notion of public decency, and even those sexual acts which everyone agrees are legitimate and desirable would be regarded as illegitimate and indecent if they were shown explicitly on television. However much notions of public decency have changed, a society which had lost all sense of differentiating between private and public behaviour would be a society which had lost all sense of human personality or sensitivity to what others feel. We do not believe that those who protest against the amount of sexual innuendo and the exploitation of sexual themes can be written off as fuddy-duddies who know little about art and less about life, and are anxious only to reimpose a caricature of Victorian values. It seems to us that caricaturists are too often to be found in the other camp. Too often producers, writers and their professional colleagues exploit sex in order to win praise from their professional colleagues for being daring and anti-authoritarian. What passes for exploration is in fact exploitation."

Many producers of films and of TV programmes exploit the voyeurist impulse in men and women in relation to violence as cynically as they exploit voyeurism in relation to sex. They know that the sight of violence, howsoever brutal and sadistic, evokes fascinated attention even from those who are normally gentle in real life. Viewers tend to identify with one or other, or alternately with both, of the adversaries in a scene of film violence, even as spectators of sports do. The beast under our skin is roused by the exhibition of violence as surely and quickly as by provocative display of the sex-body and its movements.

A paper on 'TV Violence in Asia' by Vijay Menon, circulated at the CMS seminar, quoted the following comment from an editorial in the 'Far Eastern Economic Review' of 18th August 1993 : "There is a window in most Asian homes that is totally unsecured. It is, of course, the television set. Asians are right to be concerned about intrusion through their electronic windows. With rapid change around the corner, Asians should not wait until their children have actually seen 8,000 televised murders—the norm for an American child by the time he leaves primary school—before taking precautions." But Doordarshan is not far behind in its offering of violence. A study conducted by the Asian Mass Communication Research and Information Centre, Singapore, in 1988-89 in eight countries of Asia showed that foreign-made programmes screened on television in these countries generally had more violent incidents per hour. But in India too, though Doordarshan screened only locally produced programmes during the survey period, the proportion of violent programmes was very high—72 per cent.

The Standing Committee on Communications of the present (tenth) Lok Sabha, in its seventh report dated 13th April 1994 said it "would like that Doordarshan should produce and telecast programmes which generate the spirit of patriotism, communal harmony, non-violence and respect for democratic values and institutions." It expressed regret that "the commercial approach adopted by Doordarshan has induced the telecasting of programmes which are not in consonance with the ethos and values of our society. The Committee, therefore, strongly recommend that Doordarshan should discourage the telecasting of all such programmes on its network and should also strictly follow the system of pre-view and censorship."

In its eighth report dated 27th September 1994, the Committee was more emphatic : "Doordarshan has now decided not to accept any film-based material including film songs, for telecast, unless it bears a certificate from the Central Board of Film Certification. This is welcome insofar as it goes, but with regard to Doordarshan which caters principally to family audience, the Committee expect it to exercise even greater caution about telecasting film-based material even though it may have been cleared by the CBFC...

"Today more and more films whose themes are primarily dominated by unrelated sex and excessive violence are being churned out and circulated. Crime is increasingly becoming the main theme of the story of films. It is projected in a manner giving the impression that violence, theft, robbery, etc. are normal incidents in ordinary life. Further, vice is shown in a heroic form, even though retribution follows. The Committee regret to find that the Examining Officers have not been paying required attention to the stipulations and conditions for clearing a film. Considering the fact that films play a vital role in moulding public opinion and attitudes, in imparting knowledge and in understanding of our culture and traditions, the Committee strongly recommend that the CBFC should strictly adhere to the guidelines/objectives with regard to projection of violence and sex in films and do not certify films/songs on the grounds that they have already been shown on various channels like Zee TV, etc. The Committee strongly recommend that the display of such vulgar scenes and dual meaning songs by Doordarshan should be immediately banned and such songs should also not be played on All India Radio."

Instances of 'copycat' violence including sexual attacks, imitated from films and TV programmes, are being reported with increasing frequency in the Press. The latest instance is of fatal violence against himself by a TV addict. PTI reported from Bangalore on 22nd August 1995 that a teenager had hung himself to death : "Nandeesh, a student of St. Joseph's high school, had been experimenting daredevil acts shown on TV and was in the habit of emulating such acts". The bizarre story of a film-inspired murder, in which the killer tries to exchange his identity with that of the victim, is narrated in an ensuing Chapter dealing with films. How many more such gruesome incidents must occur before the Government stops the promotion of sex-related and other crimes by state-run Doordarshan ?

Self-invited cultural subversion

The Government's statement of objects and reasons appended to Bill No. LXVIII of 1993 for regulating cable television, subsequently enacted through an ordinance, was clearly a case of the pot calling the kettle black. With a pious air which ignored Doordarshan's own consumerist advertising and vulgar exploitation of sex and violence for maximising its audience, the statement said : "There has been a haphazard mushrooming of cable television networks all over the country during the last few years as a result of the availability of signals of foreign television networks via satellites. This has been perceived as a cultural invasion in many quarters since the programmes available on these satellite channels are predominantly western and totally alien to our culture and way of life. Since there is no regulation of these cable television networks, lot of undesirable programmes and advertisements are becoming available to the viewers without any kind of censorship.

"It is also felt that the subscribers of these cable television networks, the programmers, and the cable operators themselves are not aware of their rights, responsibilities and obligations in respect of the quality of service, technical as well as content-wise, use of material protected by copyright, exhibition of uncertified films, protection of subscribers from anti-national broadcasts from sources inimical to our national interest, responsiveness to the genuine grievances of the subscribers and a perceived willingness to operate within the broad framework of the laws of the land, e. g., the Cinematograph Act, 1952, the Copyright Act, 1957, Indecent Representation of Women Prohibition Act, 1986. It is, therefore, considered necessary to regulate the operation of cable television networks in the entire country so as to bring about uniformity in their operation. It will thus enable the optimal exploitation of this technology which has the potential of making available to the subscribers a vast pool of information and entertainment."

The 'cultural invasion' referred to in the above statement (of 23rd July 1993) had begun in the early 1980s—much before the advent of cable television—and it was self-invited. None of the bilateral economic aid agreements signed by India with the U.S. and other western countries, or the agreements for credit from the World Bank and the International Monetary Fund, has ever carried a stipulation that India's state-owned television system should telecast foreign-made programmes. Yet Doordarshan began to screen foreign English-language serials—of social comedy, crime detection and clowning—on an increasing scale from 1981 and specially since the introduction of the National Programme in August 1982.

A sample survey carried out in Delhi by the Indian Institute of Mass Communication in 1983 showed that comprehension of the foreign programmes shown on the television screen had little to do with many viewers being glued to them. The survey covered 500 respondents in TV households : 100 each in Vasant Vihar, Model Town, Gole Market, Sadar Bazar and Inderpuri (localities listed in descending order in terms of level of education, income and knowledge of English). It was found that the foreign serials in English shown by Doordarshan at peak viewing time in the evening hours, were viewed by 84.2% of the respondents. The extent to which the foreign programmes were comprehended may be inferred from the following :

* Of the five localities, Inderpuri had the least proportion of residents who saw English movies in cinema halls or used English during conversation either at home or outside or both. Yet as many as 54% of the Inderpuri respondents watched foreign serials.
* More than a fifth (22.4%) of the respondents failed to identify 'Old Fox' as a detective serial.
* During participant observation conducted in 50 TV households, viewers were asked at the end of a comedy (Lucy Show or Father Dear Father) to relate two or three of the jokes which had elicited laughter from them along with the laughter from the unseen American or British audience. Neither young viewers nor elders could recollect specific exchanges of witty dialogue. They could only recall funny incidents like Lucy having a fall while learning to ski, or Father getting something funny stuck on his nose.

It proved difficult to locate homes for conducting participant observation of the sophisticated political satire serial 'Yes Minister'. It was hardly viwed in the lower and middle income localities, and participant observation could be conducted only in areas like Vasant Vihar, Safdarjung Enclave, Janakpuri and Pandara Road where most of the residents are English-educated. Even there, the programme was usually followed seriously by not more than one member of the household—in most cases a male.

Noting that the selection of Indian movies, as well as of foreign serials, reflected bad taste and poor judgment, the Working Group on Doordarshan Software said in its report : "The selection of Indian movies is supposed to be done by a selection committee chaired by the Director-General of Doordarshan. We found it impossible to believe that a group of cultured Indians can make a selection of Indian movies and foreign serials as atrociously mindless and/or vulgar as many of both the categories telecast by Doordarshan are. We can only infer that the responsibility for selection has been delegated down the line. But in a matter as serious as the selection of foreign comedy and of Indian movies, we are of the view that such delegation of responsibility is impermissible. It amounts an abnegation of intellectual and moral responsibility. The selection of foreign social comedy serials that has been done so far by Doordarshan amounts to a self-invited cultural invasion from the West."

These remarks pertain to Doordarshan of the early 1980s. Since then it has gone from bad to worse. The programmes of vulgar entertainment, both Indian and foreign, now put out by Doordarshan require no knowledge of a language, Indian or foreign, since they employ such universal non-verbal communication signs of sexual intimacy as the kiss, pawing and pelvic thrust. The words of the songs in such programmes hardly matter. In the foreign programmes such as MTV's, they are crooned or, more often, howled out merely as accompaniment to the emphatic rhythm of the percussion, wind and string instruments.

If it is western culture at its lowest level that is purveyed by Doordarshan, and by All India Radio in its metropolitan FM channels, the Indian culture—if it may be dignified by that term—exported by Doordarshan and by AIR's Vividh

Bharati is also of a shallow and mindless variety. A very large proportion of films in Hindi are being produced in India not only, or primarily, for the Indian market but with the Gulf region in view—aimed more at the affluent Muslim males starved of direct gaze at the opposite sex (burqa-clad as most of the women are in their own countries), than at the Indian expatriates working there for a living. The exchange that we now have at the level of popular 'culture' is a travesty of the vision that inspired Rabindranath Tagore to establish Visva-Bharati at Shantiniketan as an international university. Tagore wrote : "Visva-Bharati represents India where she has her wealth of mind which is for all. Visva-Bharati acknowledges India's obligation to offer to others the hospitality of her best culture, and India's right to accept from others their best." We are now exporting our worst and importing the worst from others.

This unlovely situation has not come about because of absence of warning. In its 1984 report, the Working Group on Doordarshan Software said : "Given the disparity in access, and the lack of relevance of the software of Doordarshan to the harsh living conditions of the common people, it seems ironical that television should be claimed—as it has been by a widely quoted American writer—as a medium which retribalises humankind". This retribalisation was supposed to be in contrast to the first industrial revolution, of which printing as the beginning of mass communication was part, as an agent of detribalisation. "If", the report said, "Doordarshan with its foreign social comedy serials and Indian feature films projecting the aping of western life styles is promoting a process of universal tribalisation, it is by inducting sons and daughters of television viewers and the moneyed Indian upper crust—comprising businessmen and politicians, civil servants and academics, and every other category of the privileged—into the international fraternity of rock and roll, jive and disco. The international elite of the developed and developing countries do indeed constitute one tribe, irrespective of their skin colour and geographical distribution."

Like Rabindranath Tagore, Mahatma Gandhi envisaged

cultural interaction between nations without any of them getting culturally uprooted. He said : "I want the winds of all cultures to be blown freely about my house, but I do not want to be swept off my feet by any." The danger in today's situation is that unlike the military invasions of India in the past, which overthrew local rulers and destroyed great temples that symbolised local culture, today's cultural invasion, aided and abetted by cultural compradors at whose head stands Doordarshan, is an invasion directly of Indian men and women in the mass. The low power transmitters of which there are nearly 600 now dotting the country, like the 70 high-power transmitters of Doordarshan, carry destabilising and disorienting messages, visual and verbal, to millions living on the margin of poverty in urban and rural areas who occasionally have access to television viewing. They confirm the middle and upper classes in, and whet their appetite for, a hedonistic culture of consumption of which sexual gratification is a prime component.

The effect on urban youth is summed up in these words by Sugatha Kumari, poet and social activist of Kerala : "The new generation is the Quit India generation, wanting to fly West." Concern was expressed at this trend by members of Parliament belonging to all political parties, serving on the parliamentary Standing Committee on Human Resource Development, in the 12th report on National Policy on Culture which was laid before the two Houses on 25th August 1994. Excerpts from the remarks of the standing committee are reproduced below :

"Nothing in the recent past has had such dramatic and deleterious impact on our cultural traditions as the invasion of the mass media, *both indigenous and foreign.* (emphasis added).

"An important objective of the National Policy on Culture is to evolve a creative response to this new challenge which will enable us to preserve our cultural continuity with the past, rejecting the baneful and integrating the desirable. Should we fail to evolve a sufficiently creative response to this challenge, there is every danger of India succumbing to an imitative culture and losing its indigenous creative genius. It will avail us nothing if we attain material progress but lose our soul in the bargain. There is no way in which we can shut ourselves off from the consequences of satellite technology. Retracting into a shell is not the answer. At the same time, passively succumbing to the invasion is not the answer either. Even while emphasising the need for a creative response to this invasion, the National Policy on Culture must see how we can avail ourselves of the technology to promote an understanding of our cultural heritage among the masses of our people at large, as well as to take the message of India to the outside world...It is a challenge to which our electronic media must rise, in concert with the Department of Culture whose duty it is to ensure that Indian global television does not become a pale imitation of existing Western-dominated networks.

"The Committee expresses its serious concern over the ever-increasing and reckless exhibition of violence, anti-social activities and obscenity through the cinema, the worst sufferers of which are the younger generation whose finer sensibilities are being coarsened and creative faculties dulled...The National Policy on Culture should address these issues and discourage these trends."

Acting exactly contrary to this exhortation, Doordarshan proceeded without compunction on the course of its self-invited cultural subversion by handing over to MTV two chunks of time in the Metro channel, including two hours of family viewing time from 5 p.m.

2 THE PRESS AS TWO-FACED JANUS

Oldest of the modern media of mass communication, the Press has by and large served India better than the others, both before and after independence. Films, too, played a socially purposeful role in the pre-independence period and the early years of freedom.

In contrast to the scope afforded to the socially conscious communicator by newspapers and films, both of which are in the private sector, monopoly control of radio by the Government since before independence, and of television since its advent in the 1960s, has proved stultifying.

It is the middle class that contributes most of the personnel of all the mass media. But since the Press, besides being free of government control, is relatively less market-driven than films with their large budgets and generally short life, many newspapers have from time to time exemplified the idealism that marks the more attractive of the two faces of the middle class. Jawaharlal Nehru said of the Janus-like middle class in the course of his presidential address at the Lucknow session of the Congress on 12th April, 1936 : "Being too much tied up with property and the goods of the world, it is fearful of losing them, and it is easy to bring pressure on it and to exhaust its stamina. And yet, paradoxically, it is only from the middle class intellectuals that revolutionary leadership comes, and we in India know that our bravest leaders and our stoutest comrades have come from the ranks of the middle class."

The beginnings of the Press in India revealed both the faces : newspapers as commerce and as social mission. The first printed periodical, the *Bengal Gazette,* which appeared in Calcutta on 29th January, 1780 was a commercial venture and it illustrated the nexus that often exists between newspapers and politicians. Though published on Indian soil, the weekly was meant for English-speaking foreigners residing in India, not for Indians. James Augustus Hicky, the publisher and editor, openly sided with the Governor-General, Warren Hastings, in the in-fighting between two factions in the Governor-General's Council. The opposition to Warren Hastings was led by Philip Francis, whose ambition was to become Governor-General himself. The journal would lampoon Elijah Impey, Chief Justice of the Supreme Court and a friend of Warren Hastings, as 'Poolbundy' (*pul* in Hindustani means bridge) in an obvious reference to a contract for maintaining bridges which the Chief Justice had secured for a relative. Warren Hastings and his wife were also boldly satirised. The types of Hicky's press were seized and his journal was suppressed in 1782 after Philip Francis decided to leave India. Warren Hastings for his part patronised a rival weekly, the *India Gazette,* which was given postal facilities not available to Hicky.

We have been witness, two centuries later, to a similar struggle between some journals affiliated with rival barons of industry who, in trun, enjoy the support of rival princes of the State. A conspicuous example is the campaign carried on in recent years against each other by the Ambanis of Reliance Industries who own the *Observer* group of publications and Nuslia Wadia, of Bombay Dyeing, who is a director of the *Indian Express.*

A half-way house in the emergence of a truly Indian Press was marked by the journals brought out, early in the 19th century, by Christian missionaries in Bengal. Though published by foreigners, these journals were addressed to Indians, and some of them were in Indian languages. They promoted the dual objectives of promoting the Christian religion and the British empire.

It was in order to counter the attacks on Indian religions which these missionary journals carried, and to assert national self-respect, that the first Indian newspapers, properly so called, were established by Raja Rammohun Roy (1772-1833), the initiator of India's renaissance in the modern period. Born in a well-to-do family, he represented the finer of the two faces of the middle class.

Stirring the social conscience

Rammohun Roy advocated, through the journals launched by him in the 1820s—the weeklies *Sambad Kaumidi* in Bengali and *Mirat ul Akhbar* in Persian and irregular in publication, the *Brahmunical Magazine*, a brief-lived magazine in English—many social reforms that were to become part of the plank of the nationalist movement. These included abolition of Sati or the custom, already on the wane in most parts of the country, of Sati or the burning of the widow on the funeral pyre of her husband, equality before the law, and modern education through the English medium. He did not press for representative government, it being too soon for that—with an entrenched imperial power and a people steeped in illiteracy and superstition and with little sense of a national identity; the affiliation of caste was, at that time, all that mattered for self-identity. But Rammohun Roy's readiness to assert national self-respect is evident from his courageous criticism of the brash methods of the foreign missionaries who reviled the religious beliefs and practices of Indians, both Hindus and Muslims.

The role of the Press acquired a new dimension with the advent of daily newspapers in the 19th century. Several of them were moderate or conservative, both with regard to political and social issues; some were moderate in their politics but radical in their attitude to social reform or *vice versa;* and some others were radical both in politics and on social issues without necessarily subscribing to the tactics of law-breaking in the name of Satyagraha.

The complexity of the scenario is illustrated by the instance of Annie Besant (1847-1933) and her daily newspaper *New India*. Having fought and suffered in England for many causes—as a free-thinker, trade unionist and proponent of planned parenthood—she became a theosophist, found in India her spiritual home, and settled at Adyar, in Madras, in 1907. Through *New India* which she ran from 1914, Annie Besant advocated a political line that was bold in comparison with the petitionary politics of the then Congress leadership. In 1916 the British authorities demanded a security from Annie Besant for "the better conduct of her publications". It was to protest against this action that young Jawaharlal Nehru, then practising law at Allahabad, made his first public speech in June 1916.

Annie Besant was chosen, while under internment as punishment for her advocacy of self-government for India, as president of the 1917 Congress session at Calcutta, becoming the first woman to be so honoured. But her popularity declined when she refused to endorse Gandhi's movement in 1919 against the Rowlatt Bills, his advocacy of Non-Cooperation, and support to Khilafat. She held that there was nothing in the two Bills to which an honest citizen could take exception, and that, instead of non-cooperation, the best men and women should enter the legislative councils and press for the transfer of greater power to the people's representatives. Civil disobedience, she warned, was "rearing huge obstacles in the way of the first Home Rule government."

The over-simplification and consequent misrepresentation in branding a person as a 'moderate' or a 'radical' is illustrated also by the case of Bal Gangadhar Tilak. He was a conservative in his attitude to social reform, while being a radical in politics; he coined the pledge 'Swaraj is my birthright, and I shall have it.' Though Tilak suffered imprisonment and deportation, he was for a constructive response to any move that the British were prepared to make in the direction of self-government, such as the Montagu Reforms Act of 1919.

Gandhiji was an exemplar of educative journalism. His first journalistic venture was 'Indian Opinion', a weekly brought out in 1904 in South Africa. It was published in four languages—English, Gujarati, Hindi and Tamil—in order to reach all the major elements of the Indian population in Natal and the Transvaal. It is characteristic of Gandhiji that while, on the one hand, he utilised the journal to ventilate the grievances of Indians who were grossly discriminated against by the regime of the white colonists, he also exhorted his countrymen to give up insanitary habits, to overcome feelings of difference based on caste or religion, and to observe truthfulness in their business dealings.

After returning finally to India in 1915, Gandhiji conducted three weekly journals : 'Navajivan' (1919-31) in Gujarati; 'Young India' in English (1919-32); and 'Harijan' in English from 1933 till his martyrdom in 1948. So widespread was the interest in Mahatma Gandhi's views that what he wrote in these journals was news.

"I have taken up journalism", he wrote in 1919, "not for its sake but merely as an aid to what I have conceived to be my mission in life. My mission is to teach by example the matchless weapon of Satyagraha which is a direct corollary of non-violence. To be true to my faith, I may not write merely to excite passion. The reader can have no idea of the restraint I have to exercise from week to week in the choice of topics and my vocabulary. It is a training for me." And in his autobiography : "One of the objects of a newspaper is to understand the popular feeling and give expression to it; another is to arouse among the people certain desirable sentiments ; and the third is fearlessly to expose popular defects."

A major consequence of Gandhiji for Indian journalism was the emergence of new dailies as radical alternatives to the nationalist but somewhat staid Indian-owned newspapers of long standing. These emerged as a third alternative to the loyalist newspapers, many of them British-owned, and to the newspapers which were once described by Nehru as 'immoderately moderate'.

Nationalism Muslim publicists

The first, and towering, personality who roused nationalist consciousness among the Indian Muslim community was Maulana Abul Kalam Azad (1888-1958). After the British suppressed the 1857 Uprising which aimed at restoring power and dignity to the last Mughal emperor, Bahadur Shah Zafar, who had been reduced to a figurehead by the East India Company, Muslims were in a demoralised state and withdrew into the shell of orthodoxy. Sir Syed Ahmad Khan (1817-98) advised his co-religionists to reform their social practices and take to modern education through English, but to seek their advancement through loyalty to the British rulers. He founded in 1875 the Mohammedan Anglo-Oriental College at Aligarh, later raised (in 1921) to the status of a university. The alumni of Aligarh remained by and large adherents of the founder's philosophy of a separate Muslim identity even though the great majority of Muslims in the Indian sub-continent—including present-day Pakistan and Bangladesh—are descendants of converted Hindus. Maulana Azad poured scorn and ridicule on the Aligarh School through his writings, as in the following passage from the daily *Al Hilal* founded by him in 1912 :

"The future historian will write that, ultimately, what had to happen, happened. In the 20th century no country could remain in bondage, and none remained. The British government was a constitutional entity. It was not the autocratic rule of Chengiz Khan. Therefore it did what was expected of it, and India became free. But the world will remember that this turn of events owned nothing to the Muslims; whatever happened redounded to the credit of every other community except the Muslims. History will record about seven crore people of India that there was an unfortunate and ill-fated community which always hindered the country's progress, and proved an everlasting impediment to its advancement. They were an obstacle in the path of freedom, a toy in the hands of covetous rulers, a puppet for the aliens, and a deep wound on India's brow."

Among other prominent nationalist Muslim publicists were M. Asaf Ali of Delhi, Syud Hosain, Syed Abdullah Brelvi and Shoebullah Khan of Hyderabad. The case of Asaf Ali—as of Maulana Azad and Dr. M. A. Ansari—illustrated how the pan-Islamic and anti-British sentiment generated among Indian Muslims by the attack on Turkey during World

War I matured into territorial nationalism and sympathy for all—and not only Muslim—victims of western domination. Asaf Ali, who had served the British administration till 1914, writes in his memoirs : "I was more pro-Turkey than I knew. The entire early training and home influence of sentimental attachment to the Turks sprang into the saddle of my reason and, driven by impulse, my decision was irrevocably taken. My resignation was cabled out (from London). Simla must know how war on Turkey was likely to react on Muslims, if I could chuck away what was the promise of a high career."

On returning to India in January 1915, Asaf Ali threw himself into the work of organising the Home Rule League and the Congress in Delhi. A creative writer in Urdu, he also wrote for two nationalist English newspapers, the 'Bombay Chronicle' and the 'Independent' launched by Motilal Nehru in Allahabad. A Swarajist, he advocated the entry of nationalists into the legislative councils rather than their boycott since, otherwise, loyalist elements would parade as representatives of the people. When Asaf Ali was adopted as the Congress candidate for the Central Legislative Assembly from Delhi in 1934 he received a telegram from Gandhiji published by the 'Hindustan Times' on 13th November, 1934 : "I hope every Delhi vote will be cast in your favour." On Asaf Ali winning by a large margin, Gandhiji wrote to him : "How I wish your success will lead to heart unity between the two brothers—Hindu and Mussalman."

The Mahatma's wish was not to be fulfilled. The Muslim League grew from strength to strength, thanks to Congress ambivalence towards separate electorates by which the League swore, and the negative policies pursued by the Congress during World War II beginning with the resignation of popularly elected provincial Ministries in October 1939 which left the field clear for the League to bask in the sunshine of British patronage.

However, there were brave spirits among Muslims who held to the ideal of national unity as against the League's advocacy of partition in order to create Pakistan. Among such was Shoebullah Khan.

Born in 1919 he entered journalism after graduating from Osmania University. He first worked on the weekly 'Taj'. The journal was banned for carrying an article of his criticising the Nizam's complicity in the activities of the Ittehad-ul-Muslimeen and the Razakars under Qasim Razvi's leadership. Shoebullah Khan joined the 'Rayyat', but that newspaper too was forced to stop publication because it was critical of the Nizam's administration. Shoebullah then started his own daily, 'Imroze'. His advocacy of Hyderabad's accession to India invited the anger of the Razakars. Their threats did not cow him down. On the night of 21st August, 1948, while he was returning home from office, he was pounced upon by Razakar miscreants who shot him and cut his hands. He dragged himself towards his house and collapsed when he was a few yards away. Khasa Subba Rau said in the course of the first Shoebullah Khan Memorial Lecture in 1952 : "We journalists deal in words of varying power to put our stories and ideas across to the public. But Shoebullah delivered his message in letters written with blood."

Trends after independence

Kasturi Srinivasan, of the 'Hindu', said at a meeting of the All India Newspaper Editors' Conference, of which he was president, in October 1942 that the Press could be fully free only after the country became free. But it soon turned out that, in certain respects, each State is like every other—whether it be alien and autocratic or native and democratic, capitalist or socialist. None of them will tolerate attempts at subversion through sedition and violence, or the disclosure of State secrets.

The 'Free Press Journal' of Sadanand learnt this to its cost. This Bombay newspaper disclosed in September 1947 that Indian naval and land forces were being moved towards Junagadh, a Hindu-majority State on the Gujarat coast whose Muslim ruler acceded to Pakistan and was seeking armed help from outside, sparking off vigorous popular protest. The Central Home Minister, Sardar Patel, was furious. Sadanand, who had made arrangements for starting an Indian international news agency after visiting Cairo, London and New York during 1945-46 and making arrangements with foreign news agencies and individual journalists, was denied the lease of teleprinter lines though he had placed a large order for teleprinters. This was the beginning of his financial decline and serious ill-health. He died in 1953, a heroic and tragic figure in the history of Indian journalism.

Not many newspaper editors and publishers showed thereafter the courage to publish and be damned which characterised the nationalist Press prior to independence and which Sadanand displayed in the early years of independence. One reason was the creeping commercialisation of the Press, which became more and more a business for the publisher and a profession for the journalist and less and less a mission for either.

Partly because of the desire on the part of publishers to play safe, and partly because Prime Minister Nehru was Prince Charming who bewitched not only young men and women but most of the intelligentsia including journalists, the Press was by and large uncritical in its appraisal of government policies. It is only with the benefit of hindsight that Nehru has begun to be criticised for making acceptance of the accession of Jammu & Kashmir to India conditional on—and liable to be rejected through—a plebiscite under international auspices. It was a tiny section of the Press that criticised the Indian Government's muted disapproval of Soviet colonialism in Eastern Europe in contrast to its loud denunciation of the surviving vestiges of Western colonialism in some parts of the world. In the long years of the verbal border dispute with China, hardly any Indian newspaper questioned the propriety of the authorities of free India making their own the delineation of the border with Tibet as laid down by imperial Britain, and treating as sacred Indian territory areas in Ladakh and in the North East Frontier Agency (now Arunachal Pradesh) about whose terrian New Delhi had only a hazy notion and over which its authority was next to nil. It is, again, in retrospect that Nehru is being blamed—and only by a few—for his off-the-cuff declaration in September 1962, on a halt in India during his international peregrinations (he had returned from a visit to London and was taking off for Colombo) that the Indian Army had been instructed to clear NEFA of the Chinese. India is still to recover from the ignominy of the bloody nose administered by Communist China in retaliation.

In contrast, the Press was bolder and more critical in its appraisal of the Government's domestic policies, specially in the economic sphere. Even here, however, the country might have suffered less from the horrors of insurrection and terrorism if Indira Gandhi's handling of political problems in Assam and Punjab had been subjected to investigative and candid analysis; likewise with Rajiv Gandhi's misadventure in relation to Sri Lanka.

Such deficiencies notwithstanding, the performance of the Indian Press after independence has been creditable enough to merit praise by the Second Press Commission which reported in 1982. Though the Commission was split seven-to-four on issues of newspaper ownership and of governmental regulation of newspaper economics (the majority favouring State intervention and the liberal minority dissenting), the eleven members of the Commission were unanimous in expressing their appreciation of the role played by the Press in India's public life. They said : "It is to the credit of the Indian Press that, despite its predominantly urban and middle class moorings, it has evinced interest in the problems of farmers, agricultural workers, artisans, tribal groups and other sections of the rural population. Though, judged by readership or by ownership, it is not necessary for most of our newspapers to highlight the issues of poverty, the Press has made a major contribution by reminding readers of those who live below the poverty line, and giving the ruling middle and upper classes a feeling of guilt. Many newspapers have, from time to time, drawn attention to such matters concerning the weakest sections of society as non-enforcement of minimum wages and the failure to revise them to keep pace with the fall in the purchasing power of the rupee; the persistence of bonded labour despite its abolition by law, or its emergence in a new guise as contract labour; the generation of black money and its use, frequently entailing the involvement of corrupt officials and politicians, etc. Such creditable instances deserve wide emulation."

The Press could play this role because it is much closer and open to the people than are All India Radio and Doordarshan, the proximity of whose personnel is to bureaucrats and to politicians in power. The rapport between the Press and the people—at least the literate—is illustrated by the rapid strides made by newspapers brought out in Indian languages.

The first Press Commission made an attempt to ascertain the circulation of dailies published in India. This figure, taking all languages together, came to 25 lakhs (2.5 million) in 1952, when there were an estimated 330 dailies. The data furnished annually to the Press Registrar, an institution established in terms of the first Press Commission's recommendations, show that the circulation of the reporting newspapers has gone up as follows :

1990	22.64 million
1991	24.29 million
1992	28.09 million
1993	29.49 million

Whereas the growth rate of all dailies taken together was upwards of nine times over the 1952-1990 period, the growth rate in the case of Hindi dailies was more than 21 times. This is in contrast of the growth rate of only five times in respect of English-language dailies. Other Indian languages which have recorded an impressive growth rate include Gujarati, Malayalam, Marathi, Tamil and Urdu.

An indicator of the strides made by the Indian language Press is the number of newspapers with a circulation of one lakh and above. There were only two such in any language in 1960, and both were in English. In 1979, Indian languages accounted for 20 out of the 30 dailies in this circulation category. In 1990, the number of newspapers selling more than a lakh of copies rose to 46, and out of these only 10 were in English and 36 were in Indian languages.

While noting with gratification the growth of the Indian language Press in absolute terms, the Second Press Commission drew attention to the need for assessing the state of development of the Press in an Indian language in relation to the number of persons speaking that language. "Though Hindi has the largest share in the total circulation of dailies", it said, "the circulation of Hindi dailies per 1,000 of the linguistic population is very low. It stood at 12 copies in 1979 (though it is a big increase over the figure of 2.8 copies in 1952), in contrast to the circulation of 47.9 copies of Malayalam dailies per 1,000 linguistic population."

The introduction of adult franchise after independence, the formation of linguistic provinces, the emergence of regional political parties and increasing literacy are among factors that have contributed to a considerable broadening of the readership base, and changes in the contents as well as the style of expression, in the Indian language Press. A landmark was the publication of a handbook by S. B. Adityan, editor of the highly successful 'Thanthi' chain of daily newspapers in Tamil. It provided guidance on how to write in simple language, for readers with a modicum of education. How Indian language journalism has both reflected and stimulated changes in popular usage was the theme of a Seminar on Modernisation of Indian Languages in News Media organised at Hyderabad in February 1978 by the Department of Linguistics of Osmania University.

Another major factor in the development of the Indian language Press in recent years has been the introduction of computerised typesetting technology. This has liberated the Indian language scripts from thraldom to metal typesetting which could not handle with elegance complex characters involving compound consonants and the like. It has become possible, thanks to the new technology, to combine speed in production with preservation of the identity and aesthetic appeal of the alphabets of Indian languages.

Creeping Commercialism

On the negative side, a disturbing trend in the Indian

Press after independence has been a creeping commercialisation which has eroded the concern for public interest, conceived in the broadest sense. This trend has gained momentum over the last decade, diminishing somewhat the validity of the tribute paid by the Second Press Commission, quoted earlier, to the role played newspapers. Advertisers, and the advertising agencies employed by them, are interested not only in the size of circulation of a newspaper but in the purchasing power of its readers. Many newspapers have tended to increase their appeal to the middle and upper classes by pandering to their Western-oriented interests and tastes, specially among the younger generation many of whom ape every changing Western fashion in hairdo, dress, eating habits and in the high-decibel noise that passes for music. Illustrative of this trend is the hiring of time in All India Radio's metro FM Channel by Bennett Coleman, publishers of the 'Times of India', to purvey pop and rap Western music to anglicised and Americanised youth.

Other instances of newspapers competing with Doordarshan in providing titillating fare are recent news reports such as 'Race on to find Europe's biggest bust' and 'Russian women complain they do not get enough sex.' Newspapers regularly carry pictures of exiguously clad beauty contestants, Indian and foreign, and of fashion shows featuring bizarre dresses. Such are the lengths to which even newspapers with a reputation to lose are prepared to go for maximising readership among the affluent, who have money to spend on the luxury goods and services advertised in the Press.

During the Indira Gandhi years, when the Government kept threatening the Press with enforcement of a news-to-advertisement ratio in newspaper space, even those among the radical intelligentsia who looked with disdain on conspicuous spending and consumerist advertising came to realise the importance of revenue from advertising for the survival of a free Press. Thus, an article in the 'Business Standard' supplement of 27th September, 1982, by G. N. S. Raghavan, who had just concluded his assignment as secretary of the Second Press Commission, said : "Before I had occasion to study the economics of newspaper publishing, I used to be upset by much of the advertising in our Press : the textile brand that will win the heart of the young woman or man of the reader's dreams; the portraits and eulogy of unknown founders of family-owned enterprises; the delights of bar, bed, board and swimming pool in five-star hotels (many of them in the public sector in our socialist democracy), and the matrimonial ads which seek to unite middle or upper class boy with middle or upper class girl.

"I know now that financial viability which requires substantial revenue from advertising, is essential for sustaining the freedom, and improving the quality, of a newspaper. Instead of feeling upset, I feel reassured by the profusion of ads in the best of our newspapers. Whether it is a daily or a journal of less frequent periodicity, the newspaper is the only commodity which is marketed at a price lower than the cost of production. Revenue from circulation has to be supplemented by advertising, to cover the balance of the cost and yield a surplus for growth and for qualitative improvement.

"It is useful to recall what the three Royal Commissions on the Press in Britain have had to say on advertising revenue and advertising space. The first, known as the Ross Commission after the chairman's name, said in its report of 1949 : 'As long as newspapers are sold to the public for less than they cost to produce, they will need a supplementary source of income. Of the various possible sources of income, the sale of their space to advertisers seems to us to be one of the least harmful. The income to be feared is that which comes from a concealed source and can be earned only by the sale of the editorial columns. It has been proposed that a limit should be set either to the amount of advertising a newspaper of a given size may carry, or to the amount of advertising revenue it may earn. We do not think that these proposals would necessarily achieve their ostensible object; in normal circumstances, their effect might merely be to drive advertisers to use other media than the Press.'

"The Shawcross Commission (1961-62) said : 'A diminution of Press advertising would mean that newspapers generally would economise by carrying fewer pages of editorial text.'

"The McGregor Commission (1974-77) said : 'Advertising is much the most important source of revenue for all classes of publication except for national popular newspapers and 'consumer' periodicals...Some advertising, especially classified, is as interesting to readers as editorial.'

"Finally, in the circumstances of media ownership in India, it may fairly be asked why the Press should be singled out for restrictions on advertisement revenue when State-owned radio and television have been making more and more money from commercial advertising."

While standing by all that has been stated above, the writer of the article now feels disturbed deeply by the thought that if the argument for maximising revenue is carried too far, matters might end up by the Press, too, deadening the social conscience, as Doordarshan is doing, by presenting the life style and interests of the well-to-do as the sole Indian reality.

A measure of the dualism in Indian society as reflected in the Press is the success in terms of circulation and revenue enjoyed by such periodicals meant for the leisured and affluent class as 'Femina' and 'Debonair', 'Women's Era' and 'Savvy', and 'Sports World' and 'Sports Star'. Even in daily newspapers, the emphasis is on the sensational and the transient rather than the basic problems of India such as mass poverty and mass illiteracy, and the pollution of the country's rivers and urban environment. A newspaper reader summed up the situation in a letter published in a letter to the editor published in the 'Indian Express', Delhi, of 4th August, 1995 : "Tonnes of precious newsprint are wasted daily by the Press to deify criminals, both killers and white-collar cheats like Harshad Mehta, Charles Sobhraj, Phoolan Devi, Rajan Pillai, Veerappan, Haji Mastan, Dawood Ibrahim and their ilk. But it is quick to forget Bofors or scams like the securities scandal. It only shows that the Press is in the business of entertainment, not setting the nation's agenda.

"V. P. Singh became Prime Minister on the Bofors plank, promising the nation not only to disclose the names of recipients of the kickbacks but also to recover for the national exchequer the entire bribe paid to secure the Howitzer deal. But the Press seems to have forgotten all about it.'

"P. V. Narasimha Rao had promised to punish the guilty, however high and mighty, in the securities scam. But the matter has been given a burial after the Prime Minister managed to secure a couple of contrived resignations. Not only are the scamsters going unpunished and the end users of the colossal slush funds remain unidentified, but even the allegedly guilty foreign banks have been let off the hook. And the Press in not bothered. What could be more glaring examples of doublethink and doublespeak ?"

Economism among journalists

At the individual level, among journalists, economism is the counterpart of the commercialism that has overtaken the bulk of newspaper publishers. The two trends have, between them, diminished the role of the Press in spreading knowledge and awakening the social conscience.

In the early, missionary phase of nationalist journalism, the wages and working conditions of journalists and other newspaper employees were, at best, modest. They depended on the fortunes of the patriotic publisher who was also often editor. By the 1930s, some nationalist newspapers began to do quite well : the 'Hindustan Times' for instance. Pothan Joseph as editor pressed for improvement of the emoluments of journalists, arguing that the publisher should share the newspaper's prosperity with those who made it possible. The management offered an increase in salary to the editor. Joseph, insisting that the entire journalist staff should be given a rise, walked out, accompanied by Edatata Narayanan, assistant editor.

Syed Abdullah Brelvi took the initiative to form the first association of journalists to secure improvement in wages and working conditions. The situation has changed beyond recognition after the Government sponsored the Working Journalists (Conditions of Service) Bill, which was supported by every political party on its introduction in Parliament in 1955 and was passed the same year.

The change is brought out vividly in a paper prepared for the Second Press Commission by Balraj Mehta, economic journalist. He said : "Once security of service has been assured and pay scales etc. have been made somewhat rewarding, the working journalists' movement and individual working journalists seem to have lost interest in improvement in professional work and standards in journalism. The Indian Federation of Working Journalists was essentially a trade union formation which was soon infected by the trend towards economism in the trade union movement in general.

"As part of the general trend towards divisions and splits in the trade union movement, and trade union rivalry precipitated largely by narrow political party affiliations, there emerged a rival working journalists' organisation, the National Union of Journalists (India) which, too, has been functioning in the style of the IFWJ. Working journalists now tended to operate as a lobby and not as a profession with its own standards, code of conduct and ethics. They began to hanker after privileges comparable to those of higher echelons of the bureaucracy."

This observation is even more apposite today than when it was made more than a decade ago. When, in April 1986, the Wage Board headed by Justice (Retd.) Bachawat recommended interim relief at the rate of 7.5% of basic wages, subject to a minimum of Rs. 45 per month, the Government in response to pressure from unions of journalists and others, doubled the quantum of interim relief to 15% and the minimum to Rs. 90 per month. The clamour of journalists' unions became so loud that on 22nd October, 1991, speaking at the Madras Press Club, the then I and B Minister, Ajit Kumar Panja, felt constrained to advise newspapermen to evolve their own methods to get wage board awards implemented. This was in response to suggestions from journalists' organisations that Government should withhold its advertisements and newsprint quotas to force the hands of newspaper managements. Any such attempt, the Minister said, could be interpreted as muzzling the Press.

On the part of journalists of the top level, namely editors, economism manifests itself in a fortune-hunting movement from well-paid to better-paid position, with the policy if any of the new employer being of little consequence. For promoting the publisher's interest in maximising circulation, some editors resort to sensationalism. One of its consequences is the blurring of the distinction between news and views. This imposes on the reader the task of gleaning the news from the comment. For example, the opening paragraph of the lead story in the Delhi edition of a newspaper chain on 28th March 1993 read : "The Surajkund A.I.C.C. session saw the Congress sliding back on Saturday to its days of decadent loyalism as dissent was stifled, and the nomination culture reintroduced by all the Prime Minister's men who were determined to have everything their way down the line. They put all their might together to hijack the dissidents' resolution on the one-man-one-post issue and replace it with a harebrained motion leaving it all to Mr. Narasimha Rao." Two days later : "New Delhi.—The Congress leadership, increasingly faced with allegations of wrong-doing, did a neat trick at the just concluded Surajkund meeting of the All India Congress Committee by rejecting an amendment seeking a declaration from all Ministers and Judges of their assets. The amendment to the political resolution, moved by Congress M.P. Inderjit on corruption, was rejected by Mr. Sharad Pawar, who had moved the political resolution, on the specious ground that the amendment was more appropriate to the economic resolution."

The search for enlarged circulation takes the form also of peddling soft pornography and of other forms of appealing to the lowest common denominator of popular interest such as astrological predictions, and imported cartoon strips even if they are racist like the Tarzan series, or if the words in the balloons, translated into an Indian language, sound incongruous.

These manifestations of commercialism on the part of newspaper publishers and of economism on the part of journalists have evoked anguished comment from journalists of integrity and public men concerned about the moral health of the Press as an important limb of a democratic polity. Several of them referred to the disclosure of large payments made from public funds to some journalists, and to institutions floated by them, by Mulayam Singh Yadav of the Bahujan Samaj Party during his tenure as Chief Minister of Uttar Pradesh.

In the course of the D.R. Mankekar Memorial Lecture delivered on 5th August, 1995 in New Delhi, N.A. Palkhivala, eminent jurist, expressed regret at the fact that the main aim of most journals and newspapers today is to increase circulation, which has resulted in the lowering of standards.

A columnist wrote in the *'Indian Express'*, Delhi, of 13th August 1995 : "Journalists have been getting their free lunches and free safari suits for the last couple of decades at least. The first signs of the changing nature of corruption in Indian journalism came with the rise of new industrial houses trying to make it to the top in the licence-permit raj. They needed to control both the politicians and the media...What ought to be happening in the legislatures—critically examining the government's policies, exposing its wrong doings and holding it accountable, taking it to task for the corruption of its ministers and bureaucrats—is today expected to be done by newspapers. Hence the yearning of the public for investigative reports. The Arun Shouri phenomenon is partly explained by this displacement of the political opposition."

A journalist who interviewed the new Chairman of the Press Council, Justice (Retd.) P.B. Sawant, quoted him as saying that unfortunately there have been occasions when the Press has blacked out vital information. Deploring the edging out of everything else by politics, he said : "We should look forward to the day when politics will be relegated to the second and the third position."

Mahendra V. Desai, veteran journalist who is Oxford-educated but belongs to the Gandhian school, said in the course of an article in the *'Indian Express'* of 18th August, 1995 : "Thanks to the gifts of cash and real estate by Mr. Mulayam Singh Yadav, the names of some journalists and editors in Lucknow and Delhi are mud. They have been found only too willing to be bribed...News manipulation is a legacy of the British, was resurrected during Mrs. Gandhi's Emergency, and has now been upgraded to a fine art. As a result, never has the credibility and accountability of journalists sunk so low....So it remains to be seen what the professional journalist is prepared to do to make Justice P.B. Sawant's tenure (as chairman of the Press Council) a success rather than a sinecure."

Cross-media ownership

The diversification of the business of some major newspaper houses into television is a recent development which calls for attention both as to the causes and the possible consequences of cross-media ownership. The facts relating to the share of newspapers in total advertising expenditure in the country reveal a decline (even if advertising revenue of the Press has gone up in absolute terms). This clearly points to the desire to secure a bigger slice of the advertising cake as the motivation for diversification.

In its report (1985) the Bachawat Wage Board for journalist and non-journalist newspaper employees said in para 42 of Chapter III : "With all-round growth, classified advertisements and public notices including statutory ones are bound to go up in number and volume. The apprehension about future growth of advertisement revenue in the context of competition from TV and radio are not well-founded. Experience of the West shows that, while initially print media lost some market share to TV, in recent years electronic and print media are developing together without any devastating competition. In fact, advertising market share growth of the electronic media has to some extent stagnated, and the value of newspaper as advertisement carrier is more appreciated. In India too, the share of ads of durables and industrial goods on TV has found some decline in 1987-88 over 1986-87. Furthermore, the fact remains that advertisement on TV being a costly affair is more or less a monopoly of certain leading advertisers. Others have necessarily to depend upon the print media. Superiority of print media also lies in its portability, durability and convenience. Finally, the increasing share of advertisement revenue in total revenue, as represented by rise in proportion of advertisement revenue to non-advertisement revenue, from 130.47 in 1983-84 to 143.61% in 1987-88 further testifies to the future growth potential of advertisement revenue."

This prognosis has proved to be somewhat over-optimistic. The scenario is complex. The Indian experience has been an exception to the tendency in recent years in many parts of the world for newspaper circulations to fall, parallel with the growth of television. Though the expansion of television in India has been spectacular (from 3.6 million sets in 1984, when the system of annual licensing of television sets was abolished, to 30.8 million in 1991 and nearly 50 million by mid 1995), the circulation of daily newspapers has also gone up steadily, from 22.64 million in 1990 to 29.49 million in 1993 (the latest year for which data of the Registrar of Newspapers are available). However, the growth of the advertisement revenue of Doordarshan has been faster than that of the Press. From 15.9 crores in 1982 it shot up to Rs. 136.3 crores in 1987; 300.6 crores in 1992; 360.2 crores in 1993; and Rs. 398 crores in 1994. In contrast, though the absolute figure of advertisement revenue of the Press has been higher than that of Doordarshan in each of these years, the relative share of the Press in total advertising outlay in the country has been going down while the relative share of Doordarshan has gone up. Total advertising outlay in the country was estimated to have been about Rs. 1,000 crores in 1987-88; and in 1993-94, Rs. 2,500 crores. The following table, based on figures given in 'Doordarshan 1995', a brochure produced by the Audience Research Unit of Doordarshan, brings out the relative share of the major advertising media including the Press and Doordarshan :

						(percentage share)
Year	*Press*	*DD*	*Satellite/ video*	*Radio*	*Cinema*	*Outdoor*
1985	75	12	—	4	3	6
1992	67	18	2	2.5	0.5	10
1993	66	17	4	2	—	11

There are two points to be kept in mind while appraising the above figures. First, newspapers recover only a part of the direct cost of production from their revenue through sale of copies, and advertisement revenue is what they rely on to pay their way. Doordarshan, in contrast (like All India Radio), has its hand in the taxpayers' pocket. The extent of support from public funds for Indian television will be evident from the fact that Doordarshan's budget for 1994-95 was Rs. 957.32 crores, as against the commercial earnings of only Rs. 398 crores.

Secondly, Doordarshan's earning from advertisements is not to be equated with what Indian advertisers spend in order to reach Indian audiences through the television medium. They spent nearly Rs. 150 crores on advertisements in programmes made by private producers in India and telecast by Doordarshan. This figure, however, is only a rough estimate since private producers allow discounts on the amounts shown in their rate cards. Also, Indian-owned Zee Television, uplinked abroad but addressed mainly to India via satellite channel, is estimated to have earned Rs. 130 crores during 1994-95 from Indian advertisers. It may be assumed therefore that total spending by Indian advertisers through the television medium is now of the order of at least Rs. 650 crores.

It is the pulling power of television as an advertisement medium, with its capacity for lively demonstration of the virtues of a product or service, which accounts for the edge that this medium has over the static print medium. But the newspaper has its own plus points, as S.C. Bhatt effectively brings out in the ensuing section of this Chapter.

The discerning citizen likes to have more than one Sanjaya reporting and interpreting to him the Mahabharata war that is being fought in various spheres of life, from politics and economics to sports and the battle for gender equality. The viewer who has watched the live telecast of a cricket match, and heard the expert commentators on television or radio, still likes to read the story of the contest as narrated in the next morning's newspaper, even as students of current affairs find it useful and necessary to read more than one newspaper.

Moreover, in the Indian context the Press has enjoyed the great advantage of credibility which Doordarshan, as a monopoly run by the Central Government, has sadly lacked in its news and current affairs programmes. But things can change in the not remote future. The Supreme Court directed in its judgment of 9th February, 1995 that an independent public authority should be established to regulate broadcasting in the public interest, as distinct from the interest of the government of the day. If and when this is done (the apex court set no time limit), the news and current affairs programmes of a truly autonomous Doordarshan (or Prasar Bharati if it is so rechristened) can become a real rival to newspapers.

The threat of competition from television to newspapers is likely to be even stronger if there emerge private television channels, specially at regional level. In order to pick up a share of the advertising revenue that has got diverted from the Press to Doordarshan, some leading newspaper establishments have already entered the television field : e.g. Bennett Coleman which runs the 'Times of India'; 'Hindustan Times'; and 'India Today'. These television ventures of newspaper groups have served a good purpose. They have brought a whiff of fresh air and the professional touch to Doordarshan's programmes, which are made by men and women who may not lack talent but who have to work under the watchful eyes of bureaucrats and politicians. But there is also a danger in a closer nexus between the Press and television media. It is the danger of a condominium being established over public opinion by the print and electronic wings of communication barons.

A scenario is of the 'Eenadu' group of newspapers in Andhra Pradesh opening a television channel in Telugu, offering both entertainment and news, or only news and current affairs programmes. As a television channel not dependent on government funding, and with proven professional competence, an Eenadu television channel is likely to prove quite a success in competition with the Telugu wing of a public television service. Is such a development desirable, considering that 85% of newspaper readers in Andhra Pradesh are already Eenadu readers ? This is not to say that the print and electronic wings of the Eenadu group will necessarily play favourites, or show bias, but to point to the danger inherent in such a situation. Similar scenarios can be visualised in respect of other linguistic regions.

The challenge is to find ways of ensuring that competent communication professionals can find entry into, and prove their worth in, the media whether print or electronic. This will be possible only if there are a number of competing organisations that are potential employers of men and women of talent with dedication to the public good.

There should be no monopoly, whether in the public sector or the private. A situation of near-monopoly in influencing public opinion, through cross-media ownership in the private sector, will be as bad as the government monopoly in radio and television that has prevailed so far.

Impact of Television on the Press *by S.C. Bhatt**

Like some other things in our country, the media scene has been changing fast, particularly in the past few years, and the Press is naturally affected. Until 1984, the urban middle class had the option of seeing Doordarshan programmes or beguiling themselves with listening to the radio, reading newspapers and magazines or books, or calling on one another and socialising in the traditional manner. In that year, enterprising cable TV operators in

* Excerpted from Part II of 'History of Indian Journalism' (revised and updated), being brought out by the Publications Division, New Delhi.

Bombay city and some parts of Gujarat brought the latest as well as old feature films to the viewers in the afternoon hours when Doordarshan would be availing of a long siesta. By 1990, the cable operations had spread to other parts of the country, and in the following year satellite TV made its appearance. This was through the courtesy of the cable people who, by installing a dish antenna, could get more subscribers for their services by disseminating the satellite channels; and the latter were happy that they got viewers through the cable.

The options now available to viewers made more and more people go in for a TV set even if they had to make other sacrifices in their family budget, and the TV antenna became a familiar sight in the cities and towns as well as many villages. Of the 45.68 million sets in the country by the end of 1994, urban people had 29.71 million and the rural people accounted for 15.71 million. In terms of percentage of the population, the rural areas were lagging much behind their urban counterparts, with less TV sets in villages though they hold a higher proportion of the Indian population. But the nation's half-a-million villages were trying not to be left far behind in the race.

Both DD and the satellite channels have increased their output of programmes and there is a rivarly, often assuming unhealthy proportions, between the national network and the Indian or foreign satellite channels and their cable collaborators. We are concerned here not with the ethics and other problems of this rivalry, often called a cultural invasion of India, but with the impact TV has been having on the print medium.

Newspapers have registered substantial growth in terms both of circulation and the number of publications coming out (although quite a few are also closing down.) But the growth of television is definitely faster. Will TV swamp newspapers and lead to the closure of many of them, as has happened in several Western countries ? The Indian Newspaper Society (INS) said in its 1993-94 report : "The liberalisation policies of the government have opened many avenues for the electronic media which has resulted in the commissioning of multiple channels on Doordarshan and also that of foreign TV networks in the country. This, along with video and cable TV, is a major challenge for press advertising as a good part of advertising which otherwise would have gone to the print media is being diverted to the electronic medium." The report goes on to say that the Society has launched a campaign to stress the benefits of press advertising.

Foreign print media have been kept out of India, for the time being at least, but foreign satellite TV channels are having a field day. Although the national network has taken a series of measures to meet their competition, in the process it has made quite a few compromises too. Advertising revenue, which sustains the Press as well as TV, goes out of the country through ads released on the foreign channels by Indian advertisers, including Indian brands of liquor addressed to viewrs in India watching the foreign channels. The impact of the entertainment-oriented TV medium on the Press can also be measured in terms of the reach of the two media. According to a survey, this reach is higher for TV in almost all areas of the country except Kerala where the Press has a greater reach, and radio even greater than either TV or the Press.

The easier-to-watch TV medium has also other advantages like demonstrability of the consumer durables or fast-moving consumer goods advertised on TV. You cannot show, or make a show of, the effectiveness of a brand of detergent or toothpaste as well as you can do it on the TV. So, what is the remedy and, as we asked earlier, what is the future for the print medium ?

Some stalwarts of the print medium have in a way found their own solution. For some time now, recognising the power of the visual medium, they have begun diversifying their media business and sought to get for themselves a slice of the growing TV cake. The 'Times of India' group, a front-runner in the print media, is trying hard to make a niche for itself in the television sphere too. Its Times TV has several programmes to its credit and, what is more, it has shed its adversary attitude to Doordarshan, a government organ. It marketed the live telecast of the World Cup of Football for Doordarshan in 1994 and also the three-nation one-day cricket matches among India, West Indies and New Zealand as well as the India-West Indies Series in the same year. The 'Hindustan Times', its arch rival, has also acquired a TV image with its Eye Witness programme, featured regularly on DD-2, after the video magazine experiment failed. It has other serials to its name. 'India Today' also gave up the video newsmagazine experiment and chose DD-2 for a weekly display of its 'Newstrack' programme.

The list is quite impressive although the large majority of newspapers, particularly the Indian language papers, have been untouched by the sudden spurt of TV. While most newspapers, for reasons not difficult to fathom, have not ventured into the TV arena, the more ambitious and business-minded have been casting about for collaboration with foreign channels, or owning a channel.

In many countries newspapers have entered the TV area. Rupert Murdoch, one of the big operators who owns Star TV and 49.5% of Zee, branched out into TV via newspapers. India is thus not a solitary example of this phenomenon of the print media giants, or even small ones, pushing themselves into the TV business. In some of the advanced countries the growth of TV has wiped out many a flourishing newspaper because the ad revenue was not enough to sustain both the local TV station and a modern-day newspaper. In India the share of the Press in the total budget of Indian advertisers has declined—in eight years from 1985 to 1993—by nine percentage points (from 75% to 66%), while the share of TV (taking Doordarshan and satellite/video together) has increased over the same period from 12% to 21%. Radio has lost much of its share and now has only 2% as against 4% eight years ago, while outdoor publicity has gone up from 6% to 11%, with a wide range of messages coming to you on the streets from hoardings, banners, kiosks, busboards and even from balloons up in the sky.

The Press's total advertising revenue has indeed been going up, but what should have gone to it, if the TV were not there as a rival and potentially more attractive proposition, has gone to the new medium. Over the years, if this trend continues, what will happen to newspapers ? Interestingly, the big papers have not been affected and, in fact, never had it so good. Their ad revenues have been rising substantially, so much so that in Delhi at least the big ones—'Hindustan Times', 'Times of India' and 'Indian Express'—slashed their subscription rates to just Rs. 1.50 per copy except on one day of the week. Retaining and increasing the circulation is vital, because that helps the papers to hike the ad rates again and again and thus offset decline in circulation revenue.

The spurt in the ad revenues, specially of the big papers, owes not only to the fact that the rates are higher but because they are the chosen medium for classified advertisements, company notices including announcement of new capital issues, appointments and like. The display ads may not be as repetitive as on TV, but TV can hardly put out classified ads, matrimonials, wanted ads, job announcements, property sale and car sale and the like. Television cannot announce company meetings and carry detailed speeches of company chairmen. It can at best carry motivational ads on new capital issues, but it cannot put out ads on jobs in any significant manner. Is it possible to imagine young hopefuls sitting by their TV sets and lapping up notices of job opportunities ? But you can see them checking out ads in newspapers, in a friend's house or in a library if their own paper has not carried it.

The print medium is a medium of record, and what it publishes remains there for some time. It is possible to refer to it even after a gap of time. So, TV cannot hope to take away from the newspapers ads of the kind in which there is no scope for colour, nor need for demonstration of a product as in consumer advertisements. It is this area where the print medium will continue to enjoy a distinct advantage until, of course, some more technological advance comes up with new devices (hopefully not, the papers would say.) Much of this advantage will go to the big papers, which are already reaping it in a big way.

But the decline in the proportion of the press in total advertising will become steeper if TV has more and more channels, both indigenous and foreign. The competition even among the TV channels is so strong that some of them are shedding their inhibitions about liquor ads. There is, of course, the big question of the size of the overall advertisement budget. It has gone up substantially in recent years because of the coming in of multinationals trying to sell their products to Indian consumers, and the general growth of the economy. The foreigners are in the consumer market in a big way; some of them were already here, like Hindustan Lever, and others have entered the country in the past few years of liberalisation. Already as many as six of the top ten advertisers of DD are multinationals, including marketing companies which often sell goods made by multinational companies. If the liberalisation trend continues and if the economy keeps growing at about five per cent or more, the advertising cake can only become bigger. No wonder the big newspapers are the biggest supporters of the liberalisation process.

But one may ask : will the papers not be affected by the rising trend of TV watching ? In other words, will not the newspapers decline in circulation ? At what point will a daily newspaper become redundant ? We have seen how even in advanced countries where the literacy level is very high, almost a hundred per cent, the TV habit has led to the closure of many papers, even the big newspapers. Advertisements and circulation are closely related, and if ad revenue falls this would both be an indication of decline in circulation and, by reducing the resources at the disposal of the paper, cause a fall in circulation too.

In the advanced countries the TV is largely free of government control and the viewer has the satisfaction of getting a more or less complete picture of the day's happenings and multifaceted presentation of different points of view, with visuals and interviews with the main characters of the day's drama, as only TV can. This has helped TV replace the common man's newspaper. On the other hand, the local paper, announcing the daily sales in the big department stores and supermarkets (full-page ads of price slashes in big type) is of interest to the housewife. The white-collar worker has neither the time nor the need for a newspaper. If at all, he browses through a magazine while commuting to and from office. The serious-minded reader and the intellectual, the researcher and the journalist, would certainly buy a serious-minded paper if it can support itself with adequate advertisements and is backed by a dynamic management.

Indian TV has yet to reach that stage where it leaves the viewer more or less completely satisfied about the day's coverage, so that he would not feel the need for his paper next morning. When that stage will arrive is a difficult question to answer, but the alluring options now being offered to the TV viewers, and which are being lauded by the leading English newspapers, give the audience much to enjoy and learn. DD is also throwing open its gates fairly wide and if autonomy becomes a reality and there are options and alternatives in informative and educative programmes as well as entertainment, TV can certainly look forward to the day when both the entertainment-seeker and the discerning viewer who mixes his entertainment with information may be assured of satisfaction.

The TV medium has not only arrived; it is also full of potential and the variety it offers, with strong emphasis on entertainment, cannot be matched by the print medium. The electronic media in India had long suffered from lack of competition which is the soul of good programmes, as much as competition is the soul of a good newspaper seeking to keep ahead of its rivals in bringing to readers the news first, along with interesting and entertaining features. The foreign electronic media may have sophistication but, contrary to what some of our English newspapers propound, their newscasts are, by and large, not relevant to the Indian situation biased as they are in favour of the United States, other Western nations and Pakistan in its endless quarrels with India.

Newspapers cannot hope to compete with the TV medium in the area of entertainment but newspapers can be close to the people and their lives. If some children die of defective vaccine being administered, the local press can convey the tragedy vividly. Radio and TV can do it even more effectively but neither radio nor TV have become sufficiently local, and the foreign media just do not care for such developments except carrying a few visuals on the day of the happening.

Therefore, serious newspapers with an all-India appeal can still offer features, comments, interpretative and investigative reports that no TV channel, however autonomous it may be, can hope to do. Local newspapers seeking to reflect the events in their region can also pose a challenge to the entertainment-oriented TV medium if they know how to do it.

3 FILMS THEN AND NOW

The Lumiere Brothers of France held the first cinematograph show in India at Watson's Hotel in Bombay on 7th July 1896. The admission fee was one rupee, whose value at that time was immensely more than of the rupee today.

A Synoptic Survey

Indian pioneers began to use the cinema camera from 1899 and made short films. The first silent feature film was produced in 1912, in Bombay, and the novel medium soon spread to other centres. The themes of most of the early films, as of plays on the dramatic stage of that time, were religious and mythological. Outstanding among films of the silent era was 'Satyawadi Raja Harischandra', made in 1913 by Dadasaheb Phalke. As a tribute to his memory, an annual award was instituted in 1970 by the Ministry of Information and Broadcasting to honour individuals who have made a significant contribution to the enrichment of different aspects of Indian cinema.

Sound was added to image in 1931, when India's first talkie 'Alam Ara' was made. This was in Hindi, and was followed by talkies in other languages. Around the 1940's, many memorable films were made in great studios under great banners : for example, Bombay Talkies, New Theatres, Wadia Movietone, AVM Productions and Gemini International.

Alongside mythological themes, films began to deal with

issues of social reform and of economic justice that were propagated, along with patriotism, by many leaders of the national movement. The concern with problems of society continued into the early post-independence period. Illustrative titles of such films are 'Achoot Kanya' and 'Do Bigha Zamin'.

The growth of regional cinema was most pronounced in the south. In the late 1940's the south's bugle sounded all over India with Gemini's 'Chandralekha'. And the 1950's saw Hindi cinema reaching great heights of creativity and popular appeal. The cinema-going habit became widespread. So much so that Prime Minister Jawaharlal Nehru said at a film seminar organised by the Sangeet Natak Akademi in New Delhi on 27th February 1955 : "I think it is perfectly correct to say that the influence of the films in India is greater than the influence of newspapers and books combined."

A new wave of low-budget art films began to be produced in different regions of the country since the 1970's, stimulated by the phenomenon of Satyajit Ray. It has been said that he "changed the face of the Indian film with his lyrical, humanist, uncompromising style and gave it a permanent place in world cinema." (1995 calendar, on the theme of 'Hundred years of cinema', produced by the Directorate of Advertising and Visual Publicity.)

The lyrical quality of camera work in Ray's films was enhanced by the music. Ray, who had listened to much Western classical music as a college student, went to Santiniketan for a course in fine arts. He has said : "My three years in Santiniketan opened my eyes and ears to our artistic and musical heritage so that, in addition to buying records of symphonies and concerts, I was now regularly going to concerts of Indian classical music."

This was in line with the very important place of music in the appeal of Indian films ever since the advent of talkies. In the era before the advent of playback singers, ability to sing well was an essential qualification for becoming a film hero or heroine. K.L. Saigal and K.C. Dey, K.B. Sundarambal and M.S. Subbulakshmi are among outstanding singers who have acted in films.

After the technology of film making enabled actor or actress to borrow another's voice, the quality of music continued to be high till the near-total commercialisation of the film industry from the 1980's led to a steep all-round decline in all departments of film-making. The corruption of Hindi film music forms the theme of an article contributed to this volume by Harbans Bahadur Mathur, a sensitive observer of the media scene.

Since the 1980's Indian cinema has had a mixed record, with negative features increasingly outweighing the positive. The quality of the film industry's output is as uneven as the quantity is large. (The Central Board of Film Certification scrutinises more than 800 feature films each year.) Some of them—like 'Anand', 'Garm Hawa' and 'Manthan'—deal sensitively with problems of the individual and of society, and do the country proud. Several—like 'Chalti ka nam gadi'—offer harmless even if mindless fun. Many are tear-jerking counterparts, on celluloid, of sentimental and romantic novels. Far too many are made to a formula of melodrama, sadistic violence and crude sex. They are an assault on aesthetic sensibility, and have a brutalising and vulgarising effect on viewers.

Lewd and inane love songs are a feature of films of the last category. Besides being heard inside cinema halls, they are disseminated outside through audio cassettes and television—by cable operators, through foreign satellite channels, and sometimes even by government-run Doordarshan. Citizens should undoubtedly be free to hear such songs on tape-recorders within their homes, even as they should be free to read pornographic literature or view pornographic films in privacy. But the playing of such songs in public places through loudspeakers, like Doordarshan bringing lewd scenes and music into drawing rooms where members of a family together watch television, is on an altogether different footing.

The blare of lewd music through loudspeakers in passenger buses plying on Delhi roads is a measure of the pervasiveness of vulgarity. Two years ago the Police Commissioner of Delhi issued orders prohibiting any music on loudspeakers within buses. But the ban has been flouted with impunity by drivers of the chartered buses that carry Delhi's babus, male and female, to and back from the offices of government departments and public sector undertakings, as well as the Red Line and other privately operated buses used by the general public. The most frequently played songs include : one in which a man proclaims that his pants are sexy, his shirt is sexy, etc.; another in which a girl tells her boy friend that she pretended to go to the temple and thus slipped out of her home to meet him; and yet another in which boy and girl, both college students, demand that love should be made part of the curriculum.

So much for the coarsening of sensibility, aesthetic and moral, through the propagation of sex-laden film songs. Violence is the other bane of most feature films. Fight scenes, often unspeakably sadistic, have come to be an essential part of the formula for success at the box office. The effect of violence in films, viewed in movie hall or on the television screen, has been exactly the same in India as in Western countries where society became media-saturated much earlier. It has bred copycat violence on the part of the young and immature.

Newspapers have been reporting with chilling regularity a variety of crimes—robbery, rape and murder—in which the techniques employed were learnt from films. The latest instance is a report carried by *Indian Express* (Delhi, 19th July, 1995) of the confession by a 17-year-old, who had allegedly killed another youth of the same age, that he got the idea of swapping identity with the victim from the film 'Raghuveer'. Mehboob is said to have strangled Devraj to death and proceeded to behead the victim and chop off his genitals so that he could pass off the victim as himself (absence of circumcision would have belied the assertion). According to the report, Mehboob's father identified the corpse as being his son's.

What does the Board of Film Certification have to say

to this ? The corruption rampant in this Board, and other reasons for its ineffectiveness, were frankly narrated by Kamla Mankekar and Jaya Jaitley, both of whom have been members of the Board, at the Seminar on Vulgarity and Violence in the Media conducted by the Centre for Media Studies in New Delhi in September 1994 (see Chapter VIII).

On the effect of the depiction of violence on young minds, Jawaharlal Nehru said at the 1955 film seminar to which reference has been made earlier : "Broadly speaking, one should not restrict and interfere. But the State has to interfere to an extent in some activities. I might mention the case, let us say, of what are called horror comics....A very mild type happened to be sent as a birthday gift to my grandson. Looking at it I was horrified that anyone, much less my grandson, should have that kind of literature to read. The horror comics are something which, I am absolutely clear in my mind, should be suppressed ruthlessly. They are a hundred per cent bad, and they are causing, in some countries, all kinds of sadistic impulses, like children just murdering for murder's sake, to have the pleasure of seeing a person killed. Obviously, no government or society ought to allow that kind of thing to flourish."

In contrast, Nehru's successors in the office of Prime Minister have not only been acquiescing, through a lax censorship system, in the spread of the cult of violence by commercial feature films; they have, by permitting the screening of such films by government-run Doordarshan, actively promoted the cult of violence. A nexus between politicians in power and big money in the film industry has been widely suspected. There has been criticism, in this context, of the Government's choice of a film producer to head the Central Board of Film Certification. Appointed as a member of the Board from 7th October, 1991, Shakti Samanta looked after the duties of Chairman from 1st April 1991 and has served as Chairman from 4th September 1992.

Film industry X-rayed

The economics of film production and the factors making for competitive vulgarity, on the one hand, and the nexus between big money in the film industry and some government authorities, on the other, are analysed in the eighth report (December 1994) of the Standing Committee on Communication of the Tenth Lok Sabha. Following are excerpts from the report :

"A gradual decline is manifest in the quality of commercial films, both subject-wise and content-wise. Scenes of crime, excessive violence, cruelty and unrelated sex are on the increase in Indian films, which cast an adverse influence on the people, particularly the youth. Repeated projection of such scenes creates a dehumanising effect on the people and makes them insensitive to cruelty, perversion and corruption in society.

"Film making has become a highly commercial activity, where the investor naturally seeks to recoup the finance involved in the production of a film. Prices of every commodity required for film making have been going up year after year, including the payments made to film stars. In course of evidence, the film industry has also mentioned about a host of difficulties faced by them such as high entertainment tax rates in some States, excise and other duties on raw stock and equipment as well as on film prints, the video boom and challenges posed by satellite television, etc. At the same time, cinema halls are closing down and some of them are being converted into market complexes which make them more profitable.

"Since film financing is not treated on par with other business activities which can obtain funds from financial institutions in order to attract investors, film producers are banking on 'surefire' formula, which in simple terms means projection of sex and violence so as to be assured of some returns on such huge investments incurred. It is also a general experience that the small-budget films, sometimes experimental and path-breaking, produced with less known artists, find no takers. Today, if the producer has to sell his film he has to go in for top stars by paying exorbitant fees, which forces him to raise his finance at usurious rate of interest to make big-budget production. The vicious circle almost strangulates the film producers.

"Further, there has been a lot of criticism in recent years regarding alleged nexus between the underworld, film producers, law enforcers, etc. Huge amounts of black money are being reportedly poured in, to finance film production.

"Some of the members of the film industry, in course of evidence tendered before the Committee, argued that if sex and violence can be shown through foreign television networks, Indian networks should not be barred. The Committee are unable to accept the contention of a section of the film industry that Indian films should also be allowed to show sex and violence like foreign films and television networks. Its acceptance would mean allowing competition in vulgarity. The Committee feel that some of the scenes, particularly the dance sequences in several recent films, are extremely vulgar and repulsive. In India, trends are being set which do not reflect the realities of Indian society. Box office success of a film cannot be taken as an index of popular demand, and popular demand by itself cannot confer justification on something which is patently pernicious. In the name of modernisation, one is today witnessing erosion of traditional Indian values, folk art and culture. The Committee are strongly of the view that the basic moral values of our rich Indian tradition should not be allowed to be compromised, eroded or diluted at any cost. With the opening of the skies and unrestricted beaming of TV programmes from different parts of the world, the challenge that Indian film industry faces today is how to blend the changing realities all around the world with the imperatives of Indian cultural values and traditions. There is also a larger question as to how to guard against films which may pose a danger to the social fabric and communal harmony, and encourage films which foster and harness the edifice of a pluralistic society. The task is also for checking against films which have a baneful influence on children and adolescents.

"The Committee feel that there is a need to formulate a comprehensive national film policy. Films, even as entertainment medium, must contribute to refining sensibility, elevating standards and ennobling values. The high cost of film production should not be allowed to become an alibi for lowering and debasing standards and tastes."

M.P.s' Strictures on Censors

The minutes of the Standing Committee's meeting held on 29th October, 1993 include the following : 'As regards the role and composition of the Central Board of Film Certification, the Committee showed their dissatisfaction, especially over the manner of selection of the members of the Board, the number of meetings being held by the members per year, their actual attendance, and non-adherence to the guidelines given by the Ministry while censoring films, etc."

After taking further evidence, the Standing Committee recorded in its report : "The Committee were informed that only four meetings of the CBFC (with a membership, excluding the Chairman, ranging from 22 to 27 at different points of time) have been held since 1990. The names of places of the meetings, and the number of members who attended, are given below :

1.	Bombay (April 1990)	19
2.	Bangalore (June 1990)	16
3.	Madras (March 1992)	20
4.	Hyderabad (March 1993)	14

'According to Rule 14 of the Cinematograph Rules, 1983, the Board should ordinarily meet once every quarter for the transaction of business. They regret to note that in clear violation of the rules, only four meetings of the Board were held during the past four years. The Committee desire that the provision in the rules should be strictly adhered to in future. Further, the Committee note that majority of the members who attended such meetings were the persons from film industry only.

"The Committee observe that in a large number of cases the film certifications are awarded without even any member of the CBFC having seen the film. The Regional Officer, who is a government officer, constitutes the

Examining Committee and in practice the entire powers of the CBFC are exercised by him. Therefore, more than the Chairman or any other members of the Board, the opinion of the CBFC is controlled by a government officer appointed as the Regional Officer. The Committee strongly feel that this practice needs to be improved with a view to make members of the Board and Advisory Panels more active and accountable for their decisions. The Committee therefore recommend a radical overhaul of the Rules so as to ensure that the central figure responsible for setting up of the Examining and Revising Committees is some member of the CBFC.

"During the course of evidence, the Committee were informed that the CBFC and Regional Panel members work in an honorary capacity. They are paid a token 'sitting fee'. The amount is insufficient even to cover conveyance expenses. Therefore there is no attraction for the members to attend the meetings of these committees. The Committee recommend that the amount of the fees should be suitably increased so as to give some incentive to the members to attend the meetings of these committees.

"The Committee note that quite a good number of films of one region get certification from the other regional centres. A Member of Parliament in a written note to the Committee stated : 'I remember once a lady member on the Board from north, not knowing Tamil, was viewing a Tamil film, only by inquiring about the film from her fellow-member. I do not know what justice she could have done to this invaluable job.' Keeping in view the multilingual, multi-cultural realities of Indian society, the Committee feel that the social-cultural implication of films on society can best be judged and assessed by people who understand the language of that film. It may therefore be ensured that majority of members of the Examining Committee or the Revising Committee who examine or review a film must understand the language of that film."

How corrupt practices can vitiate the work of the CBFC can be inferred from a set of DO's and DON'Ts prepared for the guidance of members of Advisory Panels and the

Board. Item 13 of the DOs reads : "Do inform the Chairman promptly if ever you are approached by any applicant in connection with the certification of a film." Items 5 and 6 of the DON'Ts read : "No member shall accept any gift or any other obligation from any producer/director or anybody having connections with films. Under no circumstances are members to grant a hearing on the telephone or grant interviews to film producers or directors or anyone else whose film is under consideration for certification by the Board."

Decline of Hindi Film Music *by H.B. Mathur*

The fierce controversy about the alleged obscenity of 'Choli Ke Peechche' and a few other songs from some Hindi films has tended to obscure the more serious crisis that has been stalking Hindi film music since the mid-eighties and has suddenly overtaken it in the course of recent years, viz. the decline and fall of film music as an art form and as a source of aesthetic delight.

Indian film music, like Indian cinema itself, had its origin in the Indian theatre that was firmly based in the classical traditions of song, dance and drama. Film music in its formative years turned to the rich heritage of the classical as well as folk streams for inspiration and found its own distinctive form in a happy blend of the two, creating a contemporary idiom for traditional Indian music.

The ascent of Hindi film music reached its peak in the fifties and sixties, helped by a propitious teaming up of some of the finest song writers, music makers and singers. The verses of poets like Sahir Ludhianvi and Kaifi Azmi, the lyrics composed by gifted musicians like S.D. Burman and Naushad and the voices of versatile songsters like Kishore Kumar and Lata Mangeshkar came dramatically together to produce a body of music that captured audiences all over the country from the teenagers of Bombay and Delhi to the tribals of Tawang. The artistic opulence of Hindi film songs coincided with, and drew sustenance from, the renaissance that Indian classical and folk music were enjoying in that period; and in turn contributed to the furtherance of this phenomenon. At its best, Hindi film music combined the rich emotional and experiential variety of the Indian folk and the depth and flight of the Indian classical music.

This marriage of Hindi film music with the classical and traditional music forms, and its identification with the higher forms of creative activity in the country, was suddenly disrupted in the mid-eighties by two developments. The departure of great music-makers like Sahir and Kishore Kumar from the Bombay film scene; and the destruction of the hunger and taste of audiences everywhere for meaning and musicality in film songs by the new craze for the visually attractive and the spectacular, fostered by the general movement away from the audio to video formats in the emerging communication and entertainment culture. This new culture looked upon all performing arts as show business. It found expression in the phenomenal popularity of the television broadcast of sports events, pop music festivals, physical fitness exercises and cabaret and disco singing and dancing.

The weakening of the creative elan in the production of Hindi film music gradually led to the present sorry state of utter poverty of meaning, and bankruptcy of aesthetic appeal, in which Hindi film music finds itself. Replacement of originality by gimmickry, and of innovation by imitation—characteristic of show business of any kind—has brought about an almost monotonous similarity between one film song and another. They try to outdo one another in lewdness and loudness and, in the process, look and sound very much alike—all of them having the same ingredients in the form of elements picked up from aerobics, fashion parades and night-club floor-shows.

Thus, poetry and melody—the two essential qualities of all good music—have rapidly disappeared from Hindi film music, thereby completing the process of its decline and fall. It now lies at the bottom of a globally lowest common denominator of popular taste. The malady of commercialisation spread by the advertising and cassette industries has affected even bhajan music. Blared out through loudspeakers during night-long *jagarans* in India's capital city, some of today's bhajan music sounds like the vulgarest cinema music.

All this leads us to a basic and alarming question. Is the decline of Hindi film music a temporary phenomenon, or does it symptomise a throw-back to unregenerate and barbaric patterns of sound and body movement, abandoning the classical and traditional sources and purposes of music and dance in Indian culture ?

Singing and dancing and other performing arts in India have been considered over the ages not as mere modes of entertainment, but rather as ways of achieving enlightenment; not as performance for providing pleasure, but as an act of soul-divine meditation and supplication to the Creator; and so have been revered, for centuries, as something sacred by generations of singers and dancers as well as their listeners and viewers. This heritage is under threat.

4 RADIO : NEGLECTED MEDIUM

A deputy director-general of All India Radio remarked recently that, with TV hogging public attention, the time had come to give serious thought to the issue of advertisements to remind urban people that All India Radio still exists, and to make known its programmes.

It has been the lot of radio since independence, as before, to be treated as a vehicle of entertainment and information for the urban middle class—a role in which it has been virtually displaced for a decade now by its younger and more attractive cousin, television—than as an instrument for transformation of rural India that it could have been, and still can be.

The choice reflected the dominant influence on Jawaharlal Nehru, who moulded free India in the formative years, of the Leninest, Soviet model of centralisation and large industries rather than the Gandhian model based on decentralisation and local self-reliance. Nehru's successors in power at the Centre have been guided by self-interest rather than either the Leninist or the Gandhian model.

Born within a year of each other, Gandhi and Lenin both recognised the potency of radio as a means of communication though they led two very different kinds of revolution. Gandhi attached importance to the cultivation of moral strength by the individual, rather than the indoctrination of men in the mass from a central source.

He made in November 1947 a brief but significant statement, about radio : "This is a miraculous power. I see Shakti, the miraculous power of God."

Lenin saw in radio a means of brainwashing the masses from a central source. He wrote to his disciple Joseph Stalin in 1922 : "It is technically quite feasible to broadcast human speech over any distance by wireless. Furthermore, it is also possible to use many hundreds of stations that could broadcast speeches, reports and lectures delivered in Moscow to many hundreds of places situated hundreds and, under certain conditions, thousands of versts (a verst is a Russian measure of distance equivalent to a little more than one kilometer) away from Moscow. I think from the standpoint of propaganda and agitation, specially for those masses of the population who are illiterate, and also for broadcasting lectures, it is absolutely necessary to carry out this plan." Lenin hailed radio as a 'newspaper without paper' and 'without distances'. He regarded radio technology as of "immense importance, for with a loudspeaker with the receiver, which has been developed in such a way that it will be easy for us to produce hundreds of receivers, all Russia will be able to hear a newspaper read in Moscow."

In the democratic set-up of free India, on the other hand, district level radio stations could have been established to provide folk entertainment and to disseminate among the rural poor, through free access to radio sets at public places, information relevant to the improvement of their condition such as laws on land redistribution, tenancy reform or minimum wages. Popular participation could have been mobilised for programmes like those for adult education, community development and the empowerment of panchayats to draw up and implement development programmes to meet local needs.

No reorientation after freedom

Instead, the pattern of expansion of All India Radio continued to be what it had been prior to independence.

It was in Bombay that the first radio station was established, in the private sector, by the Indian Broadcasting

Company in 1927. Inaugurating it, the British Viceroy, Lord Irwin, said : "India offers special opportunities for the development of broadcasting. Its distances and wide spaces alone make it a promising field. In India's remote villages there are many who, after the day's work is done, find time hang heavily enough on their hands, and there must be *many officials and others whose duties carry them into out-of-the-way places where they crave for the company of their friends* and the solace of human companionship. There are, of course, in many households those whom social custom debars from taking part in recreation outside their own homes. To all those and many more, broadcasting will be a blessing, a boon of real value." The words emphasised in this passage, and spoken more than six decades ago, apply with even greater force today to the role of Doordarshan as a sustainer of kinship and solidarity among the middle and upper classes that rule the country. It brings accustomed entertainment and familiar faces and voices to members of the civil, police, para-military and Defence services posted in various parts of the country, not to speak of the geographically mobile middle and upper levels of private and public sector enterprises. Though the expression 'national integration' is often heard over radio and television, what the two media have fostered is class integration.

After Bombay, the second radio station was opened by the Indian Broadcasting Company in Calcutta on 26th August 1927, and the third by the Madras Corporation in 1930. Brought under the control of the Government of India as the Indian Broadcasting Service from 1st April 1930, the radio system grew over the years with the opening of stations mainly at the capitals of the princely States and the British Indian provinces : Mysore in 1935; Delhi in 1936; Lucknow in 1937 (I.B.S. had been redesignated meanwhile, in June 1936, as All India Radio); Baroda and Trichinopoly in 1939. There was an interruption caused by the outbreak of the second world war. When the process of expansion was resumed after the war, partition and independence, All India Radio grew on the same pattern of lateral expansion at the level of cities and large towns.

There was a move, in 1954-55, towards giving the radio medium a mass orientation by installing facilities for community listening. Under a Centrally sponsored scheme, the Union Government gave 50 per cent subsidy to the States on the initial cost of a receiving set and ancillaries. Listening clubs were to be organised to promote discussion of programmes intended for rural listeners and to provide feedback to the programmers. At the peak of functioning of the community listening scheme, the number of community listening receivers were estimated at about 90,000—or almost one in every fifth village. But the scheme entailed the organisational problem of replacing wet batteries since the majority of villages were without electricity. Substitution by transistorised sets were not practicable either, because of the shortage of battery cells at that time.

A committee on Broadcasting and Information Media (popularly known as the Chanda Committee after the name of its chairman) recommended in its report, in April 1966, the discontinuance of community listening since the authorities in many States had failed to operate the scheme satisfactorily. When, following the general elections of 1967, non-Congress governments were formed in several States, there was a desire on their part to cut down the number of Centrally sponsored Plan schemes which had been introduced by Congress governments at the Centre without regard to differences in regional priorities. At a meeting of the National Development Council in 1969, the baby of community listening to radio was thrown out along with the bathwater of excessive centralism. The Central subsidy of 50 per cent for installing community sets was discontinued. However, in Jammu & Kashmir the scheme continued to be handled by All India Radio directly, even as Doordarshan later looked after the installation and maintenance of TV sets for community viewing of TV.

Had community listening been continued and expanded by solving the problems of maintenance of the receiving sets, instead of taking the easy and lazy course of scrapping the scheme, radio could have become relevant for the rural poor. Revival of the scheme has not been considered, on the plea that 'everybody' has a transistor. This is an instance of the urban picture being mistaken for the all-India scene. At the 1991 Census, there were 40.4 million urban households and 111.6 rural households, and the latest estimate of the population of radio sets in the country is 105 million : 32 million in urban areas and 73 million in rural. Thus, a large number of urban households have more than one radio set whereas, even assuming that there is no more than one set per rural household, more than a third of rural households are without radio. And the radio-less households would be precisely those where literacy is least and the need greatest for information that can help to overcome poverty.

Serving the well-to-do

With those living below the poverty line out of its ken, All India Radio's contribution to development understood in humane terms has been minimal. True, radio has made its contribution over the decades to the green revolution. A widely quoted instance is of a new variety of rice which was popularised by radio stations in Tamil Nadu and therefore came to be known as 'radio rice'. Another effort was the formation of radio rural forums, in which 15 to 20 listeners were expected to discuss the information and suggestions contained in the programmes on agriculture, and to decide on a plan of action. However, as Mehra Masani says in her book on *Broadcasting and the People* (National Book Trust, 1985), the project which was modelled on the Farm Radio Forums of Canada, failed : "The reasons are not far to seek. AIR lacked the resources. In Canada the forums were the joint responsibility of the Canadian Broadcasting Corporation, the Canadian Broadcasting Federation of Agriculture and the Canadian Association for Adult Education. While the broadcasts were the responsibility of the broadcasting organisation, the other two provided the money for running offices to look after the forums. Unfortunately AIR could not afford anything like this organisation. Without a close contact between the radio stations and the forums, their success was only partial at best. It is the farmers in the age group 30-50 with a middle-school level of education who are most keen on listening to radio programmes which would help them to improve their productivity and thus their standard of living. The poor and illiterate farmer fails to derive any benefit from the broadcasts." This is an instance of the dictum 'As development, so communication'. The green revolution itself is of direct relevance only to landowners and to those cultivating tenants to whom land reforms have provided security of tenure and a fair rent and thereby the incentive to invest in the increase of agricultural productivity. Landless labourers have benefited only indirectly and to a limited extent from the increased incomes and wage-paying ability of landowners. Like Doordarshan's 'Krishi Darshan', the tips broadcast daily by AIR for farmers are of benefit to farmers, not to farm-hands and to artisans who constitute the bulk of the rural population. To them AIR offers only the diversion of cheap film music.

At the other end of the spectrum of AIR's listeners are the urban affluent and middle classes, specially of the younger age group. To them AIR brings what they like : the western pop music symbolised by Michael Johnson. This fare is purveyed by private parties to whom AIR has, on payment, allotted time on its FM (Frequency Modulation) channel in the metropolitan cities. AIR derives revenue also from spots and sponsorships for its in-house programmes of the FM service, not to speak of the substantial anticipated revenue from the recently introduced FM paging service at 17 centres. All this is additional to the substantial revenue from the Vividh Bharati commercial service (Rs. 30 crore) and from advertisements in the primary channels (Rs. 28 crore.)

Since FM offers greater clarity of reception though its territorial reach is limited, it is attractive both to the advertiser wishing to reach the maximum number of potential consumers at the least cost per head, and to the well-to-do listener sensitive to the quality of reception, irrespective of whether what is received is classical Indian music or high-decibel western pop. The parties that leased FM channel time began their morning programmes in all the four metro cities with western pop, but in Madras and Calcutta they had to shift it to other hours and apply the opening transmission to devotional music. It seems to reflect the difference in cultural rootedness of the residents of the southern and eastern metros as compared to their counterparts in Bombay and Delhi.

With the mediumwave spectrum allotted to India having been exhausted, future stations of AIR have necessarily to employ FM instead of AM (amplitude modulation). Since the reach of FM signals is limited, the new stations can serve only a small area each. The Government is making a virtue of this necessity by calling them 'local' stations. The philosophy of local broadcasting is that it will serve listeners through participatory, community-based programmes. In predominantly rural districts this will be impossible without community access to radio listening in the first place. Instead of organising access and participation, AIR is planning instead to generate resources by leasing time on the new FM stations to private parties for entertainment and commercial advertising. This will be a travesty of local broadcasting.

Sad story of local broadcasting

The Chanda Committee advocated as far back as in 1966 the establishment of low-power transmitters at the headquarters of each of India's (then) 400 districts for broadcasting local-interest programmes. Each station would serve one or two million people. To ensure that the programmes would be relevant to the specific problems of people in comparatively small areas, the Committee said in its report that the local station should be allowed to modify or add to centrally planned messages about development; and news should be locally prepared. Operators of small-town radio stations in the U.S.A., Australia and elsewhere had found, the Chanda Committee pointed out, that comprehensive local news coverage is the single most attractive programme which makes listeners forsake the national networks in favour of their local station. Village folk are interested in district developments and the activities of the Taluka Panchayat Samiti, and not in those of the remote State legislative assemblies and the even remoter

Lok Sabha and Rajya Sabha. They want news of the work of co-operatives, about rural industries, irrigation rates, construction of village roads, a new bus service, problems of landholders and agricultural labourers, and all those things that affect their lives. A local station can collect such news from district officials, panchayats, social workers, teachers, traders and others, and also give timely warning of flooding of roads, breakdowns in the bus service, and so forth. Local broadcasting would be based on coordination with district authorities and with extension services.

These wise words of the Chanda Committee fell on deaf ears in the Ministry of Information & Broadcasting and the Government of India. It was not till the Congress lost power for the first time at the Centre, giving place to a Janata Party government, that local broadcasting came to be canvassed again. A Working Group on Autonomy for Akashvani and Doordarshan, appointed by the Janata Government in August 1977 with B.G. Verghese as chairman, ably summed up the principles of social education through localised electronic media : "Instructional broadcasting presupposes specific small audiences in terms of age (for example, school broadcasts) and in terms of agro-climatic and socio-cultural variables including language. Decentralised and participative development from below suggests the need for decentralised messages through local radio and television. We would envisage the Station as something more than a single studio-transmission complex, distant and seemingly exclusive, or even inaccessible to the people it is intended to serve. Instead, we envisage at the local level a small and relatively simply equipped 'mother station', with a cluster around it of small recording units and programming facilities which will help bring broadcasting to the people and the people to broadcasting. This consideration applies both to radio and television."

Reflecting this concern for local relevance, the document on the Sixth Five Year Plan (1980-85), the drafting of which was taken up by the Planning Commission as reconstituted by the short-lived Janata Government, envisaged local broadcasting for the first time. The Plan included a "pilot scheme for local radio broadcasting...radio stations with low-power transmitters for local areas to augment the development-oriented programmes for such regions. The pilot scheme visualises location of such stations in areas with large population of Scheduled Castes and Scheduled Tribes."

This seemed to hold out the promise of a revolution in Indian broadcasting. The 'working instructions' for local radio stations issued from the Directorate-General of AIR in New Delhi left little to be desired. However, as will be seen presently from the experience of the Nagercoil station in Tamil Nadu—the first to come up out of the half dozen local stations provided for in the Sixth Plan—the resources made available for local broadcasting proved too little for achieving the intended purpose.

The purpose was spelt out finely enough in the 'working instructions', which read : "Local Radio is a new concept in broadcasting in India. Each of the stations, serving a small area, will be basically a utility service and should reach right into the heart of the community, which will use the microphone to reflect and enrich its life and artistic expression. What distinguishes local radio from the regional network will be its down-to-earth, intimate and uninhibited approach. Programmes will be area-specific. They will be flexible and spontaneous, enable the station to function as the mouthpiece of the local community. It will demolish the division between the broadcaster and the audience. Local authorities, police, emergency services, adult educationists, schools, transporters, farm scientists, entertainers will all look up to the local radio for a sustained community service. Its accent will be on handling the local problems extensively, local news and views and local talent, and it will be available to a broad spectrum of the local people. Comprising predominantly field-based programmes, it will adopt a down-to-earth character and establish a two-way communication system between the listeners and the extension agencies of various government departments. Local events and functions, games and sports, exhibitions and fairs, meetings and debates, cultural or literary, will find ample coverage. Its 'access' programme will provide opportunities to distinct groups in the community to present their own programmes affording scope for the articulation of local talent and views. It will organise a number of 'helpline' services to the listeners—in employment, education, housing, law, and even family problems. Local aspirations will find fulfilment through the local radio.

"Flexibility in programming being the main characteristic of local radio, the station may take the Fixed Point Chart as a broad guideline and make deviations as and when required. Directorate may be approached only when changes involving staff and funds are made. Instead of preparation of quarterly schedules, the station may prepare fortnightly plans.

"The station's main emphasis should be on field-based programmes. It must be the objective to cover every village in the district by turn. Inadequacy of staff for Outside Broadcasts could be overcome by casual bookings. The station may use cassette recorders which could be replenished by local purchase.

"The station may devote broadcast effort mainly to programmes of farming, rural development, health, family welfare and education. The agencies engaged in these fields may be tapped for supply of materials, scripts and recordings. Programmes of education could be supplemented by obtaining recordings from neighbouring stations in the State and from the Directorate of Transcription and Programme Exchange Services.

"Programmes may be presented in the local dialect/ language by engaging, if required, casual comperes who may present the programmes in a breezy, chatty, conversational style.

"The station may make provision for programmes of special audience like women, children, youth, labour, farmers etc. and groups, associations, organisations engaged in their welfare may be encouraged to produce and present programmes.

"The station may relay one news bulletin in the local language originating from Delhi, and another from the State capital. Stations situated in the Hindi zone may take one Central Hindi news bulletin. No other news bulletin is compulsory nor recommended.

"The station will not relay any programmes from Delhi/ State capital except the broadcast of the President and Prime Minister. Mandatory relays will not apply to local radio stations.

"The stations will be free to indent programmes from other stations and use them at their discretion, keeping in view listeners' interest in such programmes."

The circular went on to deal with the question of payments : "The scale of fee payable to unauditioned artists will be on par with the fee scale for Yuva Vani artists. Station will be free to fix the fee at any point within the fee range." On travelling and daily allowances, the circular said : "The stations may make, in addition, payment towards TA/DA if the distance from the headquarters is 8 kms. and above. TA will be only second class rail fare, and DA at a flat rate of Rs. 25 per day. No fee will be payable for escorts of women artists or children." On advisory committees : "The station may have an informal advisory panel. It may comprise important persons representing different interests like education, agriculture, extension services, panchayats, cooperation, small industries, health and hygiene, women, youth and social welfare and cultural organisations. No consultancy fee is payable."

It will be noticed that there is lack of realism in the stipulation that no travelling or daily allowance may be paid to the escorts of women or children who participate in programmes. Surely this is no way to promote the participation of rural women. And why should non-officials make a free donation of their time and pay from their pocket for travel to meetings of the advisory panel ?

A serious lacuna was that the staffing pattern for district-level stations had no provision for a news unit, whereas the broadcast of news of local interest is a major factor in the service expected of a local station. As a result, Nagercoil station could put out only a fortnightly 10minute bulletin of local news.

Both the success and the limitations of the novel experiment in local broadcasting are brought out in two appraisals of the working of the Nagercoil station—the first of the five stations that were actually established out of the six envisaged in the Sixth Plan. The first review is by the Assistant Station Director who initially headed the Nagercoil station, K. Anjaneyulu. Following are salient points from his paper :

"The 'wandering mike' captures the joys and sorrows of people of different walks of life, like a wandering mendicant, a toiling labourer in a tea estate, an agricultural labourer, a worker in a cashew-nut factory, a domestic maid, etc.

"A myth centering round a temple here, the history of a church or mosque there...or the latest details pertaining to two rival groups of fishermen concerning their fishing rights sanctioned by tradition—all these are put across.

"If there is a public grievance about the drainage facility, it is presented along with the reply from the concerned municipal commissioner. Problems faced by the public in obtaining essential commodities from fair price shops are taken to the concerned civil supplies officer and his replies together with information on remedial steps are presented to the listeners."

Though the picture drawn is rosy, K. Anjaneyulu's paper also says : "The norms of staff requirements on the programme side based on the total hours of transmission, normally practised, should undergo drastic rethinking when it concerns a local radio station. A major percentage of programmes organised by a local station are expected to be field based. This requires extensive field work involving adequate infrastructural facilities."

The second and more sharply analytical appraisal was by the audience research wing of AIR, based on a study conducted in October 1985, after a year of working of the Nagercoil station. The report presented the following findings and suggestions :

(i) An analysis of the programmes over a period of three months showed that they were more or less on the same pattern as other stations, with the highest proportion being claimed by music : film, devotional, light classical and folk.

(ii) Talks formed 57.1 per cent of the programmes for women, and 50 per cent of the Farm & Home programmes (which occupied only 4.1 per cent of broadcast time, presumably because the post of Farm Radio Officer had not been filled). The programmes for industrial workers consisted entirely of talks.

(iii) Almost all programmes were studio-recorded.

(iv) Manpower was insufficient and there were no OB recording facilities.

(v) The highest listening by radio owners (the other stations they could hear being Radio Sri Lanka, Tirunelveli and Tiruchi) was between 6 a.m. and 8 a.m. and 8 p.m. to 10 p.m. The study therefore recommended the introduction of a morning transmission by the Nagercoil station (it had only a single transmission, in the evening, from 6 p.m. to 9 p.m.) and the extension of the evening transmission till 10.30 p.m.

(vi) Officials of the development departments feared that they might be violating the code of official conduct if they spoke frankly on radio. It was recommended that the Ministry of I & B should arrange for high-level clearance, by the State government, of participation by officials.

(vii) Local news should be broadcast for a duration of 15 minutes, daily. For this purpose there should be a news unit with a correspondent and a news editor.

Exceptional case of Kota

Nagercoil is one of the first lot of local radio stations operating on AM. Each with an eventual sanctioned staff strength of 64, they operate three transmissions a day. The so-called 'local' stations opened thereafter in large numbers have fared far less well. The reason is simply that the resources of manpower, finance and equipment made available to them fall far short of what is needed to enable a local radio station to function in a manner worthy of its name. With a staff strength of 23 each, they put out only one transmission, from 5 p.m. to 10 p.m.

There is a lesson for all broadcasters in the success story of Kota, in Rajasthan. This was among the five in the first lot of local stations, but uniquely among them it had the benefit of having a Development Broadcasting Unit (DBU). This was funded until recently, under a four-year project, by the Asia-Pacific Institute for Broadcast Development with its headquarters at Kuala Lumpur and by the Ryerson International Development Centre, Canada. The resources which thus became available enabled the production of researched, participative and field-based programmes.

In contrast to the standard staffing pattern, Kota's DBU alone had four programme executives. They would visit villages in the 50km. radius covered by Kota's AM transmitter, talk to the people and ascertain their problems and interests. DBU's 20minute programmes were made with the collaboration of the villagers. The language employed was the locally spoken Haroti—not standard Hindi.

The weekly programmes of DBU began to be broadcast from 7th January 1988 at the peak listening time of 7.20 a. m., before the farmers left for their fields. The series of DBU programmes were under the title 'Nai Kiran' ('New Ray of Light'). Since a one-shot broadcast could be missed by several even among radio-owners, and since many villagers might not possess a radio set, each programme was recorded on tape and cassettes were supplied to the workers of the official development agencies, as well as to voluntary workers of Non-Governmental Organisations (NGOs). They would play the cassettes for groups of villagers at any time convenient to the latter.

Among the 38 DBU programmes broadcast from Kota station till the end of September 1988 were several which helped to bring about desirable change, on the ground, among the rural communities in interaction with whom the programmes were made. For example, the people of Naigon village were suffering from guinea worm infection. They attributed it to the water from hand pumps, and therefore switched over completely to the village well. A DBU producer talked to the villagers as well as to doctors of the health department. It was found on inspection by a specialist that it was actually the well water in which the worms were breeding. This was explained to the villagers, and the well was sealed for disinfection. With treatment of worm wounds organised by the health authorities, the village was soon relieved of the affliction.

Another DBU programme was aimed at promoting cleanliness in the village of Sorgia—to serve as a model for neighbouring villages. Prizes were announced for a 'clean child' contest, and the prize-giving ceremony was followed by films and talks on hygiene and sanitation. Households were invited to participate next in a cleanliness contest, and the winners were awarded prizes.

The objective of another programme, which took the final form of a community drama, was to encourage enrolment of children in schools, instead of utilising them as child labour. The expenditure incurred on the programme was nearly Rs. 10,000, but it had a noticeable impact on school enrolment.

An indicator of audience interest in these programmes was the large number of letters received by the Kota station from village listeners. Ms. Roberta Borg, the project coordinator, said in the course of an interview that though the villagers were largely illiterate, they took the trouble to have their messages—stating a problem or requesting advice—written out for them by others. This was a measure of the interest evoked by the programmes of the Development Broadcasting Unit.

The experiment in development broadcasting at Kota should induce All India Radio to endow each local radio station with adequate resources of personnel and finance.

Also important is the example set by Kota of supplementing the broadcast of programmes promotive of rural development with audio cassettes for utilisation in the non-broadcast mode. The problem of access to radio for the rural poor can be met best by a combination of the community listening facility with audio cassettes for use by village level development workers, both in the official and in the voluntary sector.

Poorer but Freer Cousin

Notwithstanding the trenchant criticism above of AIR—not so much of those who operate it as of those who control its operations—it will be churlish not to acknowledge that, after the advent of television as an urban mass medium, the performance of AIR has been more creditable than of Doordarshan.

If only because AIR is the poorer and plainer cousin compared to TV with its meretricious appeal that brings in more and more advertisement money, AIR has been interfered with less by the Netas and Babus of the I & B Ministry. The contrast is strikingly evident in the contents of the news bulletins of the two media. AIR is still left with a code and some standards of decency and of credibility.

Being much more decentralised than Doordarshan in terms of the number of programme-making centres as distinct from transmitters (though not as vastly dispersed as the Press is), AIR has been able to keep closer to the people and to reflect the interests and taste of its audience. Even in the Vividh Bharati channels, for example, there is a stronger regional flavour in the music and other programmes broadcast by the eight regional centres in the south. There is thus a social effect on the mass media as well as the effect of mass media on society. As noticed earlier, the private commercial parties who hired time on the FM channels in Madras and Calcutta found it necessary to shift western pop from the morning transmission to make room for the devotional music that listeners preferred at that hour.

But AIR is under pressure. A senior radio functionary,

referring to the persistent question from the mandarins of I & B Ministry why AIR is lagging behind DD in resource generation, suggested wryly : 'Why don't they turn all radio stations into Vividh Bharati centres?' It would be sad if this should happen.

5 TV : SIREN AMONG THE MEDIA

A variety of forces were at work in the 1950s to bring television to India. Businessmen, politicians in power, and civil servants who went abroad and saw television in the U.S.A. and elsewhere wanted to have similar entertainment at home. Multi-national corporations in the field of television saw in India a large potential market. UNESCO was interested too, dominated as its secretariat was by experts and officials drawn from the industrialised and media-saturated countries of the west with their own ethno-centric notions of development and of communication.

A committee formed by UNESCO came up in the 1960s with a set of 'norms' by which to measure the adequacy or otherwise of mass communication facilities in a country. As an 'immediate target', the group recommended that every developing country should aim at providing for every 100 of its inhabitants ten copies of daily newspapers, five radio receivers, two cinema seats and two television receivers. This was a simplistic and quantitative approach which did not take into account the relevance of content of the mass media, or their accessibility to the common people in developing countries.

However, the commendation of a diffusion rate of ten copies of daily newspapers per hundred of the population had the merit of implicitly calling upon developing countries to raise the levels of literacy and of purchasing power necessary for meeting the target. India has failed miserably on this count. With a population of about 900 million, daily newspapers should be commanding a combined circulation of some 90 million; the figure for 1993, the latest year for which the Press Registrar has data, was only 29.5 million, or less than a third of the UNESCO target.

Of the media that are literacy-free, film is the most expensive for regular exposure, and radio the cheapest, while television provides, for a high one-time payment, regular exposure both to the aural offerings of radio and the visual delights of television. Considering that the majority of India's people are poor, it is not surprising that the number of cinema theatres is only about 13,000, translating as a little less than a third of the UNESCO target of 18 million cinema seats for a population of 900 million (the seating capacity of cinema theatres in the country varies widely, and the average might perhaps be 450).

In contrast, India has over-fulfilled the UNESCO targets in respect of radio and television. The estimated 105 million radio sets are 234 per cent of the recommended norm, and the 46 million TV sets, 256 per cent. The high incidence of TV sets is explained by two factors. One is the higher purchasing power per capita in the urban areas which account for about 30 million TV sets in contrast to only about 16 million in rural India; in contrast, of the 105 million radio receivers (90 per cent of them transistor sets), 73 million are in rural areas and 32 million in urban centres. The rural well-to-do would probably have gone in for TV in larger numbers if electricity supply were regular. In Andhra Pradesh, there in an officially declared load shedding of six hours per day in rural and three hours per day in urban areas during periods of power shortage.

The second factor is that even manual workers and the lower middle class in urban centres are so attracted by television that they will sacrifice more basic needs like children's education and decent housing. Such is the pulling power of Doordarshan with its cinema-based entertainment and other titillating fare that it may truly be described as the siren among the Indian mass media, a dangerously fascinating temptress luring the rich and the poor alike among the unwary voyagers through life.

From Pij to MTV

Looking at Doordarshan today, one would find it hard to believe that television was introduced in India in 1959 with a wholly educational and developmental intent. Jawaharlal Nehru was Prime Minister at the time, and he would not have countenanced the expenditure of rupee and foreign exchange resources on introducing television as a medium primarily of entertainment as in the affluent countries.

Television was therefore canvassed on the grounds of education and development. A transmitter was offered for sale at a reduced price to the Government by Philips (India) after they had demonstrated the use of television at an industrial exhibition in New Delhi. It was decided to employ it for an experimental service. UNESCO made a grant of $ 20,000 for the purpose, and the U.S. government provided some equipment. The service began on 15th September 1959, with a range of about 40 kms. around the capital. Programmes of rural social education were telecast twice a week for 180 teleclubs formed for viewing and discussion. UNESCO provided funds for the community viewing sets as well as for a study in 1961 which indicated that the programmes had made some impact. A service for schools was started on an experimental basis in 1961, and was in 1965 made part of the curriculum of higher secondary schools run by the Delhi Administration.

The localised and exclusively educational use of television ended on independence anniversary in 1965. Indira Gandhi, as Information & Broadcasting Minister in the Lal Bahadur Shastri Cabinet, introduced on 15th August 1965 a daily general service for Delhi's cosmopolitan population, of one hour's duration and comprising entertainment and news for those who could buy their own TV receiving sets. Doordarshan Kendras were opened thereafter in city after city and television became a means of entertainment (much of it coarse) and information (with the news part of it selective and angled), only token obeisance being paid to education and development. Consumerism began to be promoted with the introduction of commercials from 1st January 1976.

A late flicker of the educational and developmental impulse was an agreement entered into by the Indian government with the National Aeronautics and Space Administration (NASA) of the U.S.A. for a Satellite Instructional Television Experiment (SITE). In contrast to the terrestrial stations of Doordarshan which had gone bourgeois in their orientation, SITE concerned itself with the production of rural-interest programmes and also took steps for their wide-scale social consumption. Direct reception sets with 24-inch screens were installed in 2,330 villages in backward districts of six States with programmes in four languages : Oriya for Orissa, Hindi for the States of Bihar, Rajasthan and Madhya Pradesh; Telugu for Andhra Pradesh; and Kannada for Karnataka. SITE utilised ATS-6, which was made available and put into geostationary orbit by NASA. The Indian Space Research Organisation (ISRO) was responsible for all technical operations of the ground segment, including maintenance of the direct reception sets. Doordarshan was responsible for the software. SITE became operational, on this basis, from 1st August 1975.

There was a morning transmission of one and a half hours for school children, with programmes of 22½ minutes each in the four languages. The programmes covered science education, biographies of great Indians, health education, current affairs and entertainment. The evening transmission of two and a half hour was intended for the general rural population. It carried news; entertainment programmes, many of which served also to portray the unity underlying India's cultural diversity; and instructional programmes on agricultural improvement, animal husbandry, health, hygience and nutition, and family planning. A news bulletin formed part of a half-hour 'national segment', in Hindi, which was telecast in all the six districts.

The experiment was an unqualified success in terms of hardware and technical operations. SITE was, however, only a qualified success as an exercise in social education for the rural population. The main reason was that there were only three software production centres to make the bulk of the programmes for villages with varied agro-economic and cultural backgrounds, many of them more than a thousand kilometres apart. Area-specific programmes were minimal. And it is a truth apparent to common sense that decentralised and area-specific programmes, employing local speech and depicting the local agro-economic and human landscape, are necessary in any attempt to persuade people to change their attitudes and practices whether in agriculture and hygiene or—even more so—in family planning.

The common sense view on the need for localised software in development communication was borne out by the findings of a research study undertaken by ISRO. It entailed holistic studies by anthropologists in seven villages: one each in the six village clusters served by the satellite and, in addition, one village—Dadusar—served by a terrestrial transmitter at Pij in the Kheda district of Gujarat.

The Pij experiment was undertaken by a group of socially concerned space scientists of ISRO. The transmission comprised the half-hour national programme of SITE in Hindi, telecast through rediffusion, and a half-hour Gujarati programme prepared in Ahmedabad under the auspices of ISRO. In several of these Gujarati programmes, the Charautari dialect prevalent in the Kheda district, instead of standard middle-class Gujarati, was employed. The programmes themselves were research-based, and dealt with the felt needs and interests of the audience. About 500 community viewing sets were installed in 355 villages of Kheda district. Several villages thus had more than one set. This was a densification of viewing even higher than in Kashmir Valley—the other island of television relevant and accessible to the rural population.

The social anthropologists who lived for about a year and a half in the seven villages, for data collection and continuous observation, found : "The linguistic profile of these villages shows a higher use of dialects than the standard language of the region. None of the languages spoken in the villages were used on TV except in Dadusar where Charautari was utilised to some extent. Furthermore, the use of English-sounding technical names (in programmes on agriculture and animal husbandry) compounded the problem. If the programmes were entertaining enough in terms of songs and dances, language did not become a barrier. Due to this reason, recreational programmes of other clusters were viewed with enthusiasm in all the villages. The Hindi common news was almost ineffective in all villages. The problem of lip synchronisation affected the credibility of the TV medium to an extent in Andhra Pradesh and Karnataka which used one video and two audio channels."

In other words, the most effective rural development communication during the Satellite Instructional Television Experiment was achieved not via satellite but through a low-power, local, terrestrial station which interacted with the community round it and dealt with local problems in local speech.

The need for communication to be localised and participatory if it is to play a developmental role was realised by the more perceptive among western scholars of communication like Wilbur Schramm. He led a team of experts who were invited by the Indian government in 1963 to advise on the development of information infrastructure. It was on the recommendation of this team that the Indian Institute of Mass Communication was established in New Delhi in August 1965. On a visit to the Institute twelve years later, Wilbur Schramm said in the course of a remarkably candid address to the faculty and students :

"There is a confession that I have to make. It is about the book that I published, 'Mass media and national development', in 1964. Actually it was written in 1962. I want to confess now some of the things I did not see then, some of the things that I would do differently today if I were to write this book all over again.

"Number one : the concept of what mass communications can accomplish by themselves has been almost completely revised. The bullet theory, that you can shoot a message into a person and he falls over, that it has a predominant effect, died simply because it was found that people did not fall over. They would brush away some of these information bullets; they would catch it in their hand, or eat it like chocolate candy. This was not like an electric current flowing through a wire or anything like that. The receiver was as active as the sender. That is, we got away from the idea that we could do things with him by putting some information into him, without doing anything else.

"Secondly, the trickle-down theory. The idea of trickle-down development is something of which I would be less proud now than in my book in 1962. But that was how the pattern looked in 1962, when the great experts in the capital city, the government, the universities would go on radio or television and talk to the village people about how to be healthier, more prosperous or how to have small families. Well, it simply does not look any more that way. What we have found out in these last 15 years, rather painfully, is that important as communication from top to bottom is, more important is communication at the bottom—that is, communication between the people at the same level.

"Activity at the village level is the only means, I would say, of effective village change; and whereas communication has to travel down, it has got to travel up and, much more important, it has got to travel round at the village level. People have to work together and discuss together, they have got to make their changes together. Only when communication can build itself into the social structure, is it going to show any real hope of extensive results. Only when media channels can mix with inter-personal channels, and with the organisation in the village, are you going to have the kind of development that you will like. In other words, the idea of big media, of talk-down communication, is something which is not going to work."

The Indian government did not listen to the older and wiser Schramm. Had the SITE experience been properly analysed and understood, it would have pointed to the conclusion that television if it is to promote development will have to be localised, with the community being provided with access; that district-level television is much too expensive in the circumstances of India; and that local radio continues to be the best option for developmental mass communication in the broadcast mode—as distinct from audio or video cassettes.

Instead, television continued to be expanded as a medium primarily of entertainment for the well-to-do. Instead of following the model of Pij—the station was itself eventually dragged into the standard pattern of film-based entertainment—Doordarshan turned for inspiration to MTV which is vacuous and coarse when it is not sexist.

Delhi-centric news : Guidelines ignored

The electronic media operated by the Central government have both been manipulated for partisan political purpose, television more especially, over the years since independence. The misuse would have been difficult if the electoral system had been based on proportional representation, in which case there would have been coalition governments at the Centre (and in many States) much of the time. The electoral system of first-past-the-post, which often gives total power to a political party with a minority following, has led to the official media in India resembling to some extent the state propaganda of totalitarian regimes, whether communist or plain militarist.

The official media agencies are yet to recover from the distortions and gross abuse that occurred during the emergency rule which Prime Minister Indira Gandhi got the President to proclaim in 1975. Led to think by her own propaganda organs and intelligence agencies that the people were happy with what had been done during the eighteen months of emergency, she called elections, in March 1977, which she lost. On the new Janata Party government falling soon owing to internal dissension, the Congress led by Indira Gandhi returned to power in the Lok Sabha elections held in January 1980. It seemed—but only for a while—as if the Congress (Indira) had been chastened by experience and would not again manipulate the official media.

A letter was issued by the Ministry of Information and Broadcasting to the heads of its media units on 2nd July 1980 which was in the nature of a signal that a return to the ways of the emergency period was not desired or expected. Initially classified as 'Confidential', this letter setting out policy guidelines for the official media was placed before the Lok Sabha on 12th August 1980 and before the Rajya Sabha on 16th March 1981. Though by no means a charter of professional autonomy, the letter was a step in that direction. It called upon the official media to promote the national objectives of economic development, social justice and harmony "with a certain degree of creativity, originality and ingenuity so that the official media remain credible as well as interesting to all sections of the society, and specially the youth of the country."

The hope of the official media being given a credible and constructive role to play in the total flow of communication in the country was strengthened when, on 28th November 1980, the Ministry of Information & Broadcasting constituted a Media Advisory Committee to advise on "policies and programmes relating to the media units under its administrative control." The Committee was to advise also on structural changes in the different media organisations "and, if necessary, in the Ministry itself to bring about greater professional efficiency and improvement in the quality of performance of the media in response to wide-ranging national requirements and aspirations." The chairman of the Media Advisory Committee was G. Parthasarathi, former journalist, diplomat and educationist. The members included distinguished practitioners of communication in the widest sense in the non-official sector, as well as some with experience of work in the government media. They were E. Elkazi, Mulk Raj Anand, Basu Bhattacharya, E.V. Chitnis, N. L. Chowla, K. S. Duggal, B. V. Karanth, P.V. Krishnamurthy, K. Kurian, V. K. Narayana Menon, Sumati Mutatkar, N. Bhaskara Rao, and Fatima Zakaria.

A statement of news policy for the broadcast media was formulated by the Parthasarathi Committee. This document elaborated, and took much further forward in the direction of professionalism and credibility, the policy guidelines issued earlier by the Ministry of I & B. The news policy suggested by the Media Advisory Committee was approved by the Ministry of I & B and issued to All India Radio and Doordarshan on 4th May 1982, and the document was placed before the Lok Sabha in reply to an unstarred question on 13th July 1982.

Both the documents—the Ministry's guidelines for all the official media and the Media Advisory Committee's statement of news policy for the broadcast media—are reproduced in Appendix II. They continue to be of value for improving the performance of the official media in terms of objectivity, as well as relevance to Indian society as a whole and not only its elite upper crust.

Before the year 1982 was out, however, Doordarshan instead of moving closer to the people became more Delhi-centric and VIP-oriented. The technological facility of dish antennae to receive and low power transmitters to relay, throughout the country, signals uplinked from Delhi intensified the centralising tendency inherent in the power structure.

The occasion of the ninth Asian Games held in Delhi in the winter of 1982 marked the introduction of colour transmission simultaneously with installation of two dozen low power transmitters imported from the U.S.A. Software presented no problems during the course of Asiad, from 19th November to 4th December. Performing talent did not have to be spotted, trained and rehearsed by Doordarshan's programme producers. The performers were there, fully trained. And the language of their performing art was the universal language of body movement, obviating the need for dubbing or sub-titling. The camera had only to be focussed on the performers.

As Mehra Masani recalls : "In Iran, the Shah introduced colour TV to cover the coronation of Empress Farah. In Uganda, Idi Amin brought in colour TV at a cost of $ 6 million to cover a meeting of the Organisation of African

Unity and also to cover his most recent wedding in 1975. In Thailand it was introduced in a great hurry to cover a beauty competition. We, not to be outdone, started on colour TV in a hurry to relay the Asian Games."

Domestic fabrication of dish antennae and low power transmitters followed, and nearly 600 LPTs now dot far corners of the country, inflicting largely irrelevant programmes on viewers in distant parts. A paper on the 'Uses and Dangers of Networking', prepared for the Working Group on Doordarshan Software, said : "Networking via satellite can be an aid to programmes conducive to national integration. But this technology can also be counter-productive if unimaginatively used.

"Occasions like the Republic Day parade in the capital, or the Independence Day rally at Red Fort, are visually spectacular and it is a heartwarming experience for people in widely separated parts of the country to be able to view them simultaneously. However, even the impact of the Republic Day parade shown of television will be enhanced if the commentary from Delhi, in Hindi or English, is overlaid from time to time with translation in the local language.

"The prevailing concept of a 'national programme' is to put together a number of regional programmes which are largely unintelligible to viewers outside the region concerned. A recent example is the presentation of 'Pinnal Kolattam' on 4th November (Diwali Day) 1983. The words of the song sung by the women while performing this traditional Tamil dance conveyed fine humanist sentiments, but only to those who know Tamil; to the rest of the viewers in the country the words were gibberish. Discreet, unobtrusive and brief sound overlays, to explain the words of the Tamil song in the other Indian languages, would have enabled intelligent appreciation of the programme instead of its appealing only to the eye."

The Software Group came down heavily on Delhi-centrism in the report it gave early in 1984 : "The most trivial happening in Delhi becomes a national event deserving of extensive TV coverage, while important events elsewhere hardly merit a mention. To a large extent this is due to the simultaneous availability of uplink and the necessary TV equipment in Delhi. As a result, while Delhi mostly sees itself, the rest of India sees mainly Delhi and, occasionally, glimpses of the rest of India as seen by Delhi.

"It is a pity that a television system which is not only publicly funded but is also directly run by the Government, on the ground that this is necessary to make television serve the purpose of development in the direction of socialism, should show so little orientation towards the common people in its news and current affairs programmes. A witness said to us that Doordarshan's news bulletins are often like illustrated court circulars. Another witness said that while it was the Prime Minister's duty to go from place to place and convey to different audiences the messages of national unity, communal harmony, etc., it was neither necessary nor appropriate for Doordarshan news bulletins to report the same messages repetitively to the same audience.

"A distinguished sociologist, Prof. T.N. Madan, said to us : 'Delhi TV programmes seem to be addressed much more to entertainment seekers and passive information beneficiaries than to any other category of viewers. Besides, there is of course the obvious effort to have political impact through the news bulletins. It strikes me as essentially a substitute for cinema, and a political propaganda medium'."

Pointing out that those living below the poverty line formed 48.18 per cent of the population, the Software Group asked whether the news and current affairs programmes of Doordarshan were about, for, and accessible to, this half of India's population. The report said : "Viewers of Doordarshan live above the poverty line, and Doordarshan through its VIP-oriented programmes and trivial entertainment promotes complacency and a drugged indifference to issues of social transformation, rather than any self-questioning of their life-style on the part of its middle and upper class viewers."

Courts to the rescue

Fortunately, Doordarshan and its viewers are likely to become beneficiaries of the activism that has marked the higher judiciary in India in recent years. This socially activist role is not so much of the judiciary's own seeking; it has been thrust on it by the inability or unwillingness of the executive and legislative branches of the country's government to take difficult decisions.

Gone are the days when political parties in power at the Centre or in a State could blame the higher courts for striking down what they claimed to be progressive legislation—whether concerning land reforms, nationalisation and the compensation payable , or the privy purses of princes. It has become more common now for governments to shift on to the lap of the judiciary ticklish problems on which a decision one way or the other could cost the ruling party the votes of one or other section of the electorate.

A major instance is the question of reservation in college admissions and recruitment to public services for the Other Backward Classes—i.e., backward social groups other than the Seheduled Castes and Scheduled Tribes. With mounting demands from various castes to be classified as backward and to be given reservation in proportion to their population strength, a situation was developing in which caste rather than merit might determine three-quarters or more of admissions to medical and engineering colleges and selection for appointment in government departments and public sector undertakings. In this context, the Supreme Court laid down in 1963, in Balaji v. State of Mysore, that the interests of weaker sections of society had to be adjusted with the interests of the community as a whole : "Speaking generally and in a broad way, a special provision should be less than 50 per cent." In subsequent rulings the Supreme Court called for exclusion of the 'creamy layer' among backward castes from the benefit of reservation, and for restriction of reservations to initial recruitment as distinct from subsequent promotion.

While these principles are unexceptionable and have been widely acclaimed, the fact remains that in many judgments the courts have taken widely different, and questionable, decisions on the categories of persons to whom reservation may be provided. Thus, in 1964 the Kerala High Court in Jacob Mathew v. State of Kerala, upheld reservation in favour of Ezhavas, Muslims and Latin Catholics; it also upheld as valid the reservation in favour of outstanding sportsmen but struck down the reservation in favour of children of medical practitioners. In 1971, the Supreme Court held, in Chanchala v. State of Mysore, that "it is not unreasonable to extend that principle (namely, preferential treatment) to children of political sufferers and of Defence personnel and ex-Defence personnel."

Such anomalies are only to be expected if the courts are called upon to decide on issues of public policy—the proper domain of legislatures—instead of their own special field of the interpretation of the Constitution and of laws. This is illustrated by the decisions of a three-member bench of the Supreme Court, on 9th February 1995, in a case concerning Bengal Cricket Association and Board of Control for Cricket in India, on the one hand, and Doordarshan on the other. There were two concurring judgments, one delivered by Justice P. B. Sawant who spoke also for justice S. Mohan; and the other by Justice B. P. Jeevan Reddy.

Though it came in a curious context, namely the right to entertain—in the instant case, by telecasting cricket events— as part of the freedom of speech and expression, the judgment included the following momentous decision : "The broadcasting media should be under the control of the public as distinct from Government. This is the command implicit in Article 19 (1) (a). It should be operated by a public statutory corporation or corporations, as the case may be, whose constitution and composition must be such as to ensure its/their impartiality in political, economic and social matters and on all other public issues. It/they must be required by law to present news, views and opinions in a balanced way ensuring pluralism and diversity of opinions and views. It/they must provide equal access to all the citizens and groups to avail of the medium".

While this is a landmark pronouncement which has gladdened the hearts of all lovers of freedom of expression and of the citizen's right to information, there are features of the Supreme Court's judgment which some have found less than satisfactory. These are :

(1) No time limit has been set for establishment of a truly autonomous public broadcasting authority.

(2) The judgment does not affirm the right of citizens to establish broadcasting organisations in the private sector. The judgment says : "The question whether such right should be given to the citizens of this country is a matter of policy for the Parliament."

(3) The judgment makes a distinction between the Press, which enjoys freedom from pre-censorship, and the electronic media. The latter are held to be "subject to pre-censorship" on the ground that "broadcasting media is inherently different from Press or other means of communication and information. The analogy of Press is misleading and inappropriate."

Significant passages from the two judgments in this important case are reproduced in Appendix III. It will be seen that the judgment does not furnish reasoned justification for extending the government's right to pre-censor films (provided for in the Cinematograph Act of 1952 and already upheld by the judiciary) to radio and television which are very much more 'instant' media than films. It is not explained why it should not be adequate to provide for deterrent punishment post-facto for violation of a broadcast code— of for that matter of the guidelines laid down in respect of films.

Later in the year, towards the close of September 1995, came a judgment of the Delhi High Court expressing concern at the vulgar programmes telecast by foreign television agencies as well as by Doordarshan. The court directed that such programmes should be monitored and a report submitted to the court by 6th December 1995. It remains to be seen what view is finally taken as to the best method to deal with obscenity : deterrent punishment of offenders, or pre-censorship. The former will be preferred by those who are as strongly committed to freedom of expression as to decency and good taste in the products of the film industry and in the programmes of radio and television.

Instruction and Entertainment : fatal separation

by *P. C Joshi**

Is TV mainly for entertainment ? This question is raised in India and in other countries time and again. The dispute is not about having or not having entertainment but about the quality of entertainment. One must not be led into equating entertainment with mere viewing of feature films and song-dance sequences from feature films. Entertainment must acquire a new meaning in the Indian context where the life of our people does not have yet a clear division into work and play. How many in India can afford to have time exclusively for play in the sense an average American or an Englishman can afford ? But even in America and Great Britain the quality of entertainment is being emphasised. The report of the Committee on the Future of Broadcasting in the U.K., headed by Lord Annon, stresses entertainment with enrichment. It asks for programmes which "create delight and insight". In Indian classical and folk traditions entertainment has never been indifferent to quality. Art forms which degrade and not uplift have been strongly disapproved.

People's art and culture are so rich and varied, and yet these have not been captured so far by Doordarshan adequately. People's life is a peculiar blend of the useful and the beautiful. There is no distinction here between craft and art, the entertainer and the entertained, work and play. In tribal or peasant life, people work while they sing and dance, and they sing and dance while they work. The communicator has to try to bring TV closer to the life of the people in this deeper sense, and to raise the quality of

* From 'An Indian Personality for Television' (report of the Working Group on Software for Doordarshan), Publications Division, New Delhi, 1985. An economist with wide interests in mass communication and the arts, P. C. Joshi was chairman of the Working Group.

programmes in terms of authenticity to such an extent that an average peasant can say : my life is reflected here, it is my Doordarshan ! When the people begin to call TV their own, then alone the communicator should be satisfied. One must realise that the greatest artists are the people themselves as a collectivity, and India has still a very rich tradition of people's art intimately related to the process of living and working. People's art is not the product of leisured classes living alienated from the labour class. The artist is inseparable from the collective life of labouring people. Doordarshan must capture for the viewers the richness and dignity of the life of labouring classes in which the principles of work and play are harmonised; it must not romanticise the empty life of the non-labouring elites in whose case play is divorced from work.

It is pertinent to recall here what the eminent scientist J. D. Bernal said more than four decades back about the limited opportunity for active forms of play in modern life. His words are equally relevant today. To quote : "After work comes play. It is gradually becoming recognised what an important function recreation and amusement have in any community, above all in one where economic and material changes have broken up a balanced traditional order of life and provided for more widespread leisure. Leisure can be used either creatively or recreatively or can be wasted in boredom. Short of sheer boredom, today the cheapest form of leisure is the most passive wireless, cinema and the watching of sports. Uptil now the application of science to leisure has been practically confined to the diffusion of these passive forms of enjoyment; it has diminished boredom only to put phantasy in its place. All we can say is that science, free from profit-making, will be found as useful in extending our capacities for enjoyment as it is of our methods of material production. The new techniques of wireless, cinema and television have other possibilities than providing phantasy escapes from life."

Television in India has already turned into a major source of 'passive forms of recreation', and via the feature film it has also become a mechanism of 'phantasy escapes from life'. In a country where outdoor life and the world of nature offer such enormous scope for healthy, active and varied forms of play and recreation, the substitution of active by passive forms of recreation is a retrogressive development. Here are creative challenges for the Indian communicator : to adapt television to Indian needs, to tap its recreative potential, and to counteract its stultifying effects.

In far-flung, remote areas of the country, which have so far not known oppressive feudal customs and practices such as dowry and untouchability or the pernicious forms of modern commercialism and advertising, what television carries in terms of programmes is of crucial significance. Will the Communication Revolution be the carrier of the noble values and ideals of the Indian tradition and the scientific and egalitarian ethos of the modern age ? Or will it expose groups and communities hitherto untouched by modernity to its consumerism and the individualistic and hedonistic ethos which is being rapidly emulated by the new rich in India ? These are the anxieties and concerns of the thoughtful sections of Indian society in all parts of India. The Communication Revolution has connected us with the affluent world and exposed us as never before to an international 'demonstration effect'. The danger of communication being the carrier of the cultural values—or the malaise—of the affluent West to India and other developing countries is very imminent. Already in many developing countries the fact that cultural aggression from the affluent West has been destroying the cultural identity of these countries is a matter of grave concern, leading to national debate and discussion.

The cultural malaise of the developed countries is also now under discussion. Daniel Bell, a leading American sociologist, summed up the cultural contradictions of American society as follows : "The (American) culture was no longer concerned with how to work and achieve, but how to spend and enjoy. Despite some continuing use of the language of the Protestant ethic, the fact was that by the 1960s American culture had become primarily hedonistic, concerned with play, fun, display and pleasure. The world of hedonism is the world of fashion, photography, advertising, television and travel. It is a world of make-believe in which one lives for expectations, for what will come rather than what is. And it must come without effort. If, as Max Lerner once wrote, sex is the last frontier in American life, then the achievement motive in a go-go society finds its acme in sex. In the 1950s and 1960s, the cult of the Orgasm succeeded the cult of Mammon as the basic passion of American life."

The problem of India is that the new middle class has turned acquisitive and hedonistic, and is aggressively trying to utilise the agencies of the State, including the communication network, for the pursuit of what Daniel Bell calls 'play, fun, display and pleasure'. The vast masses, on the other hand, have still to fight for their economic and social survival at the level of elementary and basic needs. Will the greed of the new middle class have precedence over the basic needs of the vast masses ? Will the Communication Revolution aid the vast masses in their uplift and emancipation, or become an instrument of the upper-middle classes for their self-aggrandisement ? This is how perhaps Gandhi would have posed the issue if he were alive today.

* * *

TV programmes, it is said by anxious parents and teachers, are over-exposing the child to the glamour of modern life. Films depicting sex, crime and violence, being viewed by children with their parents, are creating new problems and new anxieties. Even in the West the issue of the impact of TV on the minds of children and the youth is a subject of great concern. Social scientists are investigating whether television has oriented children and youth towards sex, crime and violence. In this context the concept of moral responsibility of those managing TV has emerged in the developed countries.

The question of moral responsibility arises because television is very subtle in its impact, and it has invaded the home. Its influence has been compared to water dripping on a stone and eroding its hardness slowly and steadily. TV influences tastes and consciousness very slowly but steadily and without our knowing. Are the television authorities and professionals in India fully alive to their moral responsibility and to what society expects of them in terms of very high standards of their programmes, artistic as well as ethical ? The task of orienting young minds to new values while preserving respect for old ideals is a task as difficult as it is challenging and creative.

One of the major social changes of modern times is the entry of television inside the home. The fact that television has entered the home has created new problems but also vast possibilities. People are worried because TV has invaded the home which enjoyed a certain autonomy and sanctity in the past. Our primary source of education-cum-information-cum-entertainment as children was the home. Deep inside our unconscious and sub-conscious we carry the influences from inter-personal communication within the home. The nursery tales and lullabies from grandmothers and mothers, and lessons by grandfathers and fathers, gave the pre-TV generation its first orientation to the world, its social consciousness and sense of values. Now TV along with other agents of change is threatening these traditional modes of communication and socialisation. It is acquiring a great hold on the minds of children and weakening the influence of parents and teachers. This is being viewed with alarm as children have no time now for listening to their parents in their homes. Thus TV has emerged as a formidable rival to the authority of the parents over their children, and of the teachers over their pupils. The Annon Committee in England noted : "Television might in some ways be taking the place of the family, church or school in influencing children's outlook."

Will the teachers and parents find in TV a wholesome ally in shaping the consciousness of the growing child ? Or will TV result in moral and mental disorientation of children? These are the questions being asked by anxious parents in every home where TV viewing has become a way of life. New tensions are arising from the impact of the

Communication Revolution on the family, on the concept of the home, man-woman relation or relations between the old and the young, the individual and society. This impact is full of promise as well as dangers, depending on the type of programmes to which children are exposed.

Space research and social goals by *Yash Pal**

On 18th July, 1980 India launched its first satellite using its own experimental rocket, the SLV-3. There had been earlier successes in the Indian space programme, as exemplified by the Satellite Instructional Television Experiment (SITE), Aryabhatta, Bhaskara, etc. We are currently preparing for several large projects which will come to fruition in the coming years.

To a casual observer these events might appear as unconnected spurts of technological exuberance in an attempt to catch up with the Super Powers. However, this is not the case. There is a thread running through various Indian space activities, and our work is not done for glamour or show but to achieve specific societal objectives. Some of the benefits are planned and direct; others will emerge as spin-offs which can be truly realised to the extent we make attempts to convert them into useful applications.

To begin with, let me talk a bit about the global implications of the dawn of the Space Age. While doing this I will purposely assume an optimistic stance, being simultaneously aware of the fact that the best of inventions and advances in technology can be put to insidious purpose.

For many of us who work in space research, the new technology of being able to get outside the atmosphere to make our observations provides an enhanced capability to tackle many of the questions about the way the universe is put together, what makes it tick, what are the messages that come to us from various violent and non-violent happenings in stars, galaxies and the space and the matter

* Prominent among the socially concerned in the Indian scientific community, Yash Pal was director of the Space Applications Centre of the Indian Space Research Organisation and has served as chairman of the University Grants Commission.

in-between. We witness events now which are similar to those which must have occurred when the sun and the earth began, and others which tell us how our personal sun might die or fade away billions of years later. Living on this speck of moist rock we call earth, we search with great inquisitiveness, and perhaps with some humility, for the meaning and method in the great tapestry of the universe. And in doing all this, we use with great success the natural laws and rules of the game discovered here on earth through centuries of experimentation and theory making. Though scale and circumstance may be different, most of our physics seems to work; however, there are tantalising possibilities that completely unfamiliar scales and circumstances might reveal some basic traits of nature which remain hidden in our run-of-the-mill environment.

I suggest that this part of the space activity has great relevance for developing a new ethos and ethics for all humanity. This is an activity which joins us to our very origins—possibly illuminating the process through which life itself began—and could lead to a new awareness of our place in the scheme of things, including the triviality of our differences as seen against this large-scale panorama. Perhaps it even leads to a new type of religiosity, based not on revelation but on some sort of an Einsteinian god, where a close kinship between all men and between man and his environment becomes a self-evident truth. Taboos and rules of public behaviour then become more like traffic regulations to avoid collisions on the highway, rather than arbitrary constraints without reason or justification. Of course, one does not have to become a crass rationalist, disowning one's cultural heritage, because our past is also a part of the whole, being imprinted on our memory discs or encoded in our genes.

Space platforms provide us with a unique capability of seeing, and interacting with, large parts of the earth simultaneously. Through space communication, we develop a new concept of neighbourhoods which is independent of distance or physical location on the earth. To a country like India, it provides means of reaching, and being reached by, people who have been neglected during the normal process of industrialisation. The possibilities of using this enhanced capability are enormous : decentralised industrial growth, programmes in formal and non-formal education, support to activities in agriculture and family welfare and programmes of national integration. Indeed, we have already conducted a massive experiment in this area, namely SITE, with great success.

When we view large parts of the earth with space-borne sensors, we see not only things and features but also their inter-relationships. This is the basis for the newly emerging discipline of earth observation through satellite remote sensing. These techniques can provide invaluable information in the area of meteorology, hydrology, survey of natural resources, and in monitoring of crops and forests.

In terms of global implications one must remember that space is not just satellites, ground stations and instruments; or faster communication, survey of earth resources, monitoring of the weather; or better understanding of the solar system and the universe. It is also a new perspective, a new awareness of our place in the scheme of things, abolition of the old idea of neighbourhoods—the essence behind those first pictures of the beautiful earth from space, which bring home more clearly than ever before that we are all together on this earth, on a cosmic journey, tied together not only by a common ancestry but also by a common destiny. Indeed, concern about ecology then automatically becomes the first religion of all mankind. It becomes easier to appreciate that we are not only dependent on each other, but also vulnerable to each other's actions, that our home flows into the home of the most distant neighbour, and that the integrity of Spaceship Earth and the one family which resides on it is indivisible and has to be cherished, and preserved, as a cosmic imperative. There can be no religion greater than this. Viewed in this way, the emergence of the Space Age perhaps provides one of the most important ethical inputs in human history.

* * *

The scenario of large-scale poverty, illiteracy and

inadequate health care is often used as an argument that a country like India has no business playing around with a modern technology like space; that the resources spent for the purpose could be used better for digging wells and improving health services and doing a whole lot of other things. On the other hand, many of us have tended to argue that for doing precisely these very things, it is necessary to transfer the initiative and action to the people themselves and that the only way of doing this is to connect them with each other and with the resources of information, knowledge and infrastructure. To the extent the space way of establishing the connections is recognised as one of the quickest and most efficient means available, we need to use space technology even more than the developed countries because our needs are so very basic and urgent. Space for us is part of a major socio-economic mission.

It is this argument that provides a specific character to the Indian space programme and has, by and large, provided the basic motivation to both the doers and the supporters of this programme. It is clear, therefore, that while we learn to build payloads, satellites, rockets and ground stations, we have also to learn to configure the whole system in ways appropriate to our mission and, indeed, sometimes to get involved with a whole lot of other things which are normally not considered to lie within the functions and responsibilities of a space venture. Since technology, even space technology, is largely international in character, it normally wishes to follow the fashions of the metropolitan countries. Therefore, a sociologically motivated bending of this technology will continue to require significant efforts.

I would like to give you some glimpses of the process we have gone through, where we stand at the moment and what are our hopes for the future. The process has involved wide-ranging discussions, attempts to identify the most appropriate configurations and systems, and a fairly large space programme tuned to work towards its socially defined mission. It has also involved many friendly skirmishes, some life-size experiments and a continuing atmosphere of doing, questioning and internally instigated dissatisfaction with what we have achieved in developmental terms. It appears that such exercises will continue and, indeed, the searching and the arguments are likely to increase as the technological achievements mount; because the software and organisation aspects of the effort, and induction of related support systems, always tend to trail behind.

In spite of numerous visible successes in social areas, we have yet to give substance to our vision that the use of space technology for information transfer would abolish distance and eliminate discrimination against those who do not live close to the centres of existing infrastructure. Since the normal establishment of any facilities, even space facilities, tends to give more to those who have more, the concern, the restlessness and the arguments will stay with us. A policy of positive discrimination in favour of the underprivileged can remain just an empty statement unless the new technological capabilities are also accompanied by a transformation, and reorientation, of the earlier systems of information, generation and transmission, and the newly developed connectivity is invested with significant content.

Let me go back a little, and trace the basic features of the Indian space adventure. In the late 1960's, Vikram Sarabhai realised that space-based television broadcasting might be one way of quickly reaching the distant parts of the country with audio-visual messages related to developmental education. While technical studies and discussions in regard to a possible space-based system were conducted in collaboration with NASA, General Electric, etc., there was a simultaneous concern to gain experience in generation of relevant messages and evaluating their impact through a pilot experiment in a hundred odd villages around Delhi, which had the only TV transmitter of the country. It is significant that the initiative for this was taken by an Indian space enthusiast who dreamed of a future where all villages in this vast land would be connected via satellite. This programme, the Krishi Darshan, has since become a permanent feature of all our television broadcasting. I do believe that some of our most useful programmes are broadcast in this segment, in spite of the dissatisfaction of some of our urban elite.

Creative collaboration between NASA and the Department of Atomic Energy, which was then responsible for space affairs in India, led to the Satellite Instructional Television Experiment (SITE). In its magnitude and intent, also in the range of organisations and disciplines involved, SITE was a rather unique effort. It covered a few thousand secluded villages with direct reception television sets. Many of these villages had never seen a moving picture before. Besides using film crews and portable TV cameras, five studios were specially set up for the programme—this at a time when the country had only three metropolitan TV stations. There was massive involvement of social scientists for providing inputs to the programmes, a continuous feedback and extensive process-and-impact evaluation of the experiment.

The space organisations NASA and ISRO (Indian Space Research Organisation), along with other Indian participating agencies, were engaged in a rare, creative, co-operative venture. For fifteen hundred odd people directly engaged in the experiment. SITE was a deep human experience. It generated new capabilities, demystified space technology and helped to nucleate a large island of self-confidence. It generated a new kinship between technologists and the grassroot problems of the country, a common concern for the ultimate social and human goals, a situation where technical capability and intimate personal drives began to merge with social action. No wonder that Arthur Clarke called SITE the greatest communication experiment in history.

It took almost six years after the end of SITE for India to have an operational satellite which combines telecommunication, direct television broadcasting and meteorological functions. Let us first see what the induction of this satellite has done to television in the country. Perhaps no large country in the world has seen such a phenomenal increase in linking its inhabitants in so short a time. But what has become of the developmental goals of television in the midst of this tremendous new capability for distributing, through hundreds of relay transmitters, Hindi movies, coverage of cricket and hockey matches, 'Lucy', 'Star Trek', 'Yes, Minister', 'Odd Couple', etc., along with Zubin Mehta concerts, Los Angeles Olympics, classical dances and music and a lot of Hindi soap opera, to a new virgin audience never exposed to television before? Much of the new programming can be financed through increasing revenues from advertising. But is this developmental programming ?

Recently the University Grants Commission has begun a university hour on the S-band of INSAT, with retransmission by VHF transmitters. The programmes are produced by special facilities in the universities, and some selections from outside. Many of us feel that this might be the beginning of a countrywide classroom, which might expand to occupy a central role in the national educational activity, particularly in continuing education. But while the representation of everything desirable exists in the agenda, as also in the organisational set-up, there are continuous fears that our television system might have a tendency to become just like other TV networks of the industrialised West. Some might welcome it. In my view it would be a disaster. We have higher expectations and needs.

There are real challenges to be met. It was all right for the State to put in 2,500 direct reception sets during SITE. But who will pay if all 500,000 villages are to be covered ? The social behaviour of Indians does allow the possibility of serving an average population of one thousand per village through a single community receiver. But the organisation and management problems are daunting. It will be done, I am sure, because it must be done. Many of us are convinced that we have to follow the community reception approach, at least in the beginning, or else the access would be limited and the system will end up working for the powerful and the affluent, and be used primarily for diversion and titillation.

We have an additional challenge : how do you creatively use the long reach of the satellite in a country which has such diversity of languages and customs ? Yes, a tourist can get by in touristic India with a little bit of English, but English speaking and writing is confined to no more than a few—certainly less than ten per cent of our population. One has only to look at an Indian currency note to be reminded of the fact that we have fifteen officially recognised languages, each of them spoken by tens of millions. Therefore, while the satellite link-up is fine, it has been accepted that we must have local programmes using new organisational patterns and inexpensive mobile production equipment if we want to address the intimate developmental concerns of the mass of our people. But the satellite link is essential for bringing in the fresh breezes, the national and international scene, without which the local channels would become parochial and fossilised. I must confess that the movement towards this near-far combination is painfully slow.

A large fraction of the people who are, with some success, pushing for appropriate rural and developmental programming have been some time or other part of our space venture. Indeed, one of the major training facilities for rural programming staff has emerged in a unit within a space centre, and is recognised as such both nationally and internationally. A 'space ethos' has generated this feeling of care for and belonging with people, far away in geographic terms, because they are perceived to be close neighbours in communication terms.

Information transfer through broadcasting is, of course, not a true interaction : too many are exposed to too few. Therefore telecommunication is basically a better medium for social transactions and development. We are planning to increase the number of telephones, developing and installing digital exchanges, more radio links, also some fibre-optics links. And we also talk of Integrated Systems Digital Networks. But many of us feel that we must give priority to a basic needs programme in telecommunications. One basic need, in my view, is that within a few years every habitation in the country must be connected with every other through a message network, that every habitation should have access to relevant resources—computer or people based—to seek developmental information about weather, seeds, fertilisers, advice on crop management or whatever.

India's space programme is technically challenging. We buy things and components. But we also do a lot ourselves. Our space programme has had foreign collaborations. But each collaboration is to a purpose. What has been once learnt has been built upon and improved, without resorting to a re-import. First preference is given to indigenous development; but if the mission is at stake, a parallel import option of sub-systems is maintained. Finally, if the import becomes necessary, the indigenous development is not far behind and is often used in a back-up mode. The management system developed for the space programme offers challenges, room to accomplish, and is result-oriented. There is frequent redeployment and regrouping of people, and every year the whole budget is looked at anew, without concern for Plan and non-Plan divisions.

Even in the midst of nuts-and-bolts engineering and high technology, a sociological motivation pervades the programme. Technology is challenging and fun, but we are not just technology-happy—certainly not the top management. Vikram Sarabhai and Satish Dhawan were both socially concerned scientists first—space technologists second.

We need to open out the culture and the expertise developed in doing missions such as those in space, and begin to diffuse these in other sectors of our economy. We have to similarly convert our socio-economic tasks into missions, including their component science and technology missions. It has been shown that much can be achieved that way. It we look only for gadgets and one-time inputs of modernity from abroad without engaging in an equal measure of innovation ourselves, we will end up with a transient, sterile modernity. We must not look forward to becoming just pale versions of the industrialised West. That is not the destiny of a country like India. We have to be modern in our terms.

Part-II

Social Audit of the Media

6 SURVEY FINDINGS : QUANTITATIVE ASSESSMENT

The Centre for Media Studies based in New Delhi conducted during 1994-95 a country-wide social audit of the functioning of mass media which is without precedent in the relatively new field of media research in India.

Pioneering combination of methods

A review of past studies was naturally the starting point. It was found that the couple of studies of the social impact of television that are available were conducted before the spread of TV in India on a large scale, and much prior to the advent of cable and satellite television. The CMS inquiry can therefore be described as a virtual base-line study at national level.

At once large-scale and in-depth, the pioneering research effort by CMS utilised a combination of methods. One was the conventional questionnaire-based survey, which still remains the primary and indispensable tool for quantitative research. Its reliability depends on the quality of sample determination rather than on sample size. The truth of this was demonstrated by the prediction of voter behaviour and assessment of public opinion prior to the elections to various State Assemblies including Maharashtra, Gujarat and Andhra Pradesh during 1994-95, and on the eve of the fall of the N.T. Rama Rao government in Andhra Pradesh in 1995.

The survey of exposure to various media and the perceived effects of television was carried out in 2464 TV households in seven States spread across the country : Andhra Pradesh (south), Assam (north-east), Maharashtra (west), Orissa (east) and Uttar Pradesh (north), besides Delhi and Bangalore. The sample was distributed between metropolitan cities, medium and small towns as well as rural areas, broadly in the proportion of the incidence of TV viewing. About 60% of the sampled homes had access only to Doordarshan while 40% had cable TV also. One person was interviewed in each home. The respondents comprised slightly more men than women, and included, in descending order, students, housewives, employees, business men and other self-employed, and farmers.

Discussion with focus groups was the second method employed in the course of the social audit of the media. Utilising an open-ended check list affording scope to respondents for free expression, the method of discussion with small groups adds the vividness and human interest of individual experience to the statistical findings of survey research. The groups spoken to were of students, parents, teachers, and housewives. The cases of two TV 'addicts' were come across, and studied.

The third method employed by CMS was to covene colloquia at national and regional levels which brought together, for an exchange of views, persons active in public life, social scientists, legal luminaries, media critics and practitioners, administrators, academicians and, importantly, social activists including and in particular those engaged in work among women and children. Among the eminent participants were three former Ministers of Information & Broadcasting—I.K. Gujral, Vasant Sathe and P. Upendra; Ranganath Mishra, former Chief Justice of the Supreme Court; M.N. Srinivas, sociologist; Jayanti Patnaik, the then chairperson of the National Commission on Women; economists P.R. Brahmananda and P.C. Joshi. Father Shouraiah of Loyola college, Vijayawada; space scientists E.V. Chitnis and Pramod Kale; noted danseuce Mrinalini Sarabhai; Justice (retd.) Murtaza Hussain; G. Ram Reddy, chairman of the University Grants Commission and Prof. Ramlal Parikh, Gujarat Vidyapeeth.

The colloquia yielded both diagnoses of the malady of the mass media and suggested cures, from different perspectives and backgrounds of experience. The idea of organising such round-tables at regional centres outside the national capital and other metropolitan cities was mooted by N. Bhaskara Rao, chairman of CMS, at a national seminar on violence and vulgarity in the mass media organised in New Delhi on 22nd September, 1994. Within a period of three months, from 7th October, 1994 to 7th January, 1995, regional-level colloquia were organised at as many as six centres around the country : Lucknow, Bhubaneshwar, Vijayawada, Ahmedabad, Pune and Bangalore. These gatherings proved valuable in three ways : (i) as fora for exchange of views among concerned citizens in culturally homogeneous areas; (ii) as a supplement and a corrective to the Delhi-centric bias to which are liable not only the vast Central bureaucracy but many of the government-funded academic and professional bodies that have mushroomed in the capital since independence; and (iii) serving to sensitise local public opinion through Press coverage of the seminar proceedings and the personal interaction of participants with their professional peers and with friends in different walks of life.

Presented in the following section of this Chapter are the main findings of the survey that was conducted by trained investigators of the CMS in various parts of the country over the period from October 1994 to February 1995. (Detailed tables are given in Appendix IV.) The views and recommendations emerging from the focus group discussions and from the colloquia are presented in the next two Chapters.

IMPACT OF TV : A STATISTICAL OUTLINE

Time spent on different media

The average time spent on all media per day by viewers in cable households was 246 minutes (about 4 hours), and in DD-only households, 210 minutes (3½ hours). TV claimed the highest share among the media, on the part of all categories of members of a household : men, women, children and youth. It accounted for more than 50 per cent of media-time in each category.

Television has cast a shadow on all other media. The change in media habits is brought out by the following figures :

	Cable (%)	*DD-only (%)*
Newspapers		
Reduced	26.2	30.7
Increased	3.8	4.1
Radio		
Reduced	32.7	46.9
Increased	0.9	1.3
Cinema going		
Reduced	66.9	60.2
Increased	2.5	1.5

It should be noted that though cinema going has declined, watching movies has not : films are viewed more than before, but at home, on the TV screen. The biggest casualty is radio, as brought out by the data in Table 2 (Appendix IV); and reading of books/novels, magazines and dailies have all suffered, in that order. While readership of newspapers may not have declined, the time devoted to newspaper reading has come down, partly due to the attention claimed by TV in general and by its news and current affairs programmes.

That cable leads to more addictive TV viewing is suggested by the following figures of the percentage of viewers in three categories :

Category	*Hours/Week*	*Cable*	*DD-only*
Moderate	Up to 14 hrs	31.2	41.4
Heavy	15-35 hrs	63.9	55.6
TV addicts	Above 35 hrs	4.9	2.9

DD for entertainment mainly

The study findings reveal that only a third of cable viewers (35.1%) and a quarter of DD-only viewers (26.8%) watch news on Doordarshan at least once a week. In other words, nearly two-thirds of all viewers rarely watch DD news.

This suggests that the typical TV viewer is primarily interested in entertainment rather than news and current affairs, and that his exposure to the latter is incidental to TV viewing.

Effect on studies and homework

Information, education and entertainment are often stated to be the objectives of the mass media. Doordarshan is run by the Government supposedly as a public service. But the study showed that DD's direct contribution to children's education is next to nil, though its contribution to enrichment of general knowledge is rated highly.

It was found that the percentage of viewership of DD's educational programmes among children was as follows :

	Cable	*DD-only*
Yes, always	2.7	3.2
Yes, sometimes	21.8	15.9
Rarely	10.6	7.7
Never	64.8	73.2

When asked about the quality of these educational programmes, nearly two-thirds of cable viewers and three-fourths of DD-only viewers pleaded ignorance as they had never seen those programmes.

On the other hand, a very high proportion of viewers (93%) said that Doordarshan had helped them in developing an understanding of history through its historical programmes, and of India's cultural heritage. Promotion of awareness of economic development, and of health awareness through programmes like those on immunisation, was lauded. Television was also given credit for promoting awareness about consumer products through its advertisements and about sports through its live visual coverage of national and international events; but, ironically, about a third of the children who were interviewed reported that they play less due to their preoccupation with TV.

Children also study less on account of pre-occupation with TV, the study brought out. More than 25% of parents of children below 15 years said that TV had a negative impact on studies, while nearly a fifth said that they could not say. Following is the percentage distribution of the different responses regarding TV's effect on the homework habits and studies of children :

	Cable	*DD-only*
Positive	22.8	24.8
Negative	25.5	30.8
No influence	36.3	28.5
Don't know/can't say	15.2	15.9

Opinion was divided among parents on the general question whether the influence of TV on children's development has been harmful or helpful. Over a quarter of the parents felt that it was harmful :

	Cable	*DD-only*
Harming	26.5	30.5
Helping	39.7	40.4
Don't know/can't say	33.8	29.0

How do children themselves see it ? About one-third of them reported that their homework habits had been influenced by TV in one way or another, as follows :

	Cable	*DD-only*
Adjusted	9.5	9.8
Disturbed	11.2	10.3
Neglected	12.1	10.7

How parents responded to this situation was also sought to be ascertained. In a majority of TV households there is no bar on what children may watch. Only in 35.3% of cable and 36.1% of DD-only households are children prevented from seeing some programmes. Moderation of children's viewing of TV by parents was reported as follows:

	Cable	*DD-only*
Always	12.6	14.8
Sometimes	51.0	56.6
Never	36.4	28.6

Why cable and why not

One of the aspects of the study was ascertainment of reasons for having/not having cable TV. It will be seen from the following data that the majority cited 'more films' and 'wider choice of entertainment' as the reason for subscribing to cable; next came 'better news', while a sixth of the respondents cited 'pressure of children'. (The percentages exceed 100 because of multiple reasons given by many respondents.)

Reasons for cable connection

More films on cable	45.38
Wider choice of entertainment	67.31
Better news/awareness	40.61
Pressure of children	17.46
English music/serials	28.22
Sports	3.76
Inferiority of DD programmes	3.76
Cable as status symbol	2.54

Those not having cable TV were also asked to mention the reasons. 'Enough entertainment on DD', effect on children's studies and non-availability of cable in their area were the principal reasons cited. The cost factor was given as the reason only by about one-eighth of the respondents.

Reasons for not having cable

Have enough entertainment on DD	36.44
Studies will be affected	33.67
Not available in our area	30.42
Costs money	13.44
Obscenity/vulgarity	17.11
Programmes not relevant	6.63
Cannot relate	2.91
Against Indian culture	4.46
Do not have time	7.37

It was found that as many as 4% of the viewers covered in the survey had disconnected cable either permanently or temporarily. The study sought to ascertain the reason. Adverse effect on children's studies was cited as the most important reason.

Reasons for disconnecting cable

Children's studies affected	67.1
Programmes not good/obscene	18.6
No time	7.1
DD is enough	2.9
Grandparents' pressure	4.3

Individual and societal impact

The study brought out a variety of changes, to a greater or lesser degree, induced by exposure to TV in dress and food habits, sleeping hours, interaction among family members, etc. These are set out in the detailed tables 1 to

6 in Appendix IV. It will be seen that viewers rate TV's influence as only 'moderate' at the individual/family level, but consider it as intense and wide at the societal level. Perhaps it is a case of the respondents not being able to discern what is happening in their own lives while making a gloomy projection of TV's influence on society. It is also a question whether there is an element of self-justification and evasion on the part of parents in their responses, cited earlier, to questions on TV's influence on studies and children's development in general, and on parental control/ moderation of TV viewing by children : can parents who lack self-control in their own TV viewing control or guide TV viewing by their children ?

7 FOCUS GROUP DISCUSSIONS

Discussions on the social impact of TV were held by CMS-trained interviewers between the months of October 1994 and January 1995 with focus groups at fourteen places in six States across the country. These were : Hyderabad, Cuddapah and Karimnagar in Andhra Pradesh; Guwahati, Tezpur and Golaghat in Assam; Delhi; Jalgaon in Maharashtra; Allahabad and Lucknow in Uttar Pradesh; and Sundergarh, Keonjahr, Cuttack and Bhubaneswar in Orissa.

The focus groups comprised children, students and youth; teachers; and parents (including separate discussions with male and female heads of households). The participants were invited not only to report the social effects on TV experienced or observed by them but also to offer suggestions for minimising the negative effects and strengthening the positive features.

Presented below are the salient points that emerged from the focus group discussions.

Low estimate of Doordarshan news

A widely held view among discussants in all the focus groups except children is that Doordarshan news is selective and biased in favour of the Government, and suffers from inadequate visual depiction of events. The disdain, verging on contempt, was expressed in particular by English-knowing viewers with access to the BBC news channel.

A group of English-knowing parents at Hyderabad said that the news telecast on DD is not only belated but inadequate. During times of social tension, news is not given at frequent intervals as it should be. Instead, DD keeps on saying that "the situation is tense but under control", without any details—let alone visual coverage. In contrast, the news coverage on BBC, they said, is immediate, frequent, unbiased and accompanied by vivid visuals. They attributed Doordarshan's handicap to its being government-owned and being run as its mouth-piece.

A group of housewives at Mohannagar in Lucknow also said that DD news bulletins are inferior in quality, partial in their contents and often irrelevant.

Awareness programmes hailed

In contrast to the low opinion of Doordarshan's news bulletins, most of the participants in group discussions praised the programmes of general information, current affairs and science as contributing to the widening of their mental horijons and general awareness.

The group of English-speaking parents at Hyderabad said that the general knowledge of children was improved by their viewing such programmes as 'World This Week', 'Turning Point' and 'Quiz'. These programmes were also cited with approval in several other discussion groups.

A housewives' group at George Town in Allahabad referred to 'Surabhi' as an example of providing useful knowledge in an interesting way. 'Parakh' won similar praise as a news magazine during discussion with male heads of households at Vikas Nagar in Lucknow.

The programmes sponsored by the University Grants Commission won high praise, but the timing of their telecast was regarded by some as unsuitable, thereby reducing their usefulness.

Other current affairs and general knowledge programmes that received favourable comment included Eye Witness, News Track and Animal Kingdom.

Effect on children

a) As Seen by Themselves : A group of children (below 15 years) who were interviewed at Gomti Nagar in Lucknow said that they used to devote more time to their studies, and to play more games, before cable TV came into their homes. They now spent less time with others of their own age.

On the other hand, their knowledge about the outside world, which had been very limited, was now greater. Another positive feature mentioned by them was that they have been made aware of many things not mentioned in their school books.

Some said that their role model now was a film star or a sports person, rather than a historical figure, political leader or industrialist as in the past.

When probed what would happen if cable TV were removed tomorrow, one of them exclaimed : 'No, uncle! Do not do that. How will we pass our time ?' They said that, except for the BBC channel, they found something or other that was attractive in all the foreign channels.

A couple of the children said, half seriously, that when a movie or interesting programme is on, their mothers try to finish their household work quickly; as a result, the food they get is not as tasty as it used to be.

A group of children at Guwahati said that they cannot study when a cricket match is being shown on TV, even if examinations are on; similarly if some other favourite programme of theirs is on.

Some children in Bhubaneswar said that when TV telecasts fairy tales like 'Cinderella' and 'Sleeping Beauty', it motivates them to go to the library and read those stories. They enjoyed the reading as they could picturise the situations.

b) As Seen by Parents : A group of housewives in Delhi said that if TV is turned on, it is easier to get the child to eat.

At Golaghat in Assam, Mr. Duara said that, specially

after the coming of cable TV, they have to be firm with the children to the point of rudeness and forcibly turn off the TV, specially when a cricket match is being shown; otherwise they will not attend to their studies. He pleaded that Doordarshan should stop telecasting cricket matches.

A housewife in Delhi claimed that TV does not affect the care and attention bestowed by mothers on their children. Housewives go about attending to the kitchen and other work even when TV is on.

An adverse effect on children cited by housewives in Delhi is that they start singing off-colour songs, or repeating a greeting like 'meri jaan', when they meet any visitor.

In Guwahati, Mrs. Bardoloi felt that her children had some innovative talent which they have lost after beginning to spend their time before the TV set.

According to a parent in Gourinagar, Bhubaneshwar, after watching a serial 'PHIR WOHI TALASH' his daughter forced him to grant her permission to marry the boy of her choice.

c) As Seen by Teachers : The principal of a school in Bhubaneshwar complained that children in her school feel sleepy in the classroom as they sit up till late at night watching movies.

Some teachers working on the afternoon shift complained that the 2 P.M. films on the Metro Channel had led to an unmistakable drop in the attendance at school.

In the elite schools of Delhi where discussions were held with teachers—a Delhi Public School unit, Air Force Bal Bharati, Sardar Patel Vidyalaya and Kannada School and two Kendriya Vidyalayas—almost all agreed with the prognosis of a male teacher in Kannada school that in any class there are 20% toppers, 20% below average, and the remaining 60% average. The toppers know how to adjust their time between studies and TV viewing. The problem lies with the others as they are succumbing to TV.

A number of teachers said that with both parents going to work, the formative years of a child are left, much of the time, in the care of an ayah or of TV. The parents do not make the effort, when at home, to sit with the children and talk to them or read to them. From a sense of guilt, they allow the children to do what they like : and watching TV comes at the top of the list.

The teachers also blamed the film-based programmes and the sex-permeated among serials for a big increase in love affairs in the schools. Earlier such incidents used to be few and far between, and confined to students in the 11th and 12th classes. Now such things are happening even among 6th and 7th graders.

Students and Youth

At each of the fourteen cities and towns where focus group discussions were organised, CMS researchers made it a point to talk to groups of students and youth—who are considered the most vulnerable to the impact of TV and more especially of cable TV—as well as to parents. The following salient points emerged.

Positive Elements : (i) Students are improving their general knowledge by viewing programmes such as Quiz, World This Week and Turning Point.

(ii) The young are gaining in self-confidence and are able to move freely in society.

(iii) There is greater acceptance of gender equality.

(iv) Young housewives are able to spend the afternoons without boredom or recourse to gossip.

(v) There is better sports awareness and career guidance is found useful.

(vi) Young people feel confident in their ability to shape their future, after watching programmes where TV has shown stories of people in real life who have risen from the ranks by their own efforts and hard work.

Negative Elements : (i) Getting hooked to the idiot box definitely hampers the studies of school and college students.

(ii) There is neglect of sports, affecting the health of the young, and continuous TV watching leads in many cases to impairment of eyesight and the need to wear spectacles or contact lenses.

(iii) Young people are led prematurely into a world of sexual fantasy by watching TV or some of the Zee TV programmes.

(iv) Some of them practise copycat violence. It was reported in a Delhi elite school that a student mixed laxative given to horses with food, and fed it to his unsuspecting schoolmates. It almost led to the death of one of the victims. The boy who did it had seen it done in one of the movies shown on TV. Another case referred to in the discussions was of a boy in the Naval School who took to stealing cars and got nabbed after his tenth exploit.

Growth of Consumerism : Young people want to acquire whatever goods—from fancy shoes to 'Dove' soap—are advertised on TV. They are being inducted into a materialistic culture of consumerism. Soon there may be only one culture world-wide : American pop culture.

Precocious Sexual Stimulation : The pursuit of sexual gratification, which is part of the consumerist culture, is promoted prematurely among the young by exposure to titillating scenes on the TV screen, fashion shows, hot films, and film-based song-and-dance sequences. A housewife in Allahabad said that this effect of TV on the young can be neutralised in two ways : firstly, regulating their TV watching in terms of timing and of programmes; and (ii) answering satisfactorily the questions that arise in their minds after watching TV. However, she said, these measures are not easy to implement. For one thing, 'We ourselves feel like watching those programmes which we think are not good for the children.' Secondly, 'most of us are either not competent or bold enough to explain to children their questions concerning sex.'

Temptation of Small-Screen Career : During a discussion with students of Lucknow University, a girl student confessed : 'In the field of acting there are few chances in films, but one can go to the small screen without much difficulty'.

Dress and Deportment : Several respondents spoke

disapprovingly of the tendency on the part of both boys and girls to imitate western pop dress styles—jeans in particular—or the wearing of an ear-ring in one ear.

However, a focus group of parents in Andhra Pradesh noted a healthy change in the dress habit of young girls as the result of exposure to TV. In place of the traditional, provocative lehanga and half-sari, they were switching on to salwars kameez which seemed to the respondents to be more decent.

Parents' double standards

The need for parents themselves to exercise self-control if they are to regulate TV viewing by their children was highlighted by some instances, which focus-group moderators came across, of double standards on the part of elders.

In Lucknow, a doctor (name withheld) who claims to be the disciple of a 'Satsangi Baba' expressed himself against Star TV. He said that cable TV is leading to a cultural colonisation of our country. It was discovered towards the end of the discussion, however, that the doctor is himself a successful cable operator.

Such hypocrisy, it turned out, is not confined to men. A lady in her late fifties (name withheld), residing in Mohannagar, expressed herself strongly against Cable TV. She said that many of the programmes shown on the foreign channels were destructive of our cultural values. She herself watched TV rarely, she said, and only to see 'Krishna' on DD 2. But her daughter, who is a doctor by profession, came out with the revelation that her mother devoted several hours a day to TV and watched the V Channel among others.

Impact on family life : Two views

Contrasting impressions of the effect of DD and cable TV on communication and interaction between family members were voiced by discussants in focus group sessions.

Some housewives said that instead of playing cards in a club or visiting their men friends, husbands came home early in the evening because of the pull of TV. Thus more time was spent together by the husband and wife, and by both with their children, than during life before TV.

Whether this physical proximity for a greater duration meant better communication and understanding between the members of a family was a question on which views differed. Some felt that family ties were improved, while some others said that members of the family were each separately glued to the small screen, without any interaction by way of conversation taking place.

Discussants in Andhra Pradesh said that cable TV helped to keep elderly members of the family occupied. They now felt less neglected, and more cared for. This view of TV as a lollipop for the aged was expressed at more than one focus group discussion with male and female heads of households.

During discussion with a youth group in Delhi, a participant said that TV was a source of conflict within the family because of differing views on what programmes should be watched.

Case studies of TV addicts

A 20-year-old student of Osmania University (name withheld) said that he was not exposed to cable TV till he completed his 12th class, since his parents feared that it would hamper his studies. Once he got through the joint entrance examination for engineering and medical education, and was admitted to the B.E. (Chemical Engineering) course, he requested his parents to subscribe to cable TV as a reward for his good performance. They agreed, as there were no younger children in the home who were likely to be adversely affected by cable TV.

Prior to the arrival of cable, he had watched TV very little since he was busy with studies. But now his addiction began. He compared his being hooked on cable TV to becoming addicted to drugs. Except for the time he spends in the college, he is all the time with TV. The moment he gets home he turns it on if it is not already on, and watches it even while having his food. Formerly, he used to complete his meal within 15 minutes; now it takes at least 45 minutes.

He does not care about what he is eating, or how much, or the taste of the food. When news is telecast on one channel, he switches to another for entertainment programmes. He is attracted in particular to programmes that show semi-clad women. He feels that cable TV has taken away the potential to pursue any goal; it has slowly killed ambition. He had wanted to become eminent as an engineer; now he has been reduced to an addict. Realising his condition, his parents wanted to disconnect cable, but he told them he could not live without it. He might not have developed the addiction, he said, if he had viewed only Doordarshan.

A teacher in the Sardar Patel Vidyalaya, Delhi, who is married but childless, said that they have two TV sets in their home with cable. Her husband is an ardent sports fan and gets engrossed in the sports channel. She watches whatever she wants on the other set. They do not even sit together for their meals but eat separately while watching TV. Her listening to music, as well as her reading, have come down. She confesses that she has become an addict and does not know how to get out of it.

Many members of the housewives' group at George Town in Allahabad said that removal of TV would be like the death of a family member : it had become so much a part of their life. One of them asked : 'How can I cut vegetables without looking at TV ?'

Social impact of advertisements

Next only to the condemnation of vulgarity and violence depicted on the TV screen was the concern expressed by discussants, in almost all the focus groups, at the social effect of the commercial advertisements carried by TV, including Doordarshan.

Housewives in Allahabad said that often the advertisements are misleading because the product, after it has been bought, is not as good as the advertisement claimed. More serious, they said, is that some of the advertisements confuse children and when they ask for clarification of an advertisement of condoms or of female sanitary napkins, it is embarrassing. They also objected to nearly half of the time allotted for certain programmes being consumed by advertisements : it was very irritating.

At all the centres where focus group discussions were conducted, the participants said that children began to press for the purchase of things which were beyond the family's financial reach.

One participant wondered why there is no provision to complain about advertisements, and why Doordarshan does not bother to distinguish an ad from the news or a programme.

Preference for local language programmes

Telugu-speaking housewives, spoken to at Hyderabad, Cuddapah and Karimnagar in Andhra Pradesh, said that they do not understand the Hindi programmes on Doordarshan. They preferred cable TV since they could see Telugu films. Some of the discussants said that since they do not understand any language other than Telugu, it hardly mattered whether they watch programmes in Hindi, English or other foreign language : hence their exercise of the cable TV option.

Dislike of the imposition of Hindi programmes on them by Doordarshan was voiced also by English-speaking male heads of households who were spoken to in Hyderabad. These Hindi programmes were poor in quality and did not interest them, and since they could follow programmes in English equally well, they switched to cable TV.

TV as threat to culture

While many among the discussants spoke of foreign satellite channels disseminated by cable as a threat to India's cultural heritage and identity, some respondents in Assam regarded Doordarshan itself as the carrier of polluting influences.

At Tezpur, the Saikias said that they were nostalgic about life as it used to be prior to the advent of TV. They visited friends' homes, listened to radio, and went out now and then to see a movie or to eat out. All this had stopped now. Mr. Saikia compared TV to a sweet-tasting poison.

Children wanted them to buy everything advertised on TV.

Mr. Barua went further and blamed Doordarshan for making Assamese society, which used to be free of problems like dowry and drugs, aware of these aberrations of Indian culture and to be tempted by them.

The Kalitas said that cable TV is undesirable not so much because of the cost factor as the obscenity and vulgarity of the Western programmes shown on the foreign channels.

Leaves Little to Imagination : Mrs. Barkakati said that, before TV came, radio was a much better medium. She used to give close attention to radio programmes, and because radio did not provide visuals, they used to picture mentally what was referred to. This helped to improve the imaginative power of listeners. Now, this power is totally lost.

Realistic visual depiction on TV was referred to also by Pramod Mishra, a post-graduate student of Allahabad university, though without disapproval. He was sore about his parents intervening, and reminding him about his studies, when he watched 'adult' scenes. He recalled how he was rebuked when he was engrossed in a certain scene in a mythological serial in which Sakuntala was shown with the minimum of clothing.

Obscenity in 'Chitrahaar' : Many participants in the focus groups said that there was vulgarity and obscenity in Doordarshan, though on a smaller scale than in some of the foreign satellite channels. Depiction of some of the love scenes was described as provocative.

The group of housewives at George Town in Allahabad said that undesirable obscene sequences are shown by Doordarshan too, not only by the foreign channels. Obscene songs featured in 'Chitrahaar' were condemned. Some wondered how songs and son dances from yet-to-be released/censored feature films could be shown on Doordarshan so blatantly.

Towards clean fun and winder awareness

That TV has made the earth shrink and brought it to one's doorstep is a view that was shared by every focus group. But there was a price to be paid for this wider awareness : namely the vulgarity, obscenity and violence that marked many of the programmes of Doordarshan and, even more so, of the foreign channels made accessible by cable operators.

Suggestions offered for improving the situation included the following :

(1) Already, with the introduction of DD2 and its availability in more centres, the need for cable TV as an alternative source of entertainment has diminished. Let DD2 be extended to more centres.

(2) Eliminate vulgarity, obscenity and sadistic violence from Doordarshan's programmes—whether films, film-based sequences, serials or others.

(3) Let there be more programmes that improve the viewers' general knowledge and social awareness.

(4) Free Doordarshan news bulletins from the deadweight of government control and their manipulation to serve as propaganda for parties and for persons in power for the time being.

8 COLLOQUIA ON MEDIA MALADIES AND REMEDIES

CMS organised during 1994-95 a series of round-table discussions on the plus and minus points of the performance of the mass media in India and on steps necessary to enhance their contribution to nation building in the context of globe-encircling satellite TV.

Four of these colloquia were held in Delhi, and six in regional centres across the country : Lucknow, Bhubaneshwar, Vijayawada, Ahmedabad, Pune and Bangalore.

The first symposium in Delhi, on 18th February 1954, was on the emerging scene of satellite TV and India's response to the challenge.

CHALLENGE OF TRANSNATIONAL TELEVISION

Presented here are the salient points made by various participants, grouped under thematic heads.

SELF-DEFENCE THROUGH LOCALLY RELEVANT PROGRAMMING

Vasant Sathe, former Minister of I & B : India does run a serious risk of cultural invasion, information imperialism and economic colonialism. We need not cave in. We have resources enough to stand on our own legs. It is our market of 250 million well-to-do consumers whom the foreign media and investors are after. We cannot ban cable TV. Rather, we should be competitive. Let us show better programmes on Doordarshan, of local interest, so that we retain the viewership. The low power transmitters should be enabled to transmit locally made video feeds.

P. Upendra, former Minister of I & B : Neither a ban on dish antennae, nor aping, will help. MTV will always be slicker in its presentation of mindless entertainment. We should offer programmes that are at once entertaining, socially relevant and useful. The appeal of foreign TV is to the urban viewers. There is no immediate threat in rural India. If we provide programmes of interest, in the regional languages, they will hold the attention and interest of the audience.

M.V. Desai, veteran journalist : The electronic media suffer from excessive centralisation. They use English and Hindi almost exclusively, whereas the majority of our people have mother tongues other than these. Doordarshan should offer locally relevant and useful programmes in local speech. Decentralisation is the best defence against destabilisation of the Indian ethos.

P.C. Chatterji, former Director General of All India Radio: Doordarshan and AIR should acquire credibility. Both blacked out the views on the Kashmir question expressed recently by Dr. Karan Singh, though he is an important political actor and observer vis a vis Kashmir. We should not drive viewers to alternative sources of news.

N. Bhaskara Rao : There is a class division in the world of information, as of economic life. There should be citizen involvement in the media. There are now no local advisory committees for the stations of All India Radio or Doordarshan. We have to promote responsiveness of media towards the public, and create awareness of issues. I have mooted the idea of 'social audit of the media' on a continuing basis, with involvement of independent professionals.

S.S. Gill, former Secretary of I & B Ministry : If indigenous programmes are excellent and useful, no one will want to watch foreign programmes. It is not as if we lack talented programme makers. Only, we must allow them to work under conditions that will permit credibility such as the BBC has.

Brahma Kumari Asha, social worker : The mass media should help to build national character. The need to preserve family values is being realised now in the West, and 1994 has been designated as the U.N. Year of the Family.

Hanumantha Rao : Dish Antennae for direct reception of foreign programmes via satellite are not allowed in China. This is the reason why Rupert Murdoch is turning to India, the next biggest market. Countries like Malaysia and Singapore are market-oriented in their economy but are zealous to preserve their cultural identity. Only India seems to be unconcerned. Do we want to pride ourselves that we are a media democracy, whatever be its consequences to our people ?

R. Vijay, documentary producer : Though TV is primarily a visual medium, there is far too much talking on Doordarshan, specially by political VIPs.

Nori Venkateswarlu, broadcasting engineer : Many excellent films are being made in the regional languages. These can be telecast with dubbing in the local language. Each low power transmitter can be utilised for telecasting locally made video programmes of relevance and interest.

S.B. Lal, former Secretary of I & B Ministry : Our country boasts of the biggest cinema industry, and a widely appreciated Press. Why can't we have world class television too ?

OWNERSHIP, AUTONOMY, ACCOUNTABILITY

P. Upendra : No government will be willing to give up its control over the national electronic media. While the government can retain the main TV channel for its purposes ranging from information and education to propaganda, it should hand over other channels to private, competitive initiative.

Vasant Sathe : The government should retain one channel of Doordarshan and convert the others into independent commercial channels.

Kuldip Nayyar, veteran journalist : There is an increasing tendency for persons who have made money in other industries to come into newspaper publishing. This is not a healthy trend.

N. Bhaskara Rao : There is an increasing trend towards cross-media ownership. This is ominous. We should beware of its implications.

VULGAR ENTERTAINMENT, CONSUMERISM, CRIME

Rami Chhabra, active in the women's and family welfare movements, said that the low standard of Doordarshan's Chitrahaar and other filmy fare, specially on the Metro Channel, was debasing public taste. Instead of promoting gender equality and other dimensions of desirable social change, the advertisements and many of the entertainment programmes of Doordarshan present women as sex objects. This is contributing to increasing incidents of molestation of and crimes against women. The Indian mass media are shaking the foundations of Indian culture.

G.N.S. Raghavan : There have been many reports of the murder of employers by domestic servants in Delhi over the last year. This is not to be wondered at. Domestic employees watch along with members of the employing family Doordarshan's programmes, the most popular of which are punctuated by commercial advertisement of goods and services meant for the well-to-do. Why should they not aspire to the same luxuries ? The culture of consumerism spread by Doordarshan incites them to theft and murder.

H.B. Mathur, media critic, said that the visual medium is expensive and has an inherent tendency to become centralised and market-oriented. It treats the viewers as consumers rather than people to be served. The size and purchasing power of the audience determines profit. Zee TV and DD Metro tend to be oriented to the Gulf, which is now a zone of prosperity. Hindi cinema as a whole has become increasingly Gulf-oriented.

Mira Aghi, media specialist, said that the quality of

Metro channel programmes was appealling and no better than the satellite entertainment channels. It is as if India's TV system is no different in its priorities and concerns.

RADIO : THE CINDERELLA

P.C. Chatterji said that All India Radio broadcasts excellent music programmes but there is no promotion of listening through advance announcement of the day's programmes. The use of FM in Delhi for broadcasting rap music is deplorable. As for news, why should the same bulletins be broadcast on different channels of AIR ?

P. Upendra : It is a pity that we are ignoring radio which is the common man's medium.

H.B. Mathur : In contrast to TV which is expensive and centralised, radio is closer to the people in a poor nation. It speaks to them in their own languages.

Maya Daruwalas of the Ford Foundation : Listenership of radio is double the viewership of TV. The use of FM for local-interest broadcasting, over a 50-km radius, can help to democratise the medium.

Hanumantha Rao : There has been a rejuvenation of radio programmes in several countries of South East Asia, with the novelty of TV wearing off.

PRESS : 'OUR PROFIT V. THEIR PROFIT'

Some participants referred to certain statements by Justice Sarkaria (Retd.), Chairman of the Press Council of India, in which he had opposed the entry of foreign newspaper publishers into the country. One discussant said that he had spoken as if he were the circulation manager of the Indian Press, while another described the uproar over the entry of foreign print media as a case of 'our profit versus their profit'.

Kuldip Nayar : A line should be drawn, in the process of globalisation and the encouragement of foreign investment, at the entry of external capital into the print media. Can foreigners start political parties ?

I. Rammohan Rao, former Principal Information Officer:

We should guard against the manipulation of our society by foreign media.

B.B. Nagpal of UNI : Foreigners may buy out our newspaper chains.

Brij Mohan : There can be a brain drain within the country, with foreigners hiring the services of talented Indian journalists.

S. Venkat Narayan : Opposition to the entry of foreign publishers into India is illogical, considering that there is extensive and increasing movement of people and of ideas between India and the rest of the world.

Inder Malhotra, journalist and author : Why all this worry about foreign newspapers when our mainline dailies are devoting considerable space for reprinting material from those publications ?

Kuldip Nayar referred to a paper circulated in connection with the symposium, in which secularism had been cited as one of the subjects on which the Press had failed to educate the public. He strongly disagreed with the suggestion in the paper that secularism had become a 'nonsense word', thanks to its indiscriminate use by political parties.

S.B. Lal : There should be more space for local voices in our Press.

M.V. Desai referred to Article 19 of the Constitution which guarantees freedom of expression, and wondered whether this would apply to newspaper companies that might be established by foreigners, or with foreign capital participation. What did the Second Press Commission say on the subject ?

G.N.S. Raghavan, who had served as secretary of the Commission, said that in Chapter IV, on 'Constitution and Laws', the report notes that the Fundamental Right of freedom of expression (interpreted by the Supreme Court to include freedom of the Press) is available only to citizens, and not to companies. The Second Press Commission recommended that companies engaged in the business of communication, provided their shareholders are Indian citizens, should be deemed to be 'citizens' for the purpose of Article 19. However, the Government had not accepted this recommendation, taking the view that it would be discriminatory to give the status of citizen only to those companies that are engaged in the business of communication.

EDUCATION AND THE MEDIA

G. Ram Reddy, Chairman, University Grants Commission: There has been no convergence yet between the media and formal education. The media can play a big part in remedying a situation in which, out of 7600 colleges in the country, 3000 colleges are non-viable due to inadequacy of teachers, equipment and libraries. Even after the formation of the Indira Gandhi National Open University, Doordarshan gives only two hours to the programmes of the University Grants Commission in English and Hindi. There are hardly any college-level educational programmes in the regional languages. In contrast, in Japan the NHK devotes 16 hours of a dedicated channel every day to education. Only six per cent of persons in the age group 17-23 go to college in India : in no civilised country is the percentage so low. Prof. Ram Reddy expressed regret that, having started with the objectives of education and national integration, the media have lost sight of priorities. He called for a dedicated TV channel for education.

S.B. Lal : Education and rural channels were to have been funded with money earned by the entertainment channel. This has not happened.

Gangwani : Television with its fleeting visuals does not render the teacher redundant. Students will continue to need the teacher for rechecking.

TECHNOLOGY : FRIEND OR FOE ?

R. Vijay : It is not modern technology in itself that makes for centralisation but advertising and financial considerations. Video technology now enables low-cost production of local-interest programmes.

S.B. Lal : The live telecast via satellite of the Republic Day parade in Delhi in January 1994 by Star TV has revolutionised the image of India abroad by making widely known the armed strength and confidence of the country.

Kamtekar, referred to a 'dynamic lock' that can be built into TV reception to keep out what is not desired.

A.K. Lal : Intellectuals tend to be distrustful of technology. They need to get over this attitude. India, too, can 'invade' other countries with its programmes—and at low cost.

EROTICISM AND VIOLENCE : A WAR ON SOCIETY

The second round-table discussion was organised by CMS in Delhi on the theme of Vulgarity and Violence in Mass Media, on 22nd September 1994.

Ranganath Misra, former Chief Justice of the Supreme Court, said in his keynote address that Indian society faces a situation worse than war, on account of the rampant vulgarity and violence in the mass media, specially cinema and television. It was an undeclared and insidious war, an onslaught without notice. Values which had held Indian society together from Rig Vedic times, with an ethical discipline governing men and women and different segments of society, are being eroded.

Justice Misra, who now heads the national Human Rights Commission, said he had told the President and the Prime Minister that films, and the indiscriminate screening of them by Doordarshan, were hindering the creation of a culture of human rights which was a primary charge given to his Commission. Not only Indian society but also entire humanity was under threat, he said, because national boundaries had been dissolved by the communication revolution; an attempt to meet this menace was therefore necessary at the international level too.

P. Upendra, chairman of the Parliamentary standing Committee for the Ministry of Human Resources Development, came down heavily on the aping of foreign television by Doordarshan.

Jayanti Patnaik, chairperson of the National Commission for Women, deplored the exhibition of mindless violence and sex on the screen, big and small. She conceded that notions of propriety were relative to time and place. While Christian puritanism and victorian prudery were outdated, we could not afford either, she said, to adopt the modern Scandinavian attitude of permissiveness.

Kiran Bedi, Inspector-General of Prisons, Delhi, and Magsaysay Award winner, said that as a parent and as a citizen she shared the concern of participants in the seminar. Vulgarity in the media was a question not only of morality but also of public health.

G.N.S. Raghavan, said that Indian society was afflicted by a variety of obsceneties of which sexual obscenity in the media was an inter-connected part. There was the obscenity of vulgar riches in the midst of widespread poverty, and of disparities in educational opportunity—with lavish public spending on higher education when half the population remained illiterate. He also characterised as obscene the self-exhibition on Doordarshan by those in power, and called upon publicists in the non-official media to be sensitive to these aberrations and to press for corrective action.

N. Bhaskara Rao : We need 'survival kits' to protect ourselves from the 24-hour offering of cinema, within the home, by television.

Prof. Khilnani of Hindu College drew attention to an estimate that India is among the South Asian countries where the majority of the population would soon be in the age group below 39. It was important to protect this 'hot blood' from unhealthy influences through the mass media.

Jaya Jaitley, lawyer and social activist, illustrated the general decline in values by referring to the phenomenon of student politicians who remained on campuses till they were forty years old. She deplored the duplicity involved in the authorities permitting thinly disguised advertising of liquor on giant hoardings in the capital.

Moolchand Sharma, Professor of Law, Delhi University, said that competitive commercialisation is dictating media priorities. In moviews, two-and-a-half hours of violence is supposed to be justified by five or 10 minutes of goodness.

EFFECT ON CHILDREN : COPYCAT VIOLENCE

Justice Misra said that children tend to imitate in their actions what they see being done by adults. This point was illustrated by several participants who cited the findings of research, conducted in India and abroad, establishing a direct link between juvenile crime and the depiction of violence in the media.

Nandini Prasad, communication specialist, said that films depicted not only women in an objectionable way but men too. They were presented as villains, rapists, alcoholics and singers of bawdy songs. Women figured in the newscasts, by and large, only as politicians. The minorities were covered only in sectarian contexts such as their religious festivals. Child viewers were exposed along with adults to scenes of murder and rape. Copycat violence and impulsive behaviour was promoted by the exposure of children to scenes of sadism, pelvic thrust and frenzied gyrations in the name of dance.

Manorama Jafa of the Children's Book Trust spoke of the paucity of good literature for children. There was not a single bookstall offering publications solely meant for young readers, except for those run by the C.B.T. and the National Book Trust—and they put on view only their own titles. She urged that exhibition of vulgarity should be treated as a crime. In connection with the effect of violence shown on the screen, Manorama Jafa cited a study conducted in West Bengal which showed that 90% of juvenile crime went unreported.

DEPICTION OF WOMEN : WHAT IS VULGARITY ?

The relativism of morals to place and time was stressed by some participants.

Abhilasha Kumari of Jamia Millia's Mass Communication Centre added the dimension of class to the relativism of morals. She questioned the right of the urban well-to-do to lay down a code of decency and propriety for a society like India's that is highly diverse both economically and in terms of urban, rural and tribal society. She said that women constituted the single largest group of TV viewers. For them it provided a 'space' outside the home to which they were otherwise tied down.

Vijayalakshmi Bose, lecturer at the Jamia Millia's communication centre, referred to criticism of bedroom scenes shown on the screen and said : "There is no immaculate conception in India."

M.R. Dua, Professor, Indian Institute of Mass Communication recalled how the Delhi Cloth Mills had some years ago sought to promote a new textile variety with a Press advertisement inviting women to "be daringly different: drop the dupatta". It was considered vulgar at the time, but the dupatta has now been discarded by many women.

Kiran Kartik of the Consortium for Education and Communication posed the question whether pornography was not in the mind of the beholder. On the relationship between real life and 'reel life', he said it is possible that the depiction of violence serves as catharsis, helping the viewer to identify emotionally with the action without committing violence himself.

In contrast to the above, several participants felt that there was no difficulty in recognising vulgarity when one comes across it.

Vasantha Patri of the Psychology Department, Lady Sriram College, said that obscenity might be defined as "the wanton or wilful presentation of a person or situation intended to titillate the viewer or listener." Another participant said that "a scene which one would not like to share with his or her children" might be described as obscene.

Kiran Bedi : By our conscience, we know when a thing is obscene, i.e., those of us with the sensibility to feel embarrassed.

(The remarks of **Kapila Vatsyayan** on this subject have been quoted in Chapter I.)

FILM CENSORSHIP FAILURE : ALTERNATIVES

P. Upendra said that detailed prescription of "don'ts" in the recently issued revised guidelines for film censorship brought out the difficulty of a negative approach. Moreover, much depended on the selection of censors and on the integrity of the officials running the censorship machinery. It was, in his view, highly objectionable that the Government had appointed a film producer as chief of the Central Board of Film Certification. There were instances of the Regional Officers of the Censor Board being bribed by film producers to call particular persons from the panel of viewers in order to get a film passed, howsoever vulgar it might be.

Since self-regulation had succeeded, by and large, in respect of film publicity material, it could also perhaps be the basis for improving the tone of films. The example of Bengali films, many of which avoided vulgarity and were yet successful at the box office, showed the scope for self-regulation on the part of film producers.

Kamala Mankekar, journalist and member of the CBFC, narrated her five-year experience in the Board. Instead of being convened to meet two or three times a year as required, the Board had met last after an interval of eighteen months. The revised censorship guidelines were circulated towards the end of this single-day meeting, and could not obviously be discussed in any meaningful way.

Referring to the claim of film producers that they were providing what the public wanted, Kamala Mankekar expressed regret that the Censor Board had not conducted any survey of public opinion to put this claim to test; nor did the Board organise discussions such as the present symposium. She referred to a delegation of women having met the President of India on the subject of vulgarity in films, and said that the role of public opinion was most important. About the legislation prohibiting indecent representation of women, and publications harmful to young persons, she said : "We are a country where laws are made to be broken, not enforced."

Jaya Jaitley, who had served on the CBFC for a year,

said that the Board was a highly politicised body. A Joint Secretary in the Ministry of Information & Broadcasting decides who shall view a film for passing it.

COMMERCIALISATION OF THE PRESS

P. Upendra expressed regret that the canker of commercialism had spread to the Press also. Referring to sex magazines that carry lewd pictures and sell at fancy prices, he deplored the fact that such publications were being defended by some pseudo-intellectuals in the name of freedom of expression.

Anupama Mohan deplored the tendency towards titillation and fantasy in the Press, as in cinema. She said that reports on crime were being front-paged, with gory details. These had the same effect as glorification of violence on the screen. She regretted that, in addition to selling space for commercial advertisements, the Press had thus begun to commercialise news space also for increasing their circulation.

T.N. Rastogi deplored the declining standards of the fourth estate, which was now devoting a large amount of space to murder and other sensational news.

CORRECTIVES : ROLE OF EDUCATION

Anita Kohli, who teaches in the R.K. Puram branch of Delhi Public School, said that the role of parenting and of the teacher in forming the values of the young needed to be better understood and taken more seriously. Nothing is being done in the classroom to sensitise children on the media.

Abha Sahgal, who also teaches in the same school, said that there was nothing in the school curriculum to promote positive social values such as compassion or the equality and dignity of women.

Mohini Giri, social activist, stressed the need for suitable pictorial books for children of the three-to-five age group that would help to promote healthy social values.

Samyak suggested that the best way to promote positive values among the young is for parents and teachers to practise moderation themselves, so that ethical standards are set for compassion, frugality and control of desires.

Sister Asha of the Brahma Kumaris urged positive steps by way of formal and non-formal education to counter the undesirable effects of television.

G. N. S. Raghavan said that certain provisions in the Indian Constitution stand in the way of education helping to promote positive values among students. Ethical behaviour has been traditionally associated with religious teaching, but religious instruction in State-run schools and colleges, attended by the great majority of Indian students—is banned under Article 28 of the Constitution. Other Articles, however, grant to religious minorities the right to run educational institutions where religious instruction can be imparted. The two largest minority religions in India, Islam and Christianity, both happen to be monotheistic and proselytising. The result is that children belonging by birth to the minority religions are reinforced in the belief that theirs is the only true religion. All this, G. N. S. Raghavan pointed out, is in flat contradiction to the recommendation by the Radhakrishnan Commission on Education that the humanistic values common to all religions should be a compulsory part of education at every stage. He suggested that the Supreme Court could be petitioned, in the public interest, to examine these provisions of the Constitution which discriminate between citizens on the ground of their religion.

HOW RESEARCH CAN HELP

Anita Kohli urged that research should help to promote corrective action, and should not only be directed towards knowledge gain.

Vijayalakshmi Bose made a similar plea for action-oriented research. She also referred to bureaucratic delays in securing research funding from Indian government sources, in contrast to foreign agencies.

Devesh Kishore, who heads the communications wing of the Indira Gandhi National Open University, suggested the formation of a forum to coordinate research at various levels in the country on issues related to media impact. The findings should be made public in order to promote awareness among citizens.

CITIZENS' INITIATIVE : TALKING BACK TO THE MEDIA

Vasanti of CMS said that reliance only on government or its agencies would not suffice to reverse the unhealthy trends. There is need for citizen initiatives at various levels : in the schools, in homes, by teachers and by parents.

Nori Venkateswarlu refused to the agitation launched by women, in the Nellore region of Andhra Pradesh, which had forced the State Government to prohibit the sale of arrack even though it meant forgoing a large chunk of revenue. He said that women were the most affected by and in the best position to fight, undesirable trends whether in public policy or in the mass media.

N. Bhaskara Rao referred to recent protest demonstrations by teachers and by women in front of Doordarshan Kendras as a heartening development. This had, in fact, encouraged the Centre for Media Studies to convene the present symposium, participants in which included a large number of women and teachers. He announced that CMS proposed to launch a social audit of the media at national and regional levels, on a continuing basis, to analyse media trends as well as to sensitise the public. Citizens' initiative would be stimulated by convening similar gatherings outside Delhi to help articulate what citizens think of the social effects of the mass media.

VOICES FROM OUTSIDE DELHI

Following the Delhi seminar on violence and vulgarity in the media, CMS devoted the remaining months of 1994 to organise similar gatherings of concerned citizens from various walks of life, at six regional centres across the country.

Presented below is a summary of the discussion that took

place at these regional colloquia.

LUCKNOW

Motilal Vora, Governor of Uttar Pradesh, was the chief guest at the symposium on violence and vulgarity in the mass media held at Lucknow on 7th October, 1994. He said that the ideal role of the media is to popularise ideas and thoughts and human values, and to develop national character. But the cultural invasion of Indian society by foreign media has eroded traditional Indian values, and the younger generation is getting attracted towards Western culture—not at its best, but of the contemporary popular variety. There is still time, and policy-makers must ensure proper use of the media. They must stop the media from spreading values that adversely affect the minds of our citizens. The only way to counter the ill effects of the media is through purposeful education, Motilal Vora said. We should search for an educational system which promotes knowledge, science and technology and also produces citizens bound to moral values.

R. C. Tripathi, Education Adviser in the Planning Commission of India, said in his keynote speech : "We can ignore electronic media at our own peril. India missed partici- pating in the Industrial Revolution. We would not like to repeat history. We have to take the bull by the horns." Society, he said, has to concern itself with the contents and quality of the media programmes and consider their impact on different kinds of viewers. Glamour and romance of films and media are casting an almost stupefying influence on our youth, who succumb as its victims before they mature to understand the purpose or value of life. Things cannot be left entirely, he said, to the media or to their immature audience. The State and intelligentsia will have to intervene. Local groups, regional and national organisations should be set up to act as constant watch-dogs.

Mahendra Singh, Professor, Lucknow University, said that vulgarity has many definitions, and has different meanings in different contexts. In the atmosphere of openness prevailing in India today, there is definite need for frank discussion of the trends in the media.

Murtaza Hussain, former Judge, said that cultural values play a very important part in human lives. A cultural change for the worse can turn a person into a demon.

Other participants in the symposium included Upendra Vajpeyi, secretary of the National Media Centre, Dr. V. G. Joshi of the Girl Institute, Prof. Asha Awasthi from the Department of Sociology of Lucknow University, and Vikram Rao, president of the Indian Federation of Working Journalists.

BHUBANESHWAR

Chandrasekhar Rath, well-known Oriya writer, delivered the keynote address at the symposium on violence and vulgarity in mass media held at Bhubaneshwar on 22nd October, 1994. He suggested amendment of the Consumer Protection Act of 1984 to save consumers of mass media programmes from their ill effects. Commercial cinema goes by the market, not by morals, Prof. Rath said. For film makers, films are commodities—just like any other to be sold as hot stuff. Sex is a lure which the film industry exploits. He urged a holistic approach to the present situation, which would prove more useful than trying to tackle various problems in isolation.

Hara Prasad Das, Accountant General and well-known scholar of Orissa, said that we are on an extremely difficult terrain in considering the social effects of the media. It is difficult because of contradictions between Global and Local India, between public gestures and private morals. He suggested some ways by which the incidence of violence and vulgarity in the media could be curbed. One is through innovative creation of new audience interests; this is possible, as shown by the box-office failure of some big-budget films based on the sex-violence formula and the success of some elegant love stories. A second way could be to establish closer links between cinema and the print media, particularly creative works of fiction. Another way, he said, is to create mass awareness so that people refuse to see films or TV programmes that violate their aesthetic sensibility.

Jayanti Patnaik, chairperson of the National Commission

for Women and chief guest at the symposium, called for a national media policy which will help arrest the negative trends of violence and vulgarity.

Ramakanta Rath, eminent poet and former Chief Secretary of Orissa, said that vulgarity and obscenity were inevitably a part of the present social scenario in which 90 per cent of criminals are allowed to go scotfree. Public taste has taken a downswing, while the culture of irresponsibility pervaded every sphere of society. He felt that the basic need is for a regeneration of society.

Maqbool Ali, social worker, said that in India the norms of behaviour are clearly defined in our family and social life. We should guide the younger generation to watch such programmes in the media which are in conformity with those norms. Secondly, people must insist on healthy movies and serials portraying humans as humans and not as super-powerful heroes. Unfortunately, the media depend more on 'masala' than on facts. People need to be advised to stick to truth and reality and not succumb to fantasy. Finally, he suggested that while the depiction of reality is important in the media, gory reality should not be visually portrayed but should be left to the imagination.

Others who participated in the symposium included Prof. Bidhu Bhushan Das, former Vice Chancellor; Shakuntala Panda, Editor of *'Sucharita'*; Dr. Kumudini Barai, Principal of R. D. Women's College; Basant Nayak, Chairman, Orissa Film Chamber; Prof. Shanti Sahoo of Utkal University; and Dr. Sangram Jena, Editor, *'Nishant'*. They welcomed the effort of the Centre for Media Studies to promote citizen initiative for arresting negative trends in the mass media.

VIJAYAWADA

Hemalatha Lavanam, social worker, delivered the keynote address at the symposium on violence and vulgarity in mass media held at Vijayawada on 5th November 1994. She stressed the need to develop a positive attitude among children towards society. The time has come, she felt, for the public to check sex and violence on the idiot box.

Father Shouraiah, Director, Loyola College and chief guest at the symposium, said that though the aim of the mass media was supposed to be to educate, inform and entertain the people, the media were actually at war with the people by dishing out cheap entertainment catering to the baser instincts. He also said that while TV was on the one hand bringing the world together, it was, at the same time creating a wedge in family relationships.

Dr. Koteswaramma, Principal of the Montessori Mahila Kalasala who presided over the symposium, observed that the advances made in communication technology were exploited for wrong ends. Social audit of mass media, being attempted by the Centre for Media Studies, is an effective way of checking undesirable messages.

Durga Bhaskar, All India Radio station director, expressed concern at the exhibition of obscene scenes on television. To restore the cultural ethos, she said it was necessary to screen all the film-based programmes before telecast.

Dr. Sudha said that the media are a powerful weapon which should be handled carefully, like the knife in the hands of a surgeon, and not like the knife in the hands of criminals. Society is already suffering from a variety of pollutions, she said, and the media by spreading vulgarity and violence are adding another dangerous kind of 'psychological pollution'.

N. Bhaskara Rao of CMS referred to the poor working of the Film Censorship machinery. He cited as an example the fact that songs from films were being released before the films were certified for exhibition by the Board.

The large number of women participants in the Vijayawada symposium reflected the concern of women at the social impact of television. Many participants underlined the role of parents and teachers in moulding children as future citizens. It was for teachers and parents to create awareness about good and bad among the youth.

AHMEDABAD

Mrinalini Sarabhai was chief guest at the symposium on social impact of electronic media organised by CMS in cooperation with the National Commission for Women at the Chamber of Commerce & Industry hall, Ahmedabad, on 21st November, 1994. She said that not only do the media not communicate adequately, communication links have broken down—be it between citizens or between parents and children.

Manubhai Shah, chairman of the Consumer Education & Research Centre, said in his keynote address that India's culture was a repository of good dramas that reflected life with its negative as well as positive tendencies, and society should not therefore blindly oppose all violence and vulgarity. He said that despite the onslaught of TV, people after all have the choice whether to have a TV set at home, or to turn it on only for certain programmes. The real problem was that with the changes in Indian society, parents are not performing their duty towards children.

Ramlal Parikh, Vice Chancellor of Gujarat Vidyapeeth, who presided over the symposium felt that there is urgent need for a dialogue on the impact that TV has on the family, specially women and children. Electronic media should promote human values, he said. Several other participants from various fields also said that electronic media had a negative effect on society and we ought to be more concerned over the implications.

Kiran Kartik, director of the Consortium of Educational Communication, said the time has come to think individually and act collectively so far as the issues of violence and vulgarity are concerned. Though the electronic media had a tremendous potential, he said, they are not being used for social good; Doordarshan had become more of a commercial undertaking than a public service.

Other participants included Ila Bhatt, Chairperson of the Self-Employed Women's Association; Dr. Karthikbhai Sarabhai; Dr. Ashok Chatterji of the National Institute of Design; Prof. T. V. Rao of the Indian Institute of Management; Prof. Vimal Shah; Dr. Vinod Patel of the Department of Family Welfare; Ila Joshi; Preetiben Shah; Vijaya Seth and Saroj Tandola, director, Doordarshan.

N. Bhaskara Rao in his concluding remarks expressed regret at the passive attitude of both the Government and the general public in face of the threat to values from the mass media. He said a National Citizens' Forum should be formed to initiate action against those screening socially undesirable programmes.

PUNE

Mohan Dharia, president of VANARAI, was chief guest at the symposium on social impact of electronic media held at the Institute of Engineers, Shivaji Nagar, Pune, on 1st December, 1994. He said : "The electronic media can be an effective instrument of socio-economic transformation. They should be used to portray national issues like population control, environment protection and wasteland development."

He suggested that the negative impact of programmes beamed through certain channels can be neutralised by having a powerful and attractive channel to project issues concerning the common man. Democracy and discipline must go together, and the mass media should carry this message. Mohan Dharia said there was need for government control of the right kind over the mass media, and suggested that quality programmes can be promoted by harnessing talent and offering incentives.

B. G. Deshmukh, former Cabinet Secretary who presided over the discussion, said : "Sex, violence and consumerism are the negative aspects of the channels." Instead of wishing away the channels, which is not possible, we should involve people in social action to combat the negative influence of the electronic media.

E. V. Chitnis, former director of the Space Applications Centre, in his keynote remarks spoke on the advances made by television and radio and the great scope for reducing the gap between the information-rich and the information-poor through satellite communication. While stressing the need for regulation of the electronic media for the public good, he regretted that Doordarshan was forgetting the educative role it had itself tried to play in the early stages of its growth, and was falling into what he called a 'popularity trap'.

Sucheta Paranjpye, teacher at Tilak Maharashtra Vidyapeeth said : "Sex and violence have become the rule of the day." To an average Indian viewer, television by definition is commercial cinema, and people are blindly imitating the idols of the small screen. She also said that family relationships have suffered a set-back and people are becoming highly self-centred and materialistic. TV as a responsible medium must "mature fast and become more Indian", she said.

Pramod Kale, chief of the Satellite Launcb Vehicle Project, pointed out that it is within an individual's control whether to watch TV or not. He stressed the need for selectiveness in viewing programmes.

S. D. Gokhale, corporate adviser to the Sakal newspaper group, said that problems cannot be solved by banning certain channels. Instead, a good alternate model of useful and attractive local community television should be developed.

Sridhar Gupte, Vice Chancellor of Pune University, Dr. Shyamala Wanvase, Prof. Samar Nakhata, Freny Tarapore, Dr. Vasant Gowariker and Dr. Arun Nigvekar were among other concerned citizens, from various fields like education and films, who spoke at the symposium.

BANGALORE

M. N. Srinivas, eminent sociologist, was chief guest at a seminar on social impact of electronic media held at Bharatiya Vidya Bhawan, Bangalore, on 7th January 1995. He advocated more careful scrutiny of television programmes in order to restrain the overplaying of violence and sex. He said it was imperative to fine-tune the programmes since the family, which had ensured the stability of Indian society so far, is showing signs of erosion. Television was contributing to this process : with the increasing popularity of TV, there was less interaction between parents and children at home. TV has unfortunately taken over the process of socialisation, Prof. Srinivas observed.

He also highlighted the potential role of the electronic media, with the transmitter becoming a 'symbol of revolution'. The electronic media had initially played a part in social transformation in India, along with adult franchise, protective discrimination and abolition of untouchability. But now there was a close connection between television, advertising and consumerism, and populist advertisements were luring impressionable minds towards a crassly consumerist culture.

P. R. Brahmananda, eminent economist, accused Indian television of ignoring a significant section of society in its programmes : "There is an abysmal darkness about the major part of India" in Doordarshan, he said. With its elitist programmes, TV was destroying the social sensitivity of the viewers. He urged the mass media, both the Press and the electronic, to sensitise the rulers to the socio-economic conditions prevailing in the country. These conditions were grim, and the rulers' insensitivity could prove fatal, he warned.

Leela Rao, professor in the Department of Mass Communication, Bangalore University, established through statistics how children were being exploited by advertisers to promote their goods on TV. According to her, television was fast becoming a surrogate parent to children. She expressed concern over the lack of good programmes for children.

H. K. Ranganath of the Bharatiya Vidya Bhavan pointed out that reading habits were on the decline, and expressed concern at TV causing a set-back to art forms like poetry and literature, and to India's value system itself. TV, he said, was robbing the child's interface with parents. However, the electronic media in India are fortunately still young, and if we take care of the software, the adverse trends could be arrested and the media could begin to play a positive role.

Other participants included Prof. Ramaswamy, former director of the Indian Institute of Management, Bangalore; Prof. K. E. Eapen, media expert; M. A. S. Rajan, retired civil servant; Prabha Murthy and Jajie Mandanna, both consumer activists. The women participants were particularly critical of the way in which women are portrayed in TV serials as well as in films.

COMMUNICATION FOR RURAL DEVELOPMENT

As the series of six regional seminars outside Delhi neared

conclusion, CMS organised another national colloquim in the capital, on 4th January, 1995, on the theme of Communication for Rural Development.

Four major conclusions emerged from intense discussions among the colloquists consisting of field workers of non-governmental organisations from AP, Kerala, Gujarat, UP, and other parts of the country; academics; administrators; media agencies and concerned citizens from various walks of life :

(1) Centrally planned and bureaucratically administered programmes for rural development, based on the approach of doling out gifts from the government to the rural under-privileged, have signally failed.

(2) This approach must be replaced by mobilisation of the people, in which the workers of non-governmental organisations can play a major part, for formulating and implementing their own programmes, to meet locally felt needs, with official agencies playing a subsidiary role.

(3) It is necessary to reorient the official media, specially Doordarshan, by investing them with social relevance and local interest. With its titillating filmy entertainment and advertisements which promote the hedonistic culture of consumerism, Doordarshan is propagating attitudes which run counter to the social concern and readiness to share which are necessary for promoting broadbased human development.

(4) Development communication is most effective when it is practised as part of social action locally, rather than by career communicators/agencies.

Mahatma Gandhi was cited by many speakers as the outstanding exemplar of development communication in our time.

They said that his vision of a decentralised economy and self-reliant society was of great contemporary relevance.

Dr. N. Bhaskara Rao, Chairman of the Centre for Media Studies, recalled how the idea of a national colloquium on communication promotive of rural development had taken shape during discussions held last year with Dr. Lakshmidhar Mishra, who was heading the Council for Advancement of People's Action for Rural Technology (CAPART, a registered society formed in 1986, and funded by the central government, for assisting non-governmental organisations engaged in rural development work).

MALDEVELOPMENT

Dr. P. C. Joshi, economist and sociologist, in his key-note address expressed anguish at the maldevelopment that had taken place in recent decades in the name of development. The Green Revolution placed its bets on the strong and by-passed the powerless. There had been a concentration instead of diffusion of investment effort, development becoming capital and energy intensive. Citing the example of Uttarakhand, from where he hails, Dr. Joshi said that more fruit was being grown there now, but not for consumption by the local people; there was more liquor consumption; one-third of the local population worked outside; and more girls from Uttarakhand were to be found in the brothels of Kanpur and Delhi. Was all this development, he asked. According to Dr. Joshi, "Market driven development can have only market-driven communication" and only those having purchasing power will be reached. He was of the opinion that the "Mountain-top View" of development is far different from the bottom-level view, viz. people's perception of development.

Dr. Jagdish Nazareth of the Institute for Studies and Transformations, Ahmedabad, said that there was a lack of respect for rural people underlying the anti-poverty programmes of the Rural Development Ministry with their gift-giving approach and this was one of the inhibiting factors. These gifts resulted in worthless investment. By the time relief works were organised following drought, the affected people had migrated in search of livelihood. There was an international counterpart of the wasteful gift-giving approach, Dr. Nazareth said. He called for a synergistic utilisation of manpower and natural resources, through a redesigned rural administration, for creating a sustainable rural economy.

Dr. P.V. Parameshwara Rao, President of the Bhagavatula

Charitable Trust in Andhra Pradesh, said in his key-note paper for the colloquium that the landless had hardly 100 days of employment in a year, and two-thirds of rural children were without education. He asked : "How on earth can this country ever prosper even if thousands of crores are spent on various other projects?" Pointing out that voluntary organisations had a vision of their own, he said : "They may cooperate with the Government but they are not there to carry on the projects that are being dumped upon the people by the Government."

Professor S. C. Modgal, Vice Chancellor, G. B. Pant University of Agriculture, said that rural development can be said to have taken place only if changes occur in the value system, skills and behaviour of the people in such a manner that "they help themselves" to realize economic and social improvements. The process of rural development requires active and purposeful use of different channels of communication including person-to-person contacts, group interaction and the use of mass media in a planned and integrated manner.

According to **K. C. John**, there is overdominance of Government as if the motivating force for development is the Government, when in fact, it should be the motivation of people themselves.

Summing up the initiating session, **Dr. Lakshmidhar Mishra** called for a respectful rather than condescending attitude to folk wisdom and culture. He recalled his experience of seeing in interior Bihar an ex-bonded labourer sleeping outside his hut while his cattle slept inside in the winter when the temperature was 4-5 degrees C. Asked about it, the former bondsman said that the cattle could not survive the extreme cold. Dr. Mishra referred to his findings, in the course of his tours of rural areas, of the continued pledging of children for arduous labour and the payment of only a fraction of the prescribed minimum wages to women workers. Dr. Mishra cautioned against two varieties of skepticism with regard to the possibility of change for the better : the cynicism of the vested interests who would say that there has always been and always will be social injustice and inequality, and of those progressives who saw no possibility of social change till the class divide was abolished.

Dr. N. Bhaskara Rao said that there was low awareness about rural development programmes. The centralised approach of Delhi neither caters for the language specifics of various States nor are they based on local needs. The nomenclature of programmes could themselves do with some renaming, as these are not easily understood. The communication about these programmes is also propagandist in nature. He called for relocation of certain Government media units, as a number of districts in Bihar, UP and MP are outside their reach.

Dr. Lakshmidhar Mishra said that we should identify the creative forces around us and harness them. There is abundance of folk culture and folk tradition available. He said "Information poor are not communication poor". There is not a single print medium available in various parts of Rajasthan and UP but symbols, images, myths and legends could be used in large measure for communication purposes.

Dr. Mira Aghi said that technology is only a tool. You have to know how to use it. The idea of too many messages in a single video casette of half hour is utterly foolish as is being done quite often in the field.

According to **Prof. S. C. Modgal**, communication is conditioned by economic and political power structure, both internal and international. India's unique situation among the third world nations has always attracted communication experts, whether for introduction of radio broadcast, glamorous television, versatile video, computer, satellite or telecommunication.

D. K. Bose opined that hitherto there has been no 'communication', only sloganning. In all our development programmes, there was little focus on women's participation. As the reach of mass media is limited, there is need for continued exploration of new channels and their innovative use.

Dr. Devesh Kishore of Indira Gandhi National Open University referred to successful experiments conducted recently on modern communication technologies in the interactive mode and explained how the scope could be extended to educational institutions, rural research laboratories and other non-governmental organisations for development communication on a regular basis for a nominal charge.

Communication has become commercial and policy makers are not interested in development communication, according to **Usha Rai**, a development communicator.

There is dichotomy between "universal communication" and "area specific communication" said **Dr. Bhagyalakshmi**, Director in the Ministry of Rural Development. In every development programme, at least four or five ministries are involved and all of them need to co-ordinate their efforts to evolve a common strategy before the programme is launched.

Premlatha Narendra of CMS said that development is much broader than just anti-poverty programmes. It is any and every kind of programme that goes to improve the quality of the life of the rural poor. The basic point is convergence of programmes that are addressed to the problems of rural India. Communication strategies, therefore, have to take into account the people who are to benefit from the various programmes.

Satyamurthy, secretary, Bhagavatula Charitable Trust, concurred with the opinion of Usha Rai that communication is big business today and most expensive. People interested in development must interact with people interested in business. No development effort will get publicity until it is looked at from viability point of view.

USE AND MISUSE OF MASS MEDIA

Government-run Doordarshan came in for scathing criticism as a monumental example of the misuse of communication technology. Prof. E. V. Chitnis, space scientist who was prominently connected with the pioneering work in local interest rural communication through the low power terrestrial transmitter at Pij (Gujarat) during the Satellite Instructional Television Experiment (SITE), referred to the progress made by India in building Communication Satellites and asked : "But are they being used for rural development?" Referring to Gandhiji's use of Khadi and Salt as powerful symbols for rousing the people's consciousness, he referred to some recent instances of using small technology for mass communication : Dr. Nelson Mandela's tape recorded messages, while he was held in detention by the minority white regime in South Africa, that were put on long-playing records which sold millions of copies; and Ayotollah Khomeini's speeches recorded in Paris on cassettes and smuggled into Iran during the movement against the Shah's despotic regime.

Dr. Devesh Kishore described a project for interactive video conferencing using extended C Band for education and rural development.

In reply to some questions by Nori Venkateswarlu, former Chief Engineer of AIR, Professor Kishore stated that the teaching end facility at IGNOU would cost Rs. 2.5 crores and the use of INSAT transponder would cost Rs. 6,000 per hour on a commercial basis. In view of the language diversity in rural areas in the States, interaction in various languages may be on a time shared basis. Asked whether non-governmental organisations could use this facility for exchanging their experiences, Dr. Kishore said that they could do so as long as the interaction in non-political. A participant commented that this expensive exercise would bring video conferencing only to farmers benefiting from the green revolution.

Professor Chitnis referred to the report of the P. C. Joshi Committee on Software for Doordarshan, published under the title "An Indian Personality for Television", as a document that was "still very valid" because of its advocacy of socially relevant and local interest programmes instead of mindless entertainment.

Aloke Rai, active in people's theatre, made the pithy remark that the communication satellite, once hailed as 'Teacher in the Sky', had turned into a 'Monster in the Sky'.

A significant point that emerged from the discussion and presentations is that television technology could be effectively utilised to better social purpose by non-governmental organisations than by government-run Doordarshan. SEWA, Ahmedabad, was discussed as a case in point.

There was appreciation of the video programmes prepared and presented by **Neelam Dave** of Video-SEWA. In addition to getting programmes prepared for popularising smokeless 'Chulhas', oral rehydration and other themes of interest to ordinary housewives and thus putting communication technology at the service of the community, SEWA has gone a step further and put video technology literally in the hands of working women. One of the programmes screened at the colloquium showed women bidi workers, vegetable sellers and the like wielding a video camera and producing simple programmes to project problems and their solutions : e.g. to highlight the need for more municipal taps to meet the need for piped drinking water; and to teach village women how to build a smokeless stove.

Participants at the colloquium came to the conclusion that communication is most effective when it is an organic part of such social action.

The scope for utilising media other than television for development communication was discussed next.

Lamenting that policy makers are not interested in development communication efforts, **Usha Rai** narrated the decline and fall of the 'Development Page' in *Indian Express.* Initially it was printed every week opposite the editorial page and thus drew much attention. Later it was relegated to a less prominent position, its frequency was reduced and now it was being dropped on account of rise in the cost of newsprint and the priority allotted to 'hard' news.

G. N. S. Raghavan remarked that the fate of "Development Page" was inevitable because its very basis was wrong. It assumed that news and analysis pertaining to development was different from other news and analysis, whereas development consciousness on the part of the editor, reporter and sub-editor should permeate the selection and treatment of all economic and social information. If a journalist thought that the World Cup, politicians stabbing each other in the back, and beauty queens were news and not problems of development, the Press could make little contribution.

The traditional modes of communication—song, dance

and drama—also figured in the discussion. **Anu Dixit** said that professional troupes of traditional media performers were utilised during the UNICEF compaign for safe water and sanitation. But the difficulty was that these troupes had other commitments and were available only on certain dates. She said the multi-pronged approach is yielding very good results. Inter-personal contact is established by people by staying in the villages for which messages are developed. She narrated how effectively UNICEF is using trained Anganwadi workers, mothers' meetings, posters, flip charts and video films in their communication strategies.

G. N. S. Raghavan said that his experience of work in the Field Publicity Organisation, during which he collaborated closely with the Song and Drama division, had driven him to the conclusion that the best use of the traditional media for development would be by involving and motivating resident rural practitioners rather than professional troupes located in towns. This would reduce cost and increase exposure and impact.

Aloke Rai concurred with the suggestion that practitioners of the traditional media residing in villages should be drawn into the social communication effort. He regretted that India's rich oral culture in not being utilised.

Rajeshwar Dayal of Friedrich Ebert Foundation reminded the participants that traditional media have far more reach than the modern mass media among the poorest of the poor in rural India.

FUNDING VOLUNTARY WORK

Considering that development communication undertaken by the Government was largely ineffective in relation to cost, some participants urged that the government should withdraw from much of the area and hand it over to non-governmental organisations and local experts or committed workers.

This was unlikely to happen, a former I & B official said, because the ruling middle class has a vested interest in an expanding bureaucracy. He also said that, in the last analysis, the government media were there to promote the image of the Prime Minister/Chief Minister and the political party for the time being in power : witness the naming of anti-poverty schemes (Jawahar Rozgar Yojana, Indira Awas Yojana, Rajiv Gandhi Drinking Water Mission).

Dr. J. Bhagyalakshmi said that private philanthropists took full credit for anything they did, and asked why governments should not do so. Prof. Raghavan stated in reply that the money donated by private individuals came from the fruits of their enterprise, while not a paisa came out of the pockets of Prime Ministers or Chief Ministers for the many institutions named after them.

As an illustration of amateurishness and lack of imagination in government's development communication, some participants contrasted the acronym SEWA devised by an N. G. O. with the official labels ARWSP and DWCRA. More such examples were referred to : how N. T. Rama Rao in AP and the M.G. R. and Jayalalitha Governments in Tamil Nadu named some of the programmes with right kind of labels.

Yet, NGOs were starved for funds while the government departments had hundreds and thousands of crores to spend on their schemes. In the absence of adequate private financial support and because of the tardy procedures of the government, **Dr. Rajni Tandon** said, N. G. Os were constrained to "beg from multi-nationals" or depend on sponsors like cigarette manufacturers who wanted their products advertised. She suggested that in addition to the revenue stamp required to be fixed to receipts, there could be a 'development stamp' of the value of a rupee which must be added to the receipt for every transaction of a thousand rupees or more, and the same used for supporting NGOs' efforts.

Reference was made by a participant to the fact that social communication had been made part of the activity of the group of industries controlled by Siddharth Sri Ram, scion of the patriot and industrialist Lala Sri Ram of Delhi. This kind of example deserved emulation, said G. N. S. Raghavan; hesuggested the formation of a consortium of such donors who are willing to give financial assistance to young volunteers for development work. Every year, he said, thousands of young men and women were coming out of colleges with knowledge in various fields. Those of them who were imbued with idealism could avoid getting sucked into the rat race of careers in government or in business, and devote themselves instead to nation building work, if they could be assured of a living wage for their voluntary work.

Aloke Rai and others supported the proposal for a consortium to extend financial support to young persons wishing to take up public work. A recent initiative of Tata group of industries to set up a consortium for taking initiatives came in for praise, with a suggestion that they should sponsor communication/information efforts as a part of the strategy.

NEED FOR VALUE EDUCATION

Running through the entire discussion was concern at the erosion of values by the consumerist and filmy culture propagated by All India Radio and Doordarshan. "All their communication is silent subversion", said **Dr. P.C. Joshi.** "Government is undoing our things", complained **Dr. Mira Aghi.**

There was strong disagreement expressed when **Dr. Satyamurthy** said : "Literacy should be sold, like Colgate". One participant said that, on the contrary, there would be universal literacy only when those who were privileged to be educated felt it their duty to make the disprivileged literate. **Dr. Bhaskara Rao** affirmed that development communication was not a business, but corresponded to the fourth estate role which the Press at its best played.

Dr. Rajni Tandon who is active in the World Association for Value Centred Education pleaded for attention to the aesthetic element in education.

The link between ethical values and broad-based human development was stressed by **Dr. R.K. Samanta**, Head of the Transfer of Technology Systems and Policies unit at the National Academy of Agricultural Research Management, Hyderabad, in a paper circulated at the colloquium : "The urban values of individualism and material gains seem to have gained in rural areas. Ethical norms should lie at the core of national and rural development". Dr. Samanta called for "a national policy and educational approach to convince the urban consumer about the need to accept products of village and small-scale industries in the national interest. This can be compared to the upsurge during the independence struggle when the Swadeshi movement gathered momentum and formed an important plank of the fight against alien rule".

MOBILISING PEOPLE'S INITIATIVE

An experiment in self-reliant and self-propelled rural development, in contrast to the centrally planned anti-poverty programmes based on doles from the government, was narrated by **Gangadharan** who has been associated with the Gram Sastra Samithi (Village Science Forum) movement in Kerala. He described the effort initiated in local planning through the formation of non-official Jana Sabhas to supplement the work of the officially constituted Panchayats. In 25 villages, resource mapping had been undertaken. For reaching the target population, namely every household in the Panchayat, there was one elected representative in the Jana Sabha for every 25 households. They undertook studies and surveys of local problems, drew up action plans and worked for their implementation, utilising existing people's bodies like political parties, farming groups, Youth Clubs and Parent Teacher Associations. A handicap, Gangadharan said, was that "Government information was not available to us" to formulate locally relevant plans.

Another instance of mobilising people's initiative was narrated by **Anu Dixit** of UNICEF. During the campaign for promoting sanitation and safe water in Midnapore district of West Bengal, she said, village communities made contribution towards the acquisition of hand pumps and pipes, and volunteers helped to maintain them. There were now some 3,000 women hand-pump mechanics in the country, and also some women masons.

Dr. P.C. Joshi, while underlining the need for restoring the basic self-respect of the people in the interest of self-propelled development, recalled the emphasis laid by Jaya Prakash Narayan on "non-state forms of activism".

Dr. Bhaskara Rao lamented that community and individual initiatives no longer get coverage in the mass media, including Doordarshan—as if we want poor people to depend on government eternally. Media coverage itself is such that it does not reflect people's participation in development locally as a virtue.

Dr. Lakshmidhar Mishra brought out how people involved in the National Literacy Mission benefitted from local initiatives of poor people, which in turn helped to sustain the movement. NLM, he said, uniquely brings out what difference local involvement would make for the success of any development programme at the grass roots and among the poor and the information-disadvantaged.

FREEING THE AIRWAVES

Quickly in the wake of the Supreme Court's judgment of 9th February, 1995 calling for the establishment of a public authority for running radio and television in the public interest, CMS organised a round-table in Delhi, on 10th March, 1995, on the theme of Freeing the Airwaves. The participants examined critically the implications both of the judgment and of the recent legislation for regulating cable TV networks.

The Supreme Court's judgment was broadly welcomed by the discussants who included three former Ministers of Information & Broadcasting—I.K. Gujral, Vasant Sathe and P. Upendra; Dileep Padgaonkar, former editor of the Times of India now heading Asia-Pacific Communication Association; Prabhu Chawla, Editor, Financial Express and several media practitioners and social activists. Wireless Advisor to Government of India, A.M. Joshi, responsible for frequency allocation, also participated in the discussion.

However, the hope of freeing of the airwaves was tempered by three considerations : (i) the fact that no time limit has been set by the Supreme Court for the establishment of a truly autonomous public broadcasting authority; (ii) the Court's endorsement of the principle of pre-censorship in respect of films and the electronic media, in contrast to freedom from prior restraint that has been upheld by the Court in the case of the Press; and (iii) the danger of misuse by the Government of the power of pre-censorship as presaged by an ominous provision in the Cable Television Networks (Regulation) Ordinance 1994, (since replaced by Act No. 7 of 1995). Section 19 of the Act, in Chapter V entitled 'Miscellaneous', empowers any officer "not below the rank of a Group 'A' officer of the Central Government authorised by the State Government in this behalf" to "prohibit any cable operator from transmitting or retransmitting any particular programme" if it is likely in the opinion of the officer, to promote disharmony or disturb public tranquillity.

G.N.S. Raghavan initiated the discussion by outlining the legal framework of electronic media operations in India. He pointed out that the Supreme Court's judgement calling for an autonomous broadcasting authority had come in a curious context, namely the right of citizens to provide and to receive entertainment—by, in the instant case, watching cricket. The judgment was, however, a landmark in so far as it laid down the principle of the citizens' right to information and analysis from diverse source and viewpoints.

He drew attention to the court's sanction of precensorship in respect of the electronic media. Justices P.B. Sawant and S. Mohan had said : "The airwaves or frequency are a public property. This limitation is in addition to the restrictions imposed on the right to freedom of speech and expression under Article 19 (2) of the Constitution." In a separate but concurring judgment, Justice B.P. Jeevan Reddy held : "Broadcasting media is inherently different from Press or other means of communication/information. The analogy of Press is misleading and inappropriate." G.N.S. Raghavan submitted, with respect, that this distinction between the Press and other media is questionable.

He also drew attention to a puzzling provision in the legislation recently enacted to regulate cable TV operations. Sections 5 and 6 of the Act lay down that no person shall transmit or retransmit through a cable any programme or advertisement unless such programme or advertisement is in conformity with the prescribed programme code and advertisement code. (These codes, prescribed in Rules 6 and 7 made under the Act, are reproduced in Appendix V.) A proviso to these two sections reads : "provided that nothing in this section shall apply to the programmes of foreign satellite channels which can be received without the use of specialised gadgets or decoder." Since the STAR movie channel was at that time the only encrypted channel, did the Ministry of I & B find every other foreign satellite channel unexceptionable ?

Vasant Sathe stressed the need for continuity in broadcasting policy; hitherto, the policy of the Ministry of Information & Broadcasting had kept changing with different Ministers and secretaries. There could be continuity in policy only if a public authority is created to ensure that the airwaves, which are free, are in fact available for use by, and in the interest of, citizens.

While expressing himself against pre-censorship, Vasant Sathe said that market morality being a negation of value-based morals, it should be ensured that the electronic media promote the public good. On the subject of what constitutes vulgarity or obscenity, he said there is a simple test : the programme should be such that one could watch it along with the family.

P. Upendra said it was anomalous that India had no law to regulate broadcasting. The only law was the antiquated Indian Telegraph Act of 1855, which envisaged government sanction for a private party to set up a telegraph channel. The spirit of the Supreme Court judgment, Upendra said, is against a full opening up of the airwaves to allow private television stations; this was left to government policy and any private station would have to be subject to regulation by the public authority envisaged by the Court. He endorsed and emphasized the distinction drawn by the Supreme Court between public interest and the interest of the Government for the time being in power. Upendra was in favour of bringing the proposed Prasar Bharati, too, within the ambit of a Commission to oversee the working of broadcasting organisations. But he was frankly sceptical whether any Central government would implement the judgment. If and when a National Media Council is established, it should make not only the private sector media but also Doordarshan adhere to norms of decency and good taste.

Dileep Padgaonkar said that we should be mindful of certain considerations while moving from State regulation of the electronic media to their regulation by the market, from the Sutra of socialism and Licence Raj to the Mantra of demand and supply. While welcoming the distinction drawn by the Supreme Court between public property and government property, he said that private television channels too, like government channels, could succumb to pressures—commercial in one case and political in the other. The history of the functioning of statutory bodies, supposed to be autonomous, made him feel sceptical about the role of the public authority which the Supreme Court wanted to be established.

Expressing himself against pre-censorship, Padgaonkar said that it was incompatible with live reporting which is the distinguishing feature of the instant communication made possible by modern technology.

S. Narendra, Principal Information Officer of the Government of India, said that it is no longer possible to differentiate between ownership of newspapers and of other media : witness the control of Star TV by the press baron Rupert Murdoch. Media policy need not be left to be formulated by the Government; knowledgeable and concerned citizens could get together and make constructive suggestions.

I. K. Gujral said that, along with the Market and the Arms Trade, the Media had emerged as a potent third power. He posed a series of questions that needed to be pondered: for instance, if airwaves are to be freed, for whom should they be freed ? Should they be freed because of a court order, or under social pressure ?

Recalling the recommendations made by UNESCO's MacBride Commission for the democratisation of communication within and between countries, he said : "We acted on the external aspect while turning a blind eye to internal democratisation." As Minister of Information & Broadcasting, he had been in favour of All India Radio and Doordarshan gaining credibility through objective reporting and analysis. For his pains, he was sacked in 1975 by Prime Minister Indira Gandhi, who remarked that her Minister was 'credibility-crazy'. Gujral also recalled that as Minister of I & B he wanted Doordarshan's commercials to have an ear-marked fund for improving the quality of programmes. Instead, the government had, over the years, applied the vast funds from advertisements for expanding the hardware of Low Power Transmitters to relay programmes from Delhi.

In this connection he recalled that the Janta Dal in its manifesto for the 1989 Lok Sabha elections had called for liberalisation of media policy and the establishment of a Broadcasting Council to exercise control on advertisements in the social interest, and for a reorientation of the electronic media to serve the people through programmes of local relevance and interest.

Rammohan Rao, former Principal Information Officer, remarked ironically that Indian airwaves are already free of State control : programmes on all channels are being sold to commercial sponsors.

Dr. A.M. Joshi, Wireless Adviser to the Government of India, explained the prevailing legal position with regard to the regulation of broadcasting. He said that the Indian Telegraph Act of 1885, which still holds the field, both rules out and permits private participation. Clause (4) of the Act reads : "Within India the Central Government shall have the exclusive privilege of establishing, maintaining and working telegraphs : Provided that the Central Government may grant a licence, on such conditions and in consideration of such payments as it thinks fit, to any person to establish, maintain or work a telegraph within any part of India."

Thus, said, Dr. Joshi, it was up to the Government to decide what policy to follow.

G.N.S. Raghavan expressed surprise at some media critics blaming foreign television channels exclusively for degrading and corrupting popular taste. He cited Doordarshan's application of two hours of prime viewing time on one of its channels to MTV rubbish as an example of what he called 'cultural compradorism'. Much of Doordarshan's own fare—specially films, and film-based song-and-dance sequences—were also crude and mindless. Thus the choice offered by the Indian Government to TV viewers was between Swadeshi and Videshi vulgarity. Doordarshan's contribution to the removal of illiteracy and poverty was nil. He characterised the role of Indian TV, which stoked the fires of consumerist greed and thereby promoted crime, as not merely antisocial but anti-national : 'What is a nation', he asked, 'but society ?'

Kiran Karnik, of the Consortium of Educational Communication, said that the airwaves serving Indian television viewers were not free : they had been captured by market forces. Doordarshan, with its banal entertainment programmes, had 'killed' All India Radio.

Shiv Sharma, former Director General, Doordarshan recalled the halcyon days of the I & B Ministry when, with I.K. Gujral as Minister, Doordarshan could put out programmes that were two-sided, and not merely propagandist praise of the government's achievements. He wondered whether true media reform would come about, permitting full scope for professionalism.

Dr. Rajni Tandon urged the establishment of centres that could train personnel to make programmes of relevance for correcting the prevailing disparities in society.

B.B. Nagpal, of the United News of India, asked whether the Telegraph Act permits the establishment of an uplinking facility by a private media entrepreneur for disseminating television signals via a satellite. Dr. Joshi, Wireless Adviser, reaffirmed that the Act leaves it to the Government's discretion.

Joshi said in reply to another question that though the medium wave radio spectrum was heavily crowded, there was the Frequency Modulation option available to sustain about ten local radio stations in each location. They could serve an audience within 60 km. radius. Similarly adequate channels would be available in future, in the KU band, to enable local television stations to operate in different parts of India.

R.K. Jindal, speaking for cable operators, said that the post offices where they were supposed to register did not know that they were the designated registering authorities under the Cable Regulation Ordinance. He said that multinational corporations were out for making a killing, and only some fifty Indian cable operators may be left out of the several thousand who are now in the business.

He said that by not allowing private parties to uplink TV signals, the Indian government was merely diverting potential revenue to neighbouring Nepal. We have only about 500 TV transmitters, most of them relaying programmes and not originating them, as against 20,000 transmitters in a small country like Japan. We can generate employment on a large scale by allowing the setting up of local TV stations employing local talent and offering participatory programmes involving the audience.

N. Bhaskara Rao, in his concluding remarks, put forward a proposal for radical restructuring of the I & B Ministry and its media units. He suggested the replacement of the bureaucratically run Ministry by a National Communications Commission comprising experts from telecommunications, electronics and other congruent technologies. While the Commission would oversee the hardware of radio and television, the media of I & B Ministry should be handed over to a professionally managed Information Board—on the lines of the proposed Communications Commission—free of the stranglehold of the bureaucracy.

He said that CMS would continue its effort to provide to the electronic media and the Ministry of I & B the feedback—which they have lacked so far—of citizens' perceptions and needs.

Part-III

Agenda for Renewal

9 RESTORATION OF VALUES

Decline of ethical values, in public life as in personal, is at the root of the corruption on an increasing scale among sections of politicians, business men, public servants in the civil and defence services—even the judiciary—and others. The ascendancy of consumerism and eroticism in the mass media, specially TV, is part of this syndrome.

What accounts for the post-independence weakening of the moral fibre of Indian society and the Indian State ?

A major reason, in the view of competent observers, is the secularisation of education ordained by Article 28 of the republican Constitution which came into force on 26th January 1950. It reads : "(1) No religious instruction shall be provided in any educational institution wholly maintained out of State funds." In a poor country like ours, the overwhelming majority of young people who are privileged to go to school instead of entering the child labour market go precisely to schools, and the luckier among them to colleges, that are run by the State—from the panchayat and municipal board to city corporation and the State and Central governments.

This banishment of religion from formal education has had far-reaching consequences because the prime source of ethical values has been, through human history, religion. This is not to say that religious institutions, or men wearing religion on their sleeves, have been free of corruption—whether in the traditional god-based religions or in the new, godless religion of Marxism which arose in the 19th century and spread over a large part of the globe. There have been in India greedy and lecherous rogues wearing saffron robes; the English word 'nepotism' has its origin in Popes, vowed to celibacy, granting undue favour through appointments to their illegitimate sons whom they called nephews; and a powerful attraction offered by Islamic *Jihad* to the successful warrior professing the true faith is the wealth and the women of the conquered group. The post-Enlightenment religion of Marxism proved to be no more immune to human failing. Corruption was rampant in Stalinist U.S.S.R., as it continues to be in Communist China whose president, Jiang Zemin, in the course of a speech in September 1995 expressed distress at the cropping up of 'money worship' and 'pleasure seeking' and a resurgence of 'corrupt and ugly phenomena'.

There is, however, no gainsaying the fact that god-based religion and humanist ideology have been potent carriers of the values of human fellowship, compassion and sharing, calling for self-restraint and frugality.

The best insights of modern science, too, confirm those of traditional religion and of non-theological humanism. As the Indian space scientist Yaşh Pal put it while speaking at a South Asian seminar convened in 1980 by the Indian Institute of Mass Communication : "It has become clear from science that myself, all my cells, all my constituents and those in this match-box or in this table, or in a piece of stone—that all this material at some time past was cooked together in the same star. Does not this have any implications for questions like our essential relatedness, about ecology? And does it at all conflict with the very beautiful, holistic inspiration of all the great religious teachers ?"

Azad against solely secular education

Jawaharlal Nehru, moulder of independent India for nearly

two decades, as Mahatma Gandhi had been of a whole generation of fighters for freedom, strove to reconcile in his own mind religion and science, tradition and modernity. But Nehru, for the greater part of his life, was more conscious of the negative features of religious tradition than of the positive, and was much attracted by modern technology. His close friend and colleague Maulana Azad, whom he chose as free India's first Education Minister, was unashamed of humanity's religious heritage though he was not opposed to technology (Azad held the portfolio also of Natural Resources and Scientific Research).

Like Mahatma Gandhi, Maulana Azad was in favour of instructing children in the humanist values which are common to all religions at their best. Writing a decade before independence, Gandhi said in 'Harijan' in response to a correspondent's query on the place of religious instruction in his Wardha Scheme of Basic Education : "I regard it as fatal to the growth of a friendly spirit among children belonging to the different faiths if they are taught that their religion is superior to every other, or that it is the only true religion. Fundamental principles of ethics are common to all religions. These should be taught to the children."

Speaking in similar strain in February 1947, a month after assuming the Education portfolio in the Interim Government, Maulana Azad said : "The religious instruction imparted in India in private institutions is of a kind which, instead of broadening the outlook and inculcating a spirit of toleration and goodwill towards all men, produces exactly the opposite results. The aim of all religious teaching should be to make men more tolerant and broad-minded. And it is my opinion that this can be more effectively done if the State takes charge of the question than if it is left to private initiative."

In advocating instruction in the essence of all religions as part of the curriculum, Maulana Azad was at one not only with Mahatma Gandhi, the great experimenter with the practice of religion, but with Dr. Radhakrishnan, the renowned exponent of the philosophy of religion.

The Commission on University Education headed by

Dr. Radhakrishnan expressed itself, in the report it drew up in 1949, in the same terms as Maulana Azad. Religious instruction in the universities was one of the issues remitted to the Commission, which included distinguished scholars and scientists. The report of the Commission referred to the Constitution of free India that was then being drawn up, and said : "There is no State religion. The State must not be partial to any one religion. Each one is at liberty to approach the unseen as it suits his capacity and inclination. If this is the basis of our Secular State, to be secular is not to be religiously illiterate. It is to be deeply spiritual."

However, the Constitution that came into force in January 1950 contained provisions relating to religious instruction that were contrary to the advice of Mahatma Gandhi, Maulana Azad and Radhakrishnan. Section (1) of Article 28 expressly prohibits religious instruction in any educational institution wholly maintained out of State funds. But, strangely, it is permitted in privately run institutions even if they receive aid out of State funds. And Article 30 reads :

"(1) All minorities, whether based on religion or language, shall have the right to establish and administer educational institutions of their choice.

"(2) The State shall not, in granting aid to educational institutions, discriminate against any educational institution on the ground that it is under the management of a minority, whether based on religion or language."

Here is a case of unilateral secularism. The majority of Indian students (necessarily Hindus) were to be denied religious instruction; but students belonging to the minority religions—of which Islam and Christianity are the largest—are allowed to be indoctrinated in their respective monotheistic faiths according to which there is no salvation except through the teaching of Jesus Christ and Prophet Mohammad respectively.

The prohibition of religious instruction in State-run schools and its permission in those run by religious minorities runs counter to other Articles of the Constitution which guarantee non-discimination between citizens on the ground of religion. The unilateralism is reminiscent of the Khilafat years, in the early part of the century, when Gandhiji called upon Hindus to support their Muslim fellow-countrymen's fight to preserve the territorial empire and the spiritual suzerainty of the Sultan of Turkey over Muslims world-wide, but refused to ask for a quid pro quo from Indian Muslims. M. Asaf Ali, nationalist Muslim leader of Delhi, made a visit to Deoband, a centre of Muslim theological learning, to persuade the teachers and students there that Muslims in India would do well to reduce or eschew cow slaughter voluntarily, as a mark of respect for Hindu sentiment and a reciprocal gesture for Hindu support to Khilafat. But Gandhi was against anything smacking of a bargain. He wanted Hindu support for the Muslim cause of Khilafat to be unconditional. It is another matter that his hopes of enduring Hindu-Muslim unity being forged thereby went awry. India was partitioned in August 1947 to constitute Muslim-majority areas into a separate State of Pakistan.

Maulana Azad returned to the subject of moral instruction in the course of an address to the Central Advisory Board of Education in February 1948. He said : "It was at first considered that religious instruction would stand in the way of the free intellectual development of a child, but now it has been admitted that religious education cannot altogether be dispensed with. If national education was devoid of this element, there would be no appreciation of moral values or moulding of character on humane lines."

Hedonism, fanaticism, fill moral vacuum

Maulana Azad's warning has proved only too true. In the case of the majority of India's younger generation comprising those who are Hindu by the accident of birth, secular education has nurtured the pursuit of money and of pleasure, never mind the ethics of how they are secured. Jawaharlal Nehru was able to sense this danger by 1959 when, during the Azad Memorial Lecture, he said that "the passion for riches, for acquisition, for more and more wealth tends to corrupt" and cautioned against the tendency to criminality and eroticism.

On the part of many members of the Muslim community,

the constitutional sanction of indoctrination in a single religion in educational institutions run by religious minorities has kept alive and intensified the separatist mentality that resulted in the partition of India in 1947. Among the factors that have nurtured secessionist sentiment in Kashmir over the decades since the State acceded to India in 1947 is the continuous indoctrination of Muslim children in a fanatical version of Islam in madarsas run by the Jamaat-e-Islami.

This is grim proof of the soundness of the warning sounded by Maulana Azad in January 1948 : "What will be the consequence if the Government undertakes to impart purely secular education ? Naturally, people will try to provide religious education to their children through private sources. How these private sources are working today or are likely to work in future is known to you. I know something about it and can say that not only in villages, but even in cities the imparting of religious education is entrusted to teachers who, though literate, are not educated. To them religion means nothing but bigotry."

Need for inter-religious ecumenism

Ecumenism is a term used by Christians for unity of the whole Christian world, transcending differences between Christian sects. A higher vision, that of a vast inter-religious ecumenism, inspired Gandhi, Azad and Radhakrishnan. Jawaharlal Nehru came to accept this when he said in the course of the Azad Memorial Lecture delivered by him in November 1959, less than five years before his death : "Four great religions have influenced India—two emerging from her own thought, Hinduism and Buddhism, and two coming from abroad but establishing themselves firmly in India : Christianity and Islam. Science today challenges the old concept of religion. But if religion deals not with dogmas and ceremonials, but rather with the higher things of life, there should be no conflict with science or *inter se* between religions. It might be the high privilege of India to help in bringing about this synthesis."

While Nehru thus finally arrived at the truth perceived earlier by Maulana Azad among others, it did not impel him to call for a reconsideration of the provisions in the Constitution relating to religious instruction in schools and colleges which run flatly counter to inter-religious ecumenism: these provisions, as we have seen, banish religious instruction from State-run schools but permit fanatical indoctrination in a single religion in private schools run by religious minorities—including those that are recognised by and given financial aid by the Indian State.

What Jawaharlal Nehru came to see in 1959 is being gradually recognised by Nehruites. G. Parthasarathi, a protege of Nehru who distinguished himself in the fields of diplomacy and education after initial grounding in journalism, said in the course of his convocation address at the University of Hyderabad in March 1987 : "Now that the concept of a core national curriculum has been accepted, it seems to me that consideration might be given to the inclusion in it of a course covering the development of human values the world over, and with special reference to India. Such a course would cover the contributions made to the development of a humanistic outlook by the various religions, by outstanding thinkers, by Marxism and the different schools of socialist thought, as well as by modern science many of whose findings are supportive of the concepts of humankind's oneness and of the ecological relatedness of all life on earth."

Another Nehruite, Aruna Asaf Ali, approvingly quoted the above passage in the course of the Azad Memorial Lecture she delivered in 1989. She went further and called for a review and amendment of the Constitutional provisions pertaining to religious instruction in schools so as to promote the inter-religious ecumenism which the best Indian minds have commended through the ages, and of which recent advocates include Gandhi, Azad, Radhakrishnan and the later Jawaharlal Nehru.

Clarifying secularism : failure of the

Among the paradoxes of free India is that the noble concept of inter-religious ecumenism has come to be equated with and referred to as 'secularism'. This is a violation of the English language. As the Concise Oxford Dictionary tells us, secularism stands for : "concerned with the affairs of this world; not sacred or monastic or ecclesiastical; sceptical of religious truth or opposed to religious education."

Like much else in post-independence India, the confusion of thought about secularism has its origin in the development of Jawaharlal Nehru's ideas. Beginnings as a Marxist and an agnostic, he matured over the years to the advocacy, cited earlier, of inter-religious ecumenism. In between, for long years, he popularised the term 'secularism' to stand for his own vision of the good society. In a letter to Chief Ministers of States in 1956, he wrote : "We call our State a secular one. The word 'secular' perhaps is not a very happy one. And yet, for want of a better, we have used it. What exactly does it mean ? It does not obviously mean a state where religion as such is discouraged. It means freedom of religion and conscience, including freedom for those who may have no religion. The word 'secular', however, conveys something much more to me, although that might not be its dictionary meaning. It conveys the idea of social and political equality. Thus, a caste-ridden society is not properly secular."

It is a pity that, along with Nehru, the Indian Press by and large failed to see the absurdity of constitutional provisions some of which ordain equal treatment of citizens irrespective of their religion, and Articles 28 and 30 which treat citizens differently precisely on the ground of religion. The Ramakrishna Mission seeking the status of a religious minority in order to avoid State interference in the educational institutions run by the Mission, and securing legal reccgnition as such in 1985 through a judgment of the Calcutta High Court, was a reduction ad absurdum of Article 30. The Press hardly said a word about the case. Nor has there been much notice taken of the Supreme Court's reversal, in the second half of 1995, of the Calcutta High Court's judgment in the Ramakrishna Mission case.

Nehru, again, saw no violation of secularism in his confining to Hindus the reform of marriage and family laws in the 1950s. As a result, it became an offence for a Hindu to practise bigamy or polygamy, while Muslims remained free to practise bigamy or polygamy. No wonder that the Muslim vote bank, virtually controlled by the community's fanatical and male-chauvinist leaders, remained available to the Congress party for decades.

It is not only the Congress that has followed the policy of placating Muslim sentiment, while professing secularism, with an eye on the Muslim vote. On 7th June, 1969, the Community Party of India (Marxist), then ruling the State of Kerala in coalition with the Muslim League, announced that it would carve out a Muslim-majority district of Malappuram, on the eve of a by-election there. Other secularists did not criticise the politically opportunist decision aimed at securing the Muslim vote. It was left to Kelappan, an aged Gandhian, to lead an unsuccessful protest.

Many Muslims in northern India became alienated from the Congress during the emergency regime of 1975-76 because of the strong-arm methods employed by Prime Minister Indira Gandhi's second son, Sanjay Gandhi, to promote family planning through sterilisation. This was among the factors leading to Congress defeat in the Lok Sabha elections of early 1977. The post-emergency Janata Party government soon fell, due to internal squabbles for power. After returning to power in 1980, Indira Gandhi issued instructions for implementation of a 15-point programme for upliftment of the religious minorities (meaning Muslims since the second largest religious minority, the Christians, are neither educationally nor economically backward compared to the generality of the population). The special programme, which has continued to be implemented by successive governments to this day, is reminiscent of the days of British rule when the alien regime showed solicitude for the minorities in an effort to keep them away from the national movement. The Press, by and large, found nothing wrong in special favour being shown to certain citizens on the basis of their religion.

Opportunism is no monopoly of political groups professing secularism. The Bharatiya Janata Party, which accuses others of appeasing Muslims and exploiting caste feelings, has not dared to question the concept of reservation in admission to colleges and in recruitment to government services and public sector undertakings for persons—irrespective of his or her merit—belonging to a particular caste (Scheduled or 'Other Backward') or tribe. The BJP obviously values the OBC vote bank as much as every other political party does. It has been left to the judiciary to come to the rescue of a polity plagued by caste-based vote-bank politics, by placing a limit on such reservations and insisting on a means test by calling for exclusion of the 'creamy layer' which is to be found in every caste.

The Press neither noticed the BJP's call in 1989 for a system of proportional representation which will more truly reflect popular opinion in the legislatures, nor BJP's subsequent abandonment of this important item of electoral reform. Till the elections to the ninth Lok Sabha, the BJP had been securing fewer seats in the State Assemblies and the Lok Sabha than its share of the popular vote warranted. Thereafter, it became in many states a beneficiary of the prevailing electoral system of first-past-the-post.

When the Rajiv Gandhi government sponsored the disgraceful Muslim Women's Act following a howl of protest by Muslim male chauvinists against a Supreme Court judgment of 1985 which held that Muslims were as much bound as other citizens of India to provide maintenance to a divorced and needy wife, there was criticism of the opportunist legislation by a wide section of the Press. But thereafter the newspapers lost interest in the subject. The Press, by and large, did not criticise the call by the Muslim League, emboldened by the Rajiv Gandhi government's retreat, for repeal of the Directive Principle of the Constitution which calls for enactment of a uniform civil code for all citizens. In 1995, when a Supreme Court bench reminded the government of the subject and asked what the government was doing about it, Prime Minister Narasimha Rao trivialised the issue by speaking of the difficulties of enacting a uniform marriage law when there were different practices in different communities, and different parts of the country, in the matter of marriage between cousins.

Few commentators told the Prime Minister that the issue is not about marriage between cousins, but whether bigamy should be legitimate for some citizens of India and a crime for others, depending on their religion; and that equal treatment of all citizens irrespective of their religion is what secularism—which Narasimha Rao frequently swears by—is all about.

On 16th March 1995, the Press Information Bureau of the Central Government put out a news item that the Finance Corporation for Minorities, which the Narasimha Rao government established after conferring statutory status on the Minorities Commission, would extend aid on concessional terms to members of minority religious communities whose household income is TWICE the poverty level as defined by the Planning Commission from time to time. Here was a virtual laying down of two poverty line definitions, one for the Hindu majority and the other for religious minorities. There can be no more blatant violation of secularism, yet the Press has hardly taken notice of it. True, the PIB's daily output is largely of publicity puffs, but it is surely the duty of the national news agencies which supply the staple of news to newspapers of varying political persuasion, and of the special correspondents of individual newspapers, to retrieve the few needles of significant information from the haystack of PIB's output. In respect of these parodies of secularism, it was not to be expected that A.I.R. and Doordarhan, tightly controlled by the Government, would attempt critical discussion.

The failure of the Press in the cases—illustrative, not exhaustive—cited above perhaps arises from the fact that the intellegentsia manning the Press—belonging as they do to the same social, economic and educational background as the middle and higher levels of the teaching profession and the judiciary—share the general confusion of thought about secularism. Another reason could be that journalists, like academics, have been well looked after by successive governments—through Wage Boards in the case of the Press, as by the University Grants Commission in the case of the higher class of the teaching profession.

In any case, it is remarkable that the Press took hardly any notice when intellectuals sustained in comfort by the Establishment through such government-funded bodies as the Indian Council for Social Science Research, the Institute for Advanced Studies and the Indian Institute of Mass Communication, adopted a resolution at a gathering at Shimla in April 1987 which said : "Secular values should be actively promoted by judges, teachers and religious teachers." This extraordinary proposition would have been laughed to scorn anywhere except in India. Not surprisingly, intellectuals of that ilk, as well as the Indian Press by and large, have been in a state of amnesia about Prof. Mushirul Hasan who was expelled by Islamic mobs from Jamia Millia (a central university funded by the Government) in 1992. He was thus punished for suggesting that reasoned discussion is a better way of countering the views expressed in a book (in this case 'The Satanic Verses' by Salman Rushdie) than banning it. Mushirul Hasan continues to be holed up in the campus of Jawaharlal Nehru University where his wife teaches.

So devoid of meaning has the term secularism become that President Shanker Dayal Sharma has described Guru Teg Bahadur, who put his religion above his life, as a 'secularist'. According to a Press release of the PIB on 17th December, 1993, Dr. Sharma said in the course of his statement on the anniversary of the Guru's martyrdom : "May his shining example of service and secularism and the glory of his sacrifice inspire each one of us to work for national unity." Earlier, Prime Minister Narasimha Rao said in the course of his convocation address on 22nd November, 1991 at the Sathya Sai Institute of Higher Learning that the Sai Baba's "emphasis on five universal values of Sathya, Dharma, Shanti, Prema and Ahimsa is truly SECULAR in character, and these constitute the major bedrock of all the religons of the world."

No wonder that, in this climate of totally confused thinking on what secularism means, the Press did not report at any length, nor studied and discussed, the judgment delivered by the Supreme Court on 11th March 1994, upholding the dissolution of the popularly elected legislatures in four States following the demolition of the Babri Masjid in December 1992, on the ground that the Bharatiya Janata Party that ran the governments there was not committed to secularism.

In a medley of judgments that concurred on this central point, Justice A.M. Ahmadi (now Chief Justice) said in the course of his order : "The term 'Secular' (in the Preamble to the Constitution) has advisedly not been defined, presumably because it is a very elastic term not capable of a precise definition, and perhaps best left undefined." (SUPREME COURT CASES, 1994, Vol. III, page 77). Another Judge on the nine-member bench that decided the case, Justice B.P. Jeevan Reddy, remarked in the course of his order : "Both the expressions—'socialist' and 'secular'—by themselves are not capable of precise definition."

Our newspapers have hardly noticed the implications of the remarks of the two learned Judges quoted above, who held along with seven of their brother Judges that Secularism, though it is undefinable, is a basic feature of India's Constitution. Failure of the media to demand, and themselves to attempt, clarification of the concept of secularism has detracted from their social role as agencies of non-formal education.

The media and the general public will do well to ponder the advice given on this subject by Aruna Asaf Ali, heroine of the freedom struggle and a lifelong fighter for women's equality and economic justice. Pointing out that the Muslim League and the Bharatiya Janata Party claim to be secular, as do the Congress and the Left parties, she said in the course of an article in *'National Herald'*, Delhi, of 2nd October, 1993 : "Considering that all political parties have made a mockery of the concept of secularism, is it not time to drop the term from the vocabulary of our political discourse ? If what we want to advocate is equal goodwill on the part of the State towards all citizens of India irrespective of their religion, and civilised and humane treatment of each other by the citizens themselves, I would suggest that we find another word. Perhaps it could be humanism."

Humanist Education

A document that has not received the public attention it deserves, since the media have taken hardly any notice of it, is the report of a Core Group on Value Orientation of Education, set up by the Planning Commission. The group, which was headed by Dr. D. Swaminathan, member of the Planning Commission, was formed as the result of the notice taken of the subject by the Commission while formulating the Eighth Five Year Plan (1992-97). The Plan document said, in the chapter on education : "The significance of value education has been highlighted by several committees and commissions on education. The Planning Commission has recently constituted a core group on value orientation in education. The recommendations of the group will be considered for implementation in consultation with the Ministry of Human Resource Development, University Grants Commission, Association of Indian Universities and National Council for Educational Research and Training."

The core group's report, submitted in October 1992, says in the Introduction : "In post-independence India, in the name of secularism which was not correctly understood, hardly any serious efforts were made to promote value orientation of education." (para 2.06). This was a surprisingly daring statement to be found in a document emanating from the Congress establishment, even if the report abounds elsewhere in instances of equating—though it is linguistically absurd to do so—secularism with religious values. It is also of interest that most of the institutions where instruction is imparted in moral values, whose work is surveyed approvingly in the lengthy annexures to the core group's report, are associated with traditional religion, not secularism. They include : Sri Sathya Sai Institute of Higher Learning, Prasanthi Nilayam; the Banasthali Vidyapeeth, where the students recite 'Sarva Dharma Prarthana' on the lines advocated by Mahatma Gandhi; the Dayalbagh Educational Institute which was founded by the fifth guru of the Radhaswami faith, which seeks to promote an understanding of various beliefs so that students may develop an attitude of tolerance; and the Ramakrishna Institute of Moral and Spiritual Education,

Mysore, whose B. Ed. course includes compulsory study of the major religions of the world.

Much of the report of the Planning Commission's core group consists of a recital of what earlier committees and commissions said on the subject. Of special interest is the following extract from the report of the Committee on Religious and Moral Education set up by the Union Ministry of Education in 1959, with Sri Prakasa as chairman : "Many ills that our world of education and our society as a whole is suffering today, resulting in widespread disturbance and dislocation of life, are mainly due to the gradual disappearance of the hold of basic principles of religion on the hearts of the people. The only cure, it seems to us, is in deliberate inculcation of moral and spiritual values from the earliest years of our lives."

Again, the Education Commission headed by Dr. D.S. Kothari said in its report (1966) : "Modernisation does not mean, least of all in our national situation, a refusal to recognise the importance of, or to inculcate, necessary moral and spiritual values and self-discipline. While a combination of ignorance with goodness may be futile, that of knowledge with a lack of essential values may be dangerous." The weakening of social and moral values in the younger generation is creating many serious social and ethical conflicts in western societies, and there is already a desire among great Western thinkers to balance the knowledge and skills which science and technology bring, with the values and insights associated with ethics and religion at its best."

Two questions arise. Will politicians, engaged in a ceaseless battle for survival in, or capture of, power find time to implement the recommendations made by the Planning Commission's core group on value orientation in education ?

The recommendations amount to what we have described as the promotion of an inter-religious ecumenism. This raises the second question. Will the leaders of the two largest religious minority communities agree to compulsory instruction in the values common to all religions ? This will amount to an admission that Islam and Christianity are not the only true religions.

The Sufis of Islam cheerfully accepted the oneness of all religions. Thus saint Sarmad of Delhi, who hailed from west Asia, said that he had passed from Jewish faith into Islam and had wandered from Islam "into the garden of Sri Rama and Laxman". Sarmad's friend and follower, Dara Shikoh, translated some of the Upanishads into Persian. But Dara's younger brother Aurangzeb, a fanatic, caused both Sarmad and Dara to be put to death. And the dominant influence on the minds of Indian Muslims has continued to be the Shariat, and not Sufi teaching. Similarly, in the deeply humanist teaching of Jesus Christ himself there is no sectarian dogmatism, but Pauline churchianity has been a different matter. As for India's principal religion, while the history of Hinduism is not free of instances of sectarian pride and intolerance—as for instance on the part of the fanatical among Saivites and Vaishnavites—Hindu polytheism has served to make intelligible at the popular level, and thereby to sustain, such humanist insights as that truth is one though the learned call it by different names, and that different faiths are only different paths that lead to the same goal. It is this catholic strain in Hinduism that has made it possible for the people of India, most of whom are Hindus, to accept the democratic and egalitarian foundations of the Constitution which—aberrations like Articles 28 and 30 apart—treats all citizens alike.

The teaching of inter-religious ecumenism as a compulsory part of education will be as difficult to achieve, and for the same reasons, as a common civil code. But both are equally necessary for building a just and agalitarian society. The media can do a great deal, through sustained education of public opinion, to make this possible.

Cultural heritage : Role of media

The hope of the mass media drawing on the best elements in each of India's religious traditions is considerably dimmed by their present performance, which is subversive of our cultural heritage.

The threat to culture posed by the mass media was ably summed up by the Parliamentary Standing Committee on Human Resource Development, in its twelfth report presented on 25th August, 1994. After considering the approach paper on a National Policy on Culture prepared by the Ministry of HRD, the committee said it was "deeply disturbed at the virtual absence of any reference in the Approach Paper to the impact of the mass media on cultural development. Nothing in the recent past has had such dramatic and deleterious impact on our cultural traditions as the invasion of the mass media, both indigenous and foreign. An important objective of the NPC is to evolve a creative response to this new challenge which alone will enable us to preserve our cultural continuity with the past, while rejecting the baneful and integrating the desirable in the influences which are entering our country through the new electronic technology. Should we fail to evolve a sufficiently creative response to this challenge, there is every danger of India succumbing to an imitative culture and losing its indigenous creative genius. It will avail us nothing if we attain material progress but lose our soul in the bargain.

'There is no way in which we can shut ourselves off from the consequences of satellite technology. Retracting into a shell is not the answer. At the same time, passively succumbing to the invasion is not the answer either. Even while emphasising the need for a creative response to this invasion, the NPC must see how we can avail ourselves of this technology to promote an understanding of our cultural heritage among the masses of our people at large, as well as take the message of India to the outside world.

'On the domestic front, this will require the conscious and deliberate use of the electronic media for the dissemination of our many rich regional cultural and linguistic traditions within the region and in the country at large. It will also call for the deployment of numerous local T.V., Video and Radio Production centres, especially in remote and rural areas, for local communities to actively participate in Radio and T.V. programmes of their own making, instead of being reduced, as at present, to merely passive recipients of programmes produced, broadcast and telecast from elsewhere, many of which have little relevance to their lives. Such production centres, with responsibility delegated to grassroot bodies, would be the ultimate answer to the dangers of consumerism, commercialism, heedless Westemisation, and imitative cultural modes. This will also counteract the tokenism which now represents the media attitude towards both folk and classical culture. A few small slots in a crowd of commercial entertainment respect neither the artistes nor their public. The proliferation of channels on Doordarshan must be utilised to encourage both tradition and experiment in rural and urban art forms.

"At the same time, global satellite technology offers us an unprecedented opportunity of disseminating our culture to the world at large; it is a challenge to which our electronic media must rise, in concert, with the Department of Culture, whose duty it is to ensure that Indian global T.V. does not become a pale imitation of existing Western-dominated networks.

"The Committee recommends that the NPC should explore measures to make the mass media an effective instrument for the dissemination of culture. The emphasis should be on the production of serials, documentaries and films relating to important personalities, places, festivals, literature and the arts. The mass media should not promote superstitious and magical belief systems. Doordarshan should use innovative methods to attract attention to the classical arts. Children should be exposed to the diversity of India's cultural and linguistic traditions through translations into their mother tongues of the poetry and the songs of great patriots and poets.

"The Committee expresses its serious concern over the ever increasing and reckless exhibition of violence, anti-social activities and obscenity through the cinema, the worst sufferers of which are the younger generation whose finer sensibilities are being coarsened and creative faculties dulled. The Committee, therefore, recommends that the NPC should address these issues and discourage these trends."

Among the glories of India's cultural heritage is the sensitive awareness of our forbears to the relationship between human wellbeing and the environment, exemplified by veneration of the *pancha bhoota* of air, water, earth, fire and the sky. It is tragic that the mass media did not bring out, over the decades of the heedless pursuit of industrialism and of profit for contractors and industrialists, the social cost in terms of the pollution of our rivers and denudation of our forests. Environment has begun to be discussed by the media only after the subject became a fashion in the industrially developed countries of the west. This is one of the many instances of the imitativeness of western culture on the part of most of our media practitioners, arising from their ignorance of and consequent lack of pride in our own cultural heritage.

10 RESTRUCTURING ELECTRONIC MEDIA

Till recently, proposals for improving the working of All India Radio and Doordarshan focussed almost entirely on the conferment of administrative and professional autonomy. The earliest of the committees on the broadcast media, headed by A.K. Chanda, recommended in its report (1966) the formation of an autonomous corporation to run A.I.R. and the then incipient Doordarshan. The proposal was turned down by the Government headed by Indira Gandhi.

The very name of the next committee, formed by the Janata Government in August 1977 with B.G. Verghese as chairman, indicated the emphasis on autonomy : it was called the Working Group on Autonomy for Akashvani and Doordarshan. But the Verghese group, besides proposing the establishment of an autonomous Akash Bharati, concerned itself with the role that publicly owned radio and television should play in a democratic and developing country. This was as well, because experience has shown that autonomy is a necessary but not sufficient condition for making publicly funded institutions truly serve the public interest. Many autonomous bodies have functioned in fact but government departments under another name.

The Verghese group envisaged the supplementation of Akash Bharati by stations that could be franchised for broadcasting educational programmes, but did not envisage straight competition from one or more privately owned and operated broadcasting systems offering a full range of news, entertainment and educative programmes. In any case, with the fall of the Janata government owing to internal dissension, and the return of the Congress (I) to power, the Verghese group's recommendation of an autonomous structure for broadcasting became part of history.

The next Working Group, appointed in December 1982, was headed by P.C. Joshi and its terms of reference were restricted to software. But since the production of imaginative and timely programmes has budgetary and administrative implications, the Joshi group's report included a chapter on 'Reforms in structure and personnel management'. Knowing full well that there was no question of the then government countenancing an autonomous organisation for broadcasting, the Joshi group contented itself, in the report it gave early in 1984, with recommending 'functional freedom'. On software, the Joshi group reiterated and amplified the Verghese group's observations on the need for socially relevant programmes that will be at once attractive and educative.

Reference has been made earlier to a Media Advisory Committee headed by G. Parthasarathi formed by the Ministry of I & B in 1980. On the report of the Joshi group on software being referred to it, the Media Advisory Committee offered its comments in a document notable for its lucid exposition of the social role that should guide a publicly owned broadcasting system. The comments of the Media Advisory Committee, which have continuing validity, are reproduced in Appendix VI. The document is notable for the rebuke, directed by it at the Government, for not giving effect to the news policy for broadcast media that it had earlier formulated : "It is now for the authorities to bridge the gap between sound recommendations by professionals and their implementation. An example of the gap pertains to the Media Advisory Committee itself and to the guidelines prepared by us on News Policy for the Broadcast Media. This document has been endorsed by the Government in the Ministry of Information & Broadcasting and circulated by it to Akashvani and Doordarshan; it has been placed before Parliament; and has been widely welcomed by professionals connected with public affairs communication, or journalism in the broad sense, but implementation has been slow and hesitant."

It is noteworthy that the Media Advisory Committee headed by G. Parthasarathi went into hibernation soon after furnishing its comments on the Software Group's report, finding that its advice was falling on deaf ears.

With the advent of foreign satellite channels brought to viewers by cable operators, and Doordarshan trying to meet the competition by imitating the rivals' titillating entertainment, Doordarshan shifted its attention to audience ratings—and further away from social purpose. But the leasing of time on radio and TV channels to private Indian parties, in the context of the Narasimha Rao government's New Economic Policy of liberalisation, brought out the value of competition. For the first time, the possibility of allowing competing radio and TV organisations to function in the country was envisaged in a report, given in October 1991, by an inter-departmental committee on 'Introducing Competition in the Electronic Media' constituted by the Ministry of Information & Broadcasting. Not made public so far, the recommendations made by the Committee are reproduced in Appendix VII. The alternative approaches to a new and competitive broadcasting system that were considered by the Committee, and the implications of each approach, are of interest in the ongoing debate on the future of broadcasting in India.

Even more crucial than the institutional framework for autonomous functioning of publicly owned radio and TV, and competition in order to keep programmers on their toes, is the social role that should be discharged by the electronic media. Autonomy and competition should not mean that profit-making—the commercial motive is already powerfully at work—becomes the end in itself. Reproduced in the following sections of this chapter are two seminal papers : the first on broadcasting as a public service, and the second outlining the legal and institutional framework of the kind of broadcasting that the country has been waiting for.

From state to market monopoly? by *B.G. Verghese, Dilip Padgaonkar and N. Bhaskara Rao*

Addressing the Constituent Assembly in 1948, Jawaharlal Nehru had hoped that departmental control over broadcasting would gradually yield to autonomy on the lines of the "British model". Implicit in that hope was the concept of broadcasting as a public service. Successive governments have subscribed to the concept in theory. Some even set up committees to examine the question of autonomy for the electronic media. But the recommendations, contained in the reports of the committees, were not followed. The result is that, despite encouraging signs of openness in the recent past, the broadcasting system continues to be used, by and large, as a mouthpiece of the ruling dispensation, on the one hand, and, on the other, to be driven harder and harder by market forces.

The latter trend has emerged in the wake of economic liberalisation and the telecommunication revolution. Satellite broadcasting, video and cable have had some salutary effects. They have brought in a measure of pluralism in the media and, by that same token, undermined Doordarshan's monopoly. However, the "invasion from the skies" (which is in reality a misnomer since external sound broadcasting has long been commonplace) has also had a singularly debilitating effect on Indian broadcasting. Since the government's response has been more reactive than innovative, the "invaders" have merrily set the agenda for the broadcasting system as a whole.

What this means in substance is that programming is increasingly determined by reach rather than relevance. Its central aim is the generation of revenues rather than the rejuvenation of cultural and social life. Advertising and sponsorship now compete for prime-time slots. Hence the dominance of serials, soaps, film-based programmes and a variety of talk shows at the lower end of the spectrum. Indeed, as channels proliferate, choice decreases.

We are shifting, rather swiftly, from the monopoly of the State to the monopoly of the "market". The shift entails a seminal departure from past practice. Under a state monopoly, the focus of attention has been, by and large, the voter; under a market monopoly it is the consumer. Under genuinely public control, it must perforce be the citizen. All three elements are present in the broadcasting system today. Political control is most evident in news and current affairs programmes, market control in entertainment and sports programmes and public-interest-driven programmes in a handful of swadeshi high-brow variants, generally telecast in non-prime-time hours. Doordarshan, therefore, has tended to have the best of two worlds—political conformism and commercial aggrandizement—to the detriment of its "natural" constituency : the overwhelming majority of the Indian citizenry, which does not wish to be manipulated for political and commercial ends and which, at any rate, is of little or no interest to the market.

However, the market and the urge of every government to retain control over the mass media are realities which have to be reckoned with. The consumerist appeal of television and radio is growing. This will necessarily entail programming which, as a rule, tends to debase tastes and lower standards. The exceptions to the rule cannot detract attention from the fact that the broadcasting system is embarked on an emotional and intellectual trajectory deviating from the values and aspirations enshrined in the preamble of the Constitution, in its articles on the rights of citizens and in many of its directive principles—all of which, taken together, constitute the conceptual basis of Indian broadcasting.

The basis is now being openly subverted. The programmes, aired at present, might satisfy those elements of the middle class and mass who yearn for titillation. But what the Indian citizenry at large—perhaps as many as two-thirds of the population—has access to would be whatever is merely incidental, accidental or residual. This was surely not the purpose of broadcasting ever.

The market, obviously, has its place in the scheme of things. But the market is not co-terminus with the citizenry. It is not a substitute for civil society. The market might provide some space for issues of public interest. But this cannot be equated with public service. Much in the same vein, the government of the day, even though it is elected democratically, cannot be the sole arbiter of what constitutes the national interest or public interest. Pluralism, provided it functions within the ambit of the constitution, can alone guarantee that this vast, complex and diverse country is endowed with a broadcasting system it truly merits.

When he addressed the Constituent Assembly, Jawaharlal Nehru, doubtless, had in mind the British broadcasting System. As far back as the early thirties, when he set out to create the BBC, Lord Reith acted on the premise that a good broadcasting system, to realise its stated ambitions, had to be guaranteed its independence from State, Church and Mammon. He, therefore, envisaged a State-financed but independent broadcasting authority responsible solely to Parliament and not to the government of the day or to the market-driven fad of the day or to some theocratic fantasy of the day. For all its defects (and we in India have nursed genuine grievances on that score) the BBC is widely hailed as one of the truly momentous cultural creations of the twentieth century.

It is in this light that there is the need to set up a public broadcasting service (PBS). It alone can check the all-consuming passions of the political and bureaucratic masters, of sundry bigots and of the marketing wizards. A recent judgment of the Supreme Court has declared the airwaves to be 'public property' for the fulfilment of the people's right to receive and impart information under the fundamental right guaranteed them by Article 19 (1) (a) of the Constitution, subject only to "reasonable restrictions" embodied in Article 19 (2). It has struck down Government's monopoly over the airwaves and ordered the establishment of an independent public authority to license broadcasting. This does not mean blanket privatisation, though many more private channels are likely to emerge. Even if numerically large, especially when externally originated satellite channels are added on, these will still constitutes only a fraction of the primary Doordarshan (DD) and AIR channels which must be redeemed to make up the core of a strong and vibrant public broadcasting system in India.

The Prasar Bharati Act was hurriedly drafted and though passed unanimously was not enforced. It is comatose and must be pronounced dead. With that, the way will be clear to convert AIR and DD into a truly public broadcasting system, as an autonomous corporation, set up under a parliamentary charter, imbued with a social purpose, funded by the exchequer, run by professionals under a board of trustees, and accountable to Parliament through an annual report.

How will this be different from the present AIR and DD system and other independent channels ? Consider AIR Imphal. This broadcasts in six major and 18 minor dialects of Manipur, apart from Manipuri, Hindi and English. This is responding to a cultural and not a consumerist market. Extend this analogy to programmes for and on schools, science, extension, farms, women, children, tribal groups, health and family welfare, the armed forces, border areas and other far-flung regions, the handicapped and myriad cultures, traditions and publics which, together, make up that mysterious "mainstream", and something of the concept of public broadcasting emerges. It entails reaching out to inform, educate and delight all the people at all levels in all their diversity, to uplift and integrate and provide access and participation. Content and quality are always subject to improvement, but the objective is clear. The market would not sustain or even cross-subsidise much of this, except selectively and intermittently.

The market, certainly initially, tends to be centralising and concerned with ratings to ensure commercial viability. Widening the appeal of programmes entails catering to the lowest common factor. Vulgarisation often follows. The mass consumption market is also inevitably homogenising and must necessarily exclude much of India's rich diversity to breed alienation and cast out millions by the wayside. All this could be socially and politically destablishing and would be basically arrogant and undemocratic.

The present AIR-DD system is government controlled

and hence lacking in credibility in times of crisis and confrontation or on controversial issues. The environment in which it has to function inhibits professionalism and creativity, neither of which is internally lacking in its ranks. It also suffers from being over-centralised, a product of its historical top-down growth and its mistaken appropriation by the Centre in a federal structure.

The answer is not that broadcasting must now devolve from the Centre to the States and panchayats but that, properly conceived, it must be by, of and for the people and functionally operative at the national, regional and local levels, interacting with all levels of governance, and internationally too.

Broadcasting, more than print, can be a powerful development tool, as it has an instant and global reach, overcoming barriers of literacy and physical communications. Educational and extension broadcasting, in particular, needs to be local, not national or even regional, so that the target audience can identify with the issues, the dialect, the locale and the actors. The programmes must mirror their lives, else things take on an air of fantasy. Hence the importance of local broadcast stations, whether radio or TV, which originate programmes and not merely relay them as do hundreds of low-power transmitters currently dotting the country-side. These local stations can be low-budget and lightly manned, using field and factory as their studio and local people as actors and resource personnel. As at Pij (Ahmedabad) during SITE, groups and organisations would be able to air their views on a regular basis. The would effectively be engaged in a "social audit". The statute book could come handy here : e.g. the consumer protection act.

Programme advisory committees, both regional and sectoral, could aid and advise the broadcast stations and monitor quality and content, including advertising content. A strong broadcast complaints council, an independent licensing authority, and an audience research unit to pre-test social programmes and provide feedback would be other elements in the system. Market-driven channels too would then be persuaded to accept certain obligations regarding the type and timing of programmes. The work of the council for complaints can be highly facilitated by regular studies on the impact of broadcasting on individuals and groups.

How would such a public broadcasting system pay its way ? First and foremost, it must be clearly understood that while it can tap the market it cannot be dependent on it. Primary funding must come from the exchequer. One-time broadcast licence fees (built into the cost of receivers), a modest cess on film and tape, a licence fee on all independent, satellite and cable channels, and rentals on transmission facilities owned by AIR and DD should be credited as revenue for the PBS. Capital expenditure must be provided under the Plan and voted along with the annual revenue budget by Parliament.

The Broadcast Licensing Authority should have, under its ambit, all forms of broadcasting and transmission—radio, TV, satellite, cable and others. It should also be allowed to license, on a three to five-year (but extendible) franchise, selected institutions such as universities, public trusts, research establishments, cultural academies, recognised NGOs, cooperatives like the NDDB, and other responsible and reputed public and private institutions to operate local broadcast stations. These could provide specialised, innovative and instructional programmes including things such as workers' education, a variety of open learning systems, regional music, language teaching, and other niche or general interest programmes of quality. Once several franchise stations are on the air, they could be networked upwards, regionally and nationally, to constitute a second PBS system built from the bottom up as an alternative to the AIR/DD system.

In all of this, radio must not be relegated as has been the case so far. It has enormous potential, being cheap, ubiquitous and versatile. Nor should colour-compatible black and white TV be ignored alongside colour, as this is cheaper. Finally, though not least of all, external broadcasting cannot be neglected. The world has come to India. And India too can reach the world loud and clear, by satellite. None of this will be possible or sustainable without strong R & D support.

Such a concept of public broadcasting has to be embodied in an Act which sets out its Charter and structure. Governments at all levels would still have access to the PBS system. A Board of Trustees accountable to Parliament would be the interface between the professional broadcasters in AIR/DD and the viewing and listening publics. With a second franchise-based PBS system coming into being, the two together could more than face up to the challenge of market channels and choice and give India's broadcast public what it has long deserved but never got : a broadcasting system which plays its rightful role to help citizens, society and the nation to fulfil their aspirations for freedom, knowledge, justice, progress and peace.

Bharat Prasar Sewa Bill—*drafted by a group of concerned citizens*

I. OBJECTS AND REASONS

The desirability of an independent and responsive broadcast service for the country has long been accepted. Parliament passed the Prasar Bharati Act in 1990 which is pending implementation. In the intervening years, breath-taking technological developments have taken place in the field of telecommunications. They have radically transformed the broadcasting scene. Nevertheless our response to these trends has been more reactive than innovative.

We are shifting, rather swiftly, from the monopoly of the State to the monopoly of the "market". The shift entails a seminal departure from past practice. Under a State monopoly, the focus of attention has been, by and large, the voter; under a market monopoly it is the consumer. Under genuinely public control, it must perforce be the citizen. All three elements are present in the broadcasting system today.

The market has come to play a more and more prominent role in broadcasting. This has certainly generated a spirit of competition. But market has its limitations in a country such as ours. The most obvious limitation is that it does not operate in any region, or for the benefit of any class of viewers, which does not fetch profits. Also, it tends to cater to the needs of the consumer only. But the market is not co-terminus with civil society. Nor is the consumer a synonym for the citizen.

Even while the market continues to play its rightful role, the State will be called upon to re-define its responsibilities. Significant in this connection is the Supreme Court's recent (February 1995) judgment holding the airwaves to be public property and directing the government to take steps to establish an independent and autonomous public authority, representative of all segments of society. It provides an opportunity to ensure that broadcasting ceases to be a State monopoly. While restructuring the electronic media care must be taken that the State acts as a facilitator and performs a legitimate public service.

Such an autonomous entity has a challenge cut out for it : to enable the citizens of India to gain access to information which is pluralistic in nature. It would not be subjected to manipulation by commercial and partisan political interests. The autonomous entity will regulate and control the airwaves with these ends in view.

Since the issue of autonomy for AIR and Doordarshan was the explicit legislative intention of the Prasar Bharati Act, which received the presidential assent in September 1990, the same is ensured in the proposed comprehensive Broadcasting Bill. As such, it should perhaps be possible to go ahead with the implementation of the Act by forming Prasar Bharati Corporation (Public Broadcasting Corporation).

II. SCOPE OF THE BILL

The proposed comprehensive Broadcasting Bill takes into account the more recent technological developments and provides for market-driven as well as community-service broadcasting.

Educational and extension broadcasting needs to be community-based, not national or even regional, so that the target audience can identify with the issue, the dialect, the locale and the actors. These local stations can be low-budget and lightly manned, using field and factory as their studio and local people as actors and resource personnel with citizens' groups and organisations being enabled to air their views on a regular basis. The Bill provides for it.

A strong broadcast complaints council, an independent licensing authority, and a standards council, with ethical concerns, are also provided in the Bill. There is provision for programme advisory committees, both regional and sectoral, to aid and advise the broadcast stations and monitor quality and content. The licensing authority would strive to ensure that the market-driven channels too are persuaded to accept certain obligations regarding the type and timing of programmes, as well as responsiveness to community or audience.

The Bill seeks to bring all forms of broadcasting and transmission—radio, TV, satellite, cable and others—under the ambit of the Broadcast Licensing Authority. The BLA is proposed to be authorised to license, on a three-year (but renewable) franchise, selected institutions such as universities, research establishments, public trusts, cultural academies, recognised NGOs, co-operatives like the NDDB, and other responsible and reputed public and private institutions to operate local broadcast stations. These could provide specialised, innovative and instructional programmes, including workers' education, a variety of open learning systems, regional music, language teaching, and other niche or general interest programmes of quality. Once several franchise stations are on the air, they could be networked upwards, regionally and nationally, to constitute a second PBS system built from the bottom up, as an adjunct to Prasar Bharati. The Bill seeks to give due importance to radio broadcasting.

The Bill seeks to protect the present staff of AIR and DD by providing them the option to continue with it or leave it on terms to be decided by the Boards/Prasar Bharati. While both Doordarshan and AIR shall be free to raise money through advertisements and any other source deemed fit by the trust, a percentage of its channels and programmes shall compulsorily be devoted to a discussion of public issues. Neither Doordarshan nor AIR shall have editorial opinion and shall be content with airing plurality of opinions, subject only to restrictions mentioned in Article 19 (2) of the Constitution.

III. Indian Broadcasting Services Bill : Suggested Features

1. The Bill is called Bharat Prasar Seva Bill (Indian Broadcasting Services Bill).

2. The Bill provides for restructuring and regulation of the various broadcasting services available in the country in the light of technological developments and constitutional obligations, as laid down by the Supreme Court, particularly in its recent judgment of 9th February 1995 on airwaves.

3. The Bill will be a comprehensive legislation on broadcasting and would cover a) Radio, b) Television, c) Satellite (domestic and foreign), d) Cable, e) Interactive TV multi-media, f) Terrestrial including MMDS, and g) the Telegraph Act as relevant to broadcasting.

4. The broadcasting services under the proposed Bill will have three streams of broadcasting in the country : a) a public broadcasting service (Prasar Bharati) mostly funded by the State, b) market-driven broadcasting including cable, satellite operations and other terrestrial services and c) community service broadcasting by autonomous citizen groups, academies, trusts and NGOs, individually or as part of a network, mostly at local and regional level.

5. The Bill provides for the establishment of an autonomous Broadcasting Commission of India (BCI) with responsibility for licensing operators, setting up of Prasar Bharati Corporation, and constituting two Councils on a statutory footing, one for ensuring certain standards in broadcasting and the other for promoting audience involvement and examination of complaints from the public. It will also constitute two Boards, one for coordinating cable, satellite and other channels and the other for coordinating community-service broadcasting.

6. The Broadcasting Commission of India (BCI), appointed

by the President of India, will supervise and regulate the functioning of various broadcasting systems in the country. It will have three wings, each operating on a statutory basis. These are : a) a Broadcasting Standards Council (BSC), b) Broadcasting Complaints Council (BCC) and c) Broadcasting Licensing Authority (BLA).

7. The Bill provides for constituting a Public Broadcasting Corporation (Prasar Bharati), to ensure programmes of quality, keeping in view the information, educational and entertainment aspects and needs of people at all levels, but without succumbing to compulsions of commercial and competitive TV. Prasar Bharati will have two Boards under it, one for AIR and another for Doordarshan, both fully or partially funded by the State.

8. Under the Bill, the market-driven broadcasting, as well as community-service broadcasting, will operate within the broad parameters set by the BCI and Broadcasting Licensing Authority and within the purview of the Broadcasting Complaints Council and advertising and programme codes of the Standards Council. The Standards Council will also have the responsibility for impact research and broadcasting ethics. The Complaints Council will ensure that guidelines are followed by all operators, by monitoring the operations and encouraging viewer feedback and involvement in the process.

9. Licensing Authority issues and renews licenses to operate radio, TV, cable, satellite and related services in India under specified obligations, terms and conditions and with certain fees as prescribed by the BCI. Each time the license will be valid for 3 years. The Authority will be empowered to cancel a license under certain circumstances, like violation of guidelines or conditions. It will have the authority, in the larger public interest, to issue warning to any service operator, as and when he deviates from the codes and guidelines.

10. Ensuring the plurality of opinion within the ambit of Article 19 (2) of the Constitution, the bill provides for Advertising and Programme Codes applicable for all the

three streams of broadcasting in the country, responsibility resting with the Standards Council. The Standards Council would also prescribe limits for commercials (duration, type, etc.), some community responsibility obligations to market-driven channels—like making certain broadcast time or programmes compulsory and also certain public response obligations—as part of licensing terms.

11. The Complaints Council will be responsible for review, analysis and follow up action where called for, and license renewals will always be after clearance by the Complaints Council. The Complaints Council will have State-wise or regional chapters. The decisions of the council on the complaints received by it shall be broadcast by the concerned operator for the information of the public and as a redressal of the grievance of the affected person or group.

12. The BCI and both the Councils (BSC and BCC) ensure, through their guidelines, that national interests are not threatened and both would be given sufficient powers to determine the nature and quality of broadcasting service in the country. The two Councils will operate independently but in tandem in such a way that they would set the base for the Licensing Authority's decisions and ensure transparency in its operations. Apart from reports incorporated in the BCI's annual reports to the Parliament, they would inform the public as often as necessary so that a discerning viewership and listenership is built up over time.

13. Keeping in view the objectives of setting up of an independent BCI, a three-member committee headed by Vice President of India (Chairman, Rajya Sabha) and consisting of the Speaker, Lok Sabha and the Chief Justice of India, will select the Chairman and seven Members from different disciplines for the Broadcasting Commission of India (BCI). The Chairmen of the two Councils, the Chairman of Prasar Bharati and the two Boards would be ex-officio members of Broadcasting Commission of India. In addition, the Chairman, UGC and the Chairman, Press Council will also be ex-officio members of BCI. At least one member of the Complaints Council and Standards Council will be

members of the licensing authority.

14. The State will provide funding for the operations of the Broadcasting Commission of India and its other wings. The market driven as well as the community service operators will be levied certain fees, annual as well as for license renewal, on the basis of certain criteria linked with the extent of the service. So also certain registration one-time fees from TV sets will be collected. These revenues will go to BCI.

15. There will be two Boards to guide and coordinate the market-driven as well as community-service broadcasting operations, other than those under Prasar Bharati. The Board on community services will have prominent representatives of NGOs, trusts, local bodies and public men from education, development, health, etc. It will coordinate all such outlets/ operations, and facilitate networking nationally. The BCI will appoint the Chairman and Members of these Boards.

16. A Cable & Satellite Board of India will be formed and made responsible for overseeing cable and satellite operations at local and regional levels and by local boards, citizen groups, NGOs etc. Cable operations will be brought under the purview of this Board. It will be responsible for registering, monitoring and analysing cable and satellite operations. The conditions for registration/operation would include responding to public complaints, restrictions and restraint on duration and nature of advertisements. The cable operations will be conducted under local or regional chapters of the Complaints Council and within the parameters of the Standards Council.

17. Prasar Bharati (Public Broadcasting Corporation), with AIR and Doordarshan having their own executive Boards, will be funded annually by the State as in the case of other social sector obligations of the State. Advertising, even when falling within the code restrictions, should not be made as a source for sustenance or as criteria for judging performance or popularity. Deficit, if any, would be borne by the State. Both the Boards will have Programme Advisory Committees for each originating Kendra (of AIR and DD) for

2-3 years each time.

18. Satellite operations will be by and large moderated by Cable and Satellite Board via cable operators. There would be certain provisions in the case of Direct Broadcasting Services (DBS) from satellites in respect of advertising flows, and there would be citizen awareness compaigns to prompt citizen level (viewer-end) initiatives by way of black-listing channels/programmes, while availing of DBS by households. The State will also issue warnings where the provisions of the Constitution are under threat. The Cable and Satellite Board will process proposals for uplinking facility and recommend to the Licensing Authority of India.

19. The print media establishments will not be allowed to start and operate broadcasting services. No broadcasts of foreign services are relayed, live or otherwise, without prior approval of BCI, which will be the deciding authority on all such issues and will direct the concerned agency suitably.

20. As a public Trust, the Broadcasting Commission of India is accountable to the Parliament for its budget and annual report, review, etc.

INDIAN BROADCASTING OPERATIONS : The System

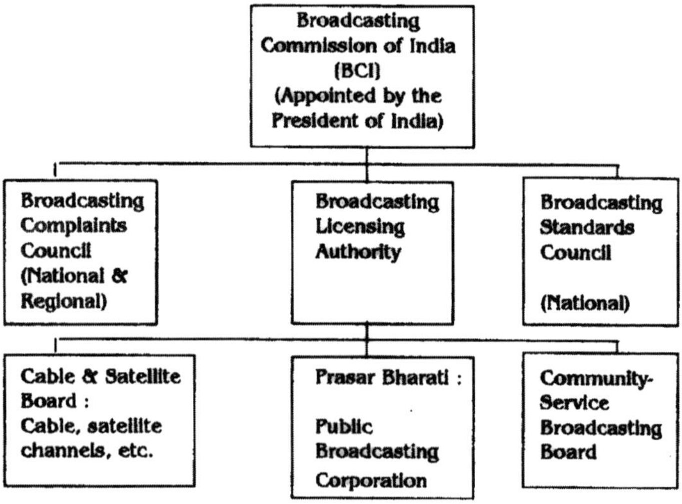

11 CITIZEN AWARENESS AND INITIATIVE

A people, it has been said, get the government they deserve. To the extent that this saying brings out the importance of awareness and vigilance on the part of the people, it applies to the mass media too.

People as victims and accomplices

A passive citizenry makes for irresponsible government and for irresponsible media. Reference was made in an earlier Chapter to the loud, rhythm-dominant, mindless and often lewd music played through loudspeakers in many passenger buses in Delhi, in defiance of orders by the Police Commissioner of the National Capital Territory.

Laws and orders are not self-executing, and the police cannot be omnipresent for checking violations—assuming that none of the police can be bribed into condoning violations. It is for citizens to demand adherence to the prescribed code whether by drivers and conductors of commercially run buses or the organisers of the chartered buses that are in the nature of cooperative enterprise. But the majority of commuters in a bus do not object to the playing of film songs in violation of the police ban. If a few passengers object, the conductor pays no heed because the protest is not widely backed. Indeed, several of the passengers enjoy the music—however silly the words and elementary the tune and the rhythm—and keep time, tapping with the hand or foot. Citizens, as victims of vulgarity and the lowering of public taste, thus become accomplices.

The findings of the survey conducted by CMS have brought out how persons of all ages have been attracted by the tinsel entertainment of film music and dance offered by radio and TV. Such is the compelling attraction of this fare that even those parents, and other older members of a family who know that it is not healthy for young palates (let alone their own) do not turn off the source. They permit children to watch even scenes of obscenity and sadistic violence on TV since they are not prepared to forgo their own amusement.

Talking back to the media

But not all is lost. There have lately been signs of citizen awareness and protest, alongside citizen acquiescence.

Letters to the Editor is a hoary feature of newspapers. It is a column that reflects not only the views and feelings of some of the readers, but the taste and philosophy of the editorial staff who scan and select from the large mail that is received. They also furnish the captions under which the selected letters are published. The Press has rendered a public service by conveying the distress and disgust of their readers at Doordarshan's performance, and publishing news of the consequences of violence depicted on the TV screen. Reproduced below are some illustrative instances from a couple of Delhi newspapers :

> TV HAVOC AT NIGHT
>
> "Is it not common sense that 11.30 is not the time to start TV programmes for students, small or grown-up ? Many families are in a dilemma. Grown-up children cannot tolerate a family time-table which wants them to go to bed by at least 11.30 p.m....."—*'Patriot'*, 3rd June, 1995.
>
> TV SERIAL LEADS TO SUICIDE
>
> "Bangalore : Apparently influenced by a suicide scene in a television serial, Nandeesh, a teenager, hanged himself to death at his residence here on Sunday, the

police said. A student of St. Joseph' high school, Nandeesh had been experimenting daredevil acts shown on TV and was in the habit of emulating such acts.—PTI"—*'Indian Express'*, 23rd August, 1995.

TELESERIALS DRAW FLAK FROM WOMEN'S GROUPS

"New Delhi, Sept. 6—Women's groups are disturbed at the images of girls projected by several television serials. Issues such as teenage pregnancy, molestation, rape and abortion are often exaggerated or shown in a facile manner that downplays the seriousness of the problem, it is felt.

"Clips from serials on ZEE TV and Doordarshan were monitored and viewed by women's groups, and their impact on young girls analysed at a discussion organised recently by the Media Advocacy Group in which the participants were several health workers from Action India who work in the middle and lower income housing colonies in Delhi....It is felt that while incidents of rape, molestation and incestuous rape do occur, TV serials only show part of the reality. TV serials often exaggerate what is happening and this further encourages men to commit such acts....In many TV serials, abortion is shown as a quick and easy option. In one clip, the girl is shown simply walking into the clinic with her brother and then walking out and going home. Women pointed out that contrary to what is depicted, abortion can be painful."—*'Indian Express'*, 7th September, 1995.

PEDDLING OBSCENITY

"Doordarshan, it appears, is competing in obscenity with foreign television networks. DD is wooing the youth away from foreign networks by airing vulgar song sequences from films....Our censors do not allow a kissing scene in Indian films, but they seem to have no problem about clearing sexually suggestive song sequences."—*'Indian Express'*, 11th September, 1995.

The protest action organised by nurses' organisations all over the country over the objectionable depiction of their profession in the film 'Dil ka doctor' is a recent instance of citizens' initiative against indecent representation of women in the media. Thousands of nurses have been reporting for work in ordinary clothing, since the uniform prescribed for them, and symbolising their profession, has been grossly insulted. Earlier, angry residents in a high-rise apartment building in Bombay served by cable operators threw down a TV set from the terrace as a symbolic act of protest.

Women members of parliament have from time to time raised the issue of vulgarity in television on the floor of both the Houses. Members of the standing committees attached to the I & B and Human Resource Development Ministries have also expressed themselves vigorously on the subject in their reports, as noted earlier. Outside parliament, women teachers from Delhi schools have led demonstrations against vulgarity on the Doordarshan screen and there have been similar expressions of protest elsewhere. A Delhi newspaper reported on 8th December, 1995 that Sadhvi Ritambhara, who heads Durga Vahini, women's wing of the Bharatiya Janata Party, plans to mobilise school and college girls against the growing menace of pornographic advertisements, obscenity on TV, and of sexual harassment. These are welcome indications of a groundswell of public opinion.

Human dignity and women's equality are issues that transcend differences on other matters between political parties. Surely they should all come together to force the Government to act firmly for stopping vulgarity and violence in the mass media. Time was when the exposure to sexism and sadism in the media affected the behaviour of some individuals; with the advent of television, video and cable, whole communities have begun to be affected as instanced by the sex scandal in Jalgaon a couple of years ago.

To demonstrate their strong feeling on certain issues, political parties resort from time to time to forms of protest which inconvenience the public and cost the taxpayer heavily, such as *bandh* and storming the well of legislatures and forcing their adjournment. Without taking recourse necessarily to such methods, cannot political parties find ways to bring strong pressure to bear on the Government which runs Doordarshan and has armed itself with a cable reulation law ?

Research can make its own contribution to the stirring of public awareness of the social effects of the mass media. This was recognised by the Standing Committee of M.P.s on Communications (1994-95). It strongly recommended in its eighth report (December 1994), on the I & B Ministry's Central Board for Film Certification, "long-term behavioural and scientific studies and audience research to gauge the impact of screen images and messages on different sections of society, and in particular on children and youth. Findings of such studies should be made available to the members of the Central Board of Film Censors and its Advisory Panels."

The present work is precisely such a behavioural and scientific study. Its publication, the authors hope, will generate pressure of public opinion on a scale sufficient to bring about a change for the better not only in film certification but in the running of Doordarshan and Akashvani and in the regulation of the cable networks that deliver satellite TV channels.

An important point made during one of the colloquia organised by the Centre for Media Studies in Delhi was that communication research should not only add to knowledge but should help to stimulate action for improving the functioning of the mass media. It is with this aim that CMS has initiated an ongoing social audit of the mass media, the findings of which in the preliminary round are set out in this work. The presentation is action-oriented to the point that it includes the draft of a Bill for the regulation of radio and television in the public interest that could be considered for adoption by Parliament.

Motivating media personnel

While restructuring of the legal and administrative framework of broadcasting is essential, it is in the last analysis the human factor that will determine whether radio and television, which have hitherto been in the public sector, develop on the right lines in our country. The human factor is equally crucial in respect of the Press and films which are in the private domain.

Whatever the nature of ownership and of superintendence, whether in publicly or privately owned media, the personnel operating them have a certain elbow room which can be utilised for the good or ill of society. Much depends on the self-image of the communicator : whether he sees himself as a mere cog in the wheel of a machine controlled by a Minister or a private business man as the case may be, or as a citizen with obligations towards fellow-citizens. The point about autonomy in terms of the individual's elbow room under any system may be illustrated by two incidents.

Jawaharlal Nehru invited C.D. Deshmukh, not long after and despite the latter's resignation from the Cabinet over the question of Bombay City as part of Maharashtra, (during the process of States reorganisation in the mid-1950s) to take up chairmanship of the University Grants Commission. Deshmukh wanted to be assured that the commission could function autonomously. Jawaharlal Nehru wrote in reply to the effect that it was for him (Deshmukh) to exercise autonomy, and for him (Nehru) to respect it. It takes autonomous individuals to exercise autonomy.

Similarly, no 'crawler' can exercise autonomy in a future autonomous broadcasting corporation. This was the expression used by L.K. Advani, Information Minister in the brief-lived Janata government during 1977. He said at a meeting with journalists : "They (authorities during the emergency regime) wanted you to bend; some of you chose to crawl."

We have drawn attention in the course of this work to the unenviable position of India—a half-century after independence—as the country carrying the largest numbers of the world's poor and the illiterate. The present work will, we hope serve as a motivating influence on personnel at various levels to exercise their individual autonomy, however limited, so as to make the media socially relevant and promotive of development understood in human terms.

Appendix

Appendix I

FILM CENSORSHIP : SUPREME COURT'S RATIONALE

On 30th March 1989, in the case of S. Rangarajan V. P. Jagjivan Ram (Civil Appeal No. 1668 and 1669 of 1988), the Supreme Court observed as follows while upholding censorship of films by prior restraint :

"11...The movie cannot function in a free market place like the newspaper, magazine or advertisement. Movie motivates thought and action and assures a high degree of attention and retention. It makes its impact simultaneously arousing the visual and aural senses. The focusing of an intensive light on a screen with the dramatizing of facts and opinion makes the ideas more effective. The combination of act and speech, sight and sound, in semi-darkness of the theatre with elimination of all distracting ideas will have an impact in the minds of spectators....It has as much potential for evil as it has for good. It has an equal potential to instil or cultivate violent or good behaviour. With these qualities, and since it caters for mass audience who are generally not selective about what they watch, the movie cannot be equated with other modes of communication. Censorship by prior restraint is, therefore, not only desirable but also necessary."

S.O. 836-(E), 6TH DECEMBER 1991

In sanctioning films for public exhibition, the Board of Film Certification shall be guided by the following principles:

1. The objectives of film certification will be to ensure

that:

(a) the medium of film remains responsible and sensitive to the values and standards of society;

(b) artistic expression and creative freedom are not unduly curbed;

(c) certification is responsive to social change;

(d) the medium of film provides clean and healthy entertainment; and

(e) as far as possible, the film is of aesthetic value and cinematically of a good standard.

2. In pursuance of the above objectives, the Board of Film Certification shall ensure that :

(i) anti-social activities such as violence are not glorified or justified;

(ii) the *modus operandi* of criminals, other visuals or words likely to incite the commission of any offence are not depicted;

(iii) scenes—

(a) showing involvement of children in violence as victims or as perpetrators of or as forced witness to violence, or showing children as being subjected to any form of child abuse;

(b) showing abuse or ridicule of physically and mentally handicapped persons; and

(c) showing cruelty to, or abuse of, animals

are not presented needlessly;

(iv) pointless or avoidable scenes of violence, cruelty and horror, scenes of violence primarily intended to provide entertainment and such scenes as may have the effect of desensitising or dehumanising people are not shown;

(v) scenes which have the effect of justifying or glorifying drinking are not shown;

(vi) scenes tending to encourage, justify or glamorise drug addiction are not shown;

(vii) human sensibilities are not offended by vulgarity, obscenity or depravity;

(viii) such dual meaning words as obviously cater to baser instincts are not allowed;

(ix) scenes degrading or denigrating women in any manner are not presented;

(x) scenes involving sexual violence against women like attempt to rape, rape or any form of molestation, or scenes of a similar nature, are avoided, and if any such incident is germane to the theme, they shall be reduced to the minimum and no details are shown;

(xi) scenes showing sexual perversions shall be avoided and if such matters are germane to the theme, they shall be reduced to the minimum and no details are shown;

(xii) visuals or words contemptuous of racial, religious or other groups are not presented;

(xiii) visuals or words which promote communal, obscurantist, anti-scientific and anti-national attitudes are not presented;

(xiv) the sovereignty and integrity of India is not called into question;

(xv) the security of the State is not jeopardised or endangered;

(xvi) friendly relations with foreign States are not strained;

(xvii) public order is not endangered;

(xviii) visuals or words involving defamation of an individual or a body of individuals, or contempt of court, are not presented. *Explanation* : Scenes that tend to create scorn, disgrace or disregard of rules or undermine the dignity of court will come under the term 'contempt of court'; and

(xix) national symbols and emblems are not shown except in accordance with the provisions of the Emblems and Names (Prevention of Improper Use) Act, 1950 (12 of 1950).

3. The Board of Film Certification shall also ensure that the film :

   (i) is judged in its entirety from the point of view of its overall impact; and

   (ii) is examined in the light of the period depicted in the film and the contemporary standards of the country and the people to which the film relates, provided that the film does not deprave the morality of the audience.

4. Films that meet the above-mentioned criteria but are considered unsuitable for exhibition to non-adults shall be certified for exhibition to adult audience only.

5.(1) While certifying films for unrestricted public exhibition, the Board shall ensure that the film is suitable for family viewing, that is to say, the film should be such that all the members of the family including children can view it together.

(2) If the Board, having regard to the nature, content and theme of the film, is of the opinion that it is necessary to caution the parents/guardians to consider as to whether any child below the age of twelve years may be allowed to see such a film, the film shall be certified for unrestricted public exhibition with an endorsement to that effect.

(3) If the Board, having regard to the nature, content and theme of the film, is of the opinion that the exhibition of the film should be restricted to members of any profession or any class of persons, the film shall be certified for public exhibition restricted to the specialised audiences to be specified by the Board in this behalf.

6. The Board shall scrutinise the titles of the films carefully and ensure that they are not provocative, vulgar, offensive or violative of any of the above mentioned guidelines.

Appendix II

NEWS POLICY FOR BROADCAST MEDIA

News policy suggested by the Media Advisory Committee, approved by the Ministry of I & B and issued to All India Radio and Doordarshan on 4th May 1982.

"There has to be a clear understanding of the difference between news and views. The reporting of news has to be factual, accurate and objective and only such views as make news should find a place in news broadcasts. There can be no editorialising in broadcast news.

"Each news story should be judged strictly on the basis of its news value.

"In the selection of news received from wide ranging sources and in news editing, AIR and Doordarshan should be guided by the highest possible professional standards. While newsworthiness will determine the selection of news, its treatment and presentation should be directly related to the special characteristics and potential of each medium as well as the target audiences.

"Apart from treating news factually and objectively AIR and Doordarshan should provide, where necessary, a background to the events and happenings in order that listeners in any part of the country are able to place such events and happenings in proper perspective.

"The broadcast news should satisfy the highest criteria of accuracy and responsibility. AIR and Doordarshan cannot indulge in speculative stories of the type which appear in certain journals. They should develop their own sources for the verification of events.

"In a developing country like ours, a special function of broadcasting should be the coverage of development : its significance, achievements and problems. Development news covers a wide range of activities—economic, technological, social and cultural. It should not be confined to mere statements and plans but explain their significance. For this purpose news gathering operations of AIR and Doordarshan should be expanded and properly dispersed. In other words, the news gathering apparatus should make a deliberate effort to explore new areas of development and nation building news. People's participation in such activities should be duly highlighted as also significant work being done by voluntary agencies. Thereby the broadcast media should not only supplement the work normally undertaken by the news agencies but put out well backgrounded stories on their own.

"With the limitation of time, the vast audiences reached and the presentational demands, AIR and Doordarshan cannot be expected to follow the pattern of news coverage followed by the newspapers. The range and scope of news gathering and selection will have to be suited to the media.

"The style and method of news reporting should reinforce the fundamental principles including territorial integrity, national integration, secularism, maintenance of public order and upholding the dignity and prestige of Parliament, State legislatures and the judiciary.

"Ministerial statements on policy matters, particularly those of the Prime Minister, are important in as much as they enable the people to understand national policies. Similarly implementation of government programmes should be given proper place in the news. The focus should be on information rather than on individuals. It is also necessary that views critical of official policies and the manner of their implementation should find adequate time.

"In reporting on political controversies the broadcast media should be guided by objectivity and fair play. Due representation of differing viewpoints should be the aim. If a variety of viewpoints cannot be projected in the same bulletin, the balance should be achieved within a reasonable period of time.

"In the choice of international events the objective should be to keep the people informed of world developments. A special effort should be made to give proper background of events. In the selection of news, greater attention should be given to events in developing countries, particularly our neighbours. Apart from strictly pruning and editing the copy from the world agencies which have an overload of news from advanced countries and also a subtle bias, it would be desirable for AIR to use copy from the Non-aligned News Pool and other third world agencies on news merits. What is most essential is for AIR to increase the number of its foreign correspondents and carefully select their location and area of news coverage so that we can project a view of world developments as seen by India and other non-aligned developing countries. AIR and Doordarshan should aim at creating informed public opinion on international events and developments. In preparing programmes in news and current affairs, the national interest must be kept in mind. The national policy of peace and peaceful co-existence, non-alignment, friendship with all countries, support for people fighting for independence and freedom and the struggle against racism and racial discrimination and for an international order based on justice and equality should be highlighted. This does not exclude the reporting of any significant criticism of Government's foreign policy, either in the content or in its implementation.

"The primary purpose of the current affairs programmes should be to enlighten the people on various aspects of political, economic, social and cultural developments. The treatment of the subject should be comprehensive, projecting different viewpoints. It should aim at providing adequate background for a proper understanding and interpretation of events and issues.

"The current affairs programmes should be broadbased in the selection of topics and participants. The interests of various sections of the people should be taken into account. The formats should be innovative and suited to the medium. There is scope for experimentation in this respect.

"Internal evaluation of news and current affairs programmes after their broadcast should be a regular exercise on a daily basis. A panel of outside experts for news and current affairs in a particular language should be considered.

"The characteristics and potential reach of the broadcast media necessitate the drafting of news items in spoken style. The language should be addressed to the ear, unlike the printed word in a newspaper or journal which is meant to be read.

"The constraint of time also calls for precision and brevity. The differences in the level of comprehension of listeners are yet another factor to be taken into account. Simplicity and clarity are essential. Reporters and those who give talks should aim at easy communication with the people, and not parade their literacy skills. AIR and Doordarshan should develop their own idiom and style.

"There should be provision for evaluation from time to time of the language of the bulletins. There has to be a much greater emphasis on specialisation and training of the news personnel within AIR and Doordarshan. A style book in each language should be prepared without delay.

"The implementation of these policies and norms will depend upon the professional capacity of the people who run the news and current affairs programmes. The choice of personnel is most important. A professional must have had training in news work. He should be able to choose items well and to rewrite the stories to suit the medium. Professional training and appreciation of the role of the media in a democratic society will give him the confidence to take the right decisions."

Appendix III

SUPREME COURT JUDGEMENT OF 9TH FEBRUARY 1995 CONCERNING DOORDARSHAN

Following are some significant passages from the two judgements, concurring, delivered by Justice P.B. Sawant, speaking also for Justice S. Mohan; and by Justice B.P. Jeevan Reddy :

P.B. SAWANT AND S. MOHAN

The law on the subject discussed earlier makes it clear that the fundamental right to freedom of speech and expression includes the right to communicate effectively and to as large a population not only in this country but also abroad, as is feasible. There are no geographical barriers on communication. Hence every citizen has a right to use the best means available for the purpose. At present, electronic media, viz., TV and radio, is the most effective means of communication. The restrictions which the electronic media suffers in addition to those suffered by the print media are that :

(i) the airwaves are a public property and they have to be used for the benefit of the society at large;

(ii) the frequencies are limited; and

(iii) media is subject to pre-censorship.

The other limitations, viz., the reasonable restrictions imposed by law made for the purpose mentioned in Article 19 (2) is common to all the media. In the present case it was not and cannot be the case of the NIB that the telecasting of the cricket matches was not for the benefit of the society at large or not in the public interest and, therefore, not a proper use of the public property. It was not the case of the NIB that it was in violation of the provisions of Article 19 (2). There was nothing to be pre-censored on the grounds mentioned in Article 19 (2). As regards the limitations of resources, since the DD was prepared to telecast the cricket matches but only on its terms, it could not plead that there was no frequency available for telecasting. The DD could also not have ignored the rights of the viewers which the High Court was at pains to emphasise while passing its order and to which we have also made a reference. The CAB/BCCI being the organisers of the event had a right to sell the telecasting rights of its event to any agency. Assuming that the DD had no frequency to spare for telecasting the matches, the CAD could certainly enter into a contract with any agency, including a foreign agency, to telecast the said matches through that agency's frequency for the viewer in this country (who could have access to these frequencies) as well as for the viewers abroad. The orders passed by the High Court in effect gave a right to DD to be the host broadcaster for telecasting in this country and for the TWI for telecasting for the viewers outside this country who have an access to the TWI frequency. The order was eminently in the interest of the viewers, whatever its merits on the other aspects of the matter.

The order passed by the High Court have to be viewed against the backdrop of the events and the position of law discussed above. The circumstances in which the High Court passed the orders and the factual and legal considerations which weighed with it in passing them speak for themselves. However, since the cricket matches have already been telecast, the question of the legality or otherwise of the orders has become academic and it is not necessary to pronounce our formal verdict on the same. Hence we refrain from doing so.

We therefore, hold as follows :

(i) The airwaves or frequencies are a public property. Their use has to be controlled and regulated by a public authority in the interests of the public and to prevent the invasion of their rights. Since the electronic media involves the use of the airwaves this factor creates an in-built restriction on its use as in the case of any other public property.

(ii) The right to impart and receive information is a species of the right of freedom of speech and expression guaranteed by Article 19 (1) (a) of the Constitution. A citizen has a fundamental right to use the best means of imparting and receiving information and as such to have an access to telecasting for the purpose. However this right to have an access to telecasting has limitations on account of the use of the public property, viz., the airwaves, involved in the exercise of the right and can be controlled and regulated by the public authority. This limitation imposed by the nature of the public property involved in the use of the electronic media is in addition to the restrictions imposed on the right to freedom of speech and expression under Article 19 (2) of the Constitution.

(iii) The central Government shall take immediate steps to establish an independent autonomous public authority representative of all sections and interests in the society to control and regulate the use of airwaves.

(iv) Since the matches have been telecast pursuant to the impugned order of the High Court, it is not necessary to decide the correctness of the said order.

(v) The High Court will now apportion between the CAB and the DD the revenues generated by the advertisement on TV during the telecasting of both the series of the cricket matches, viz., the Hero Cup and the International Cricket Matches played in India from October to December 1994, after hearing the parties on the subject.

B.P. JEEVAN REDDY

While I agree broadly with the conclusion arrived at by my learned brother Sawant, J. I propose to record my views and conclusions on the issues arising in these matters in view of their far-reaching importance.

Summary

In this summary too, the expression "broadcasting media" means the electronic media now represented and operated by AIR and Doordarshan and not any other services.

1 (a) Game of cricket, like any other sports event provides entertainment. Providing entertainment is implied in freedom of speech and expression guaranteed by Article 19 (1) (a) of the Constitution subject to this rider that where speech and conduct are joined in a single course of action the free speech values must be balanced against competing societal interests. The petitioners (CAB and BCCI) therefore have a right to organise cricket matches in India, whether with or without the participation of foreign teams. But what they are now seeking is a license to telecast their matches through an agency of their choice—a foreign agency in both the cases and through telecasting equipment brought in by such foreign agency from outside the country. In the case of Hero Cup Matches organised by CAB, they wanted uplinking facility to INTELSAT through the government agency VSNL also. In the case of later international matches organised by BCCI they did not ask for this facility for the reason that their foreign agent has arranged direct uplinking with the Russian satellite Gorizon. In both cases, they wanted the permission to import the telecasting equipment along with the personnel to operate it by moving it to places all over the country wherever the matches were to be played. They claimed this license, or permission, as it may be called, as a matter of right said to be flowing from Article 19 (1) (a) of the Constitution. They say that the authorities are bound to grant such license/permission, without any conditions, all that they are entitled to do, it is submitted, is to collect technical fees wherever their services are availed, like the services of VSNL in the case of Hero Cup Matches. This plea is in principle no different from the right to establish and operate private telecast-

ing stations. In principle, there is no difference between a permanent TV station and a temporary one; similarly there is no distinction in principle between a stationary TV facility and a mobile one; so also is there no distinction between a regular TV facility and a TV facility for a given event or series of events. If the right claimed by the petitioners (CAB and BCCI) is held to be constitutionally sanctioned one, then each and every citizen of this country must also be entitled to claim similar right in respect of his event or events as the case may be. I am of the opinion that no such right flows from Article 19 (1) (a).

(b) Airwaves constitute public property and must be utilised for advancing public good. No individual has a right to utilise them at his choice and pleasure and for purposes of his choice including profit. The right of free speech guaranteed by Article 19 (1) (a) does not include the right to use airwaves, which are public property. The airwaves can be used by a citizen for the purpose of broadcasting only when allowed to do so by a statute and in accordance with such statute. Airwaves being public property, it is the duty of the state to see that airwaves are so utilised as to advance the free speech right of the citizens which is served by ensuring plurality and diversity of views, opinions and ideas. This is imperative in every democracy where freedom of speech is assured. The free speech right guaranteed to every citizen of this country does not encompass the right to use these airwaves at his choosing. Conceding such a right would be detrimental to the free speech rights of the body of citizens in as much as only the privileged few—powerful economic, commercial and political interests—would come to dominate the media.

By manipulating the news, views and information by indulging in misinformation and disinformation, to suit their commercial or other interests, they would be harming and not serving the principles of plurality and diversity of views, news, ideas and opinions. This had been the experience of Italy where a limited right, i.e., at the local level but not at the national level was recognised. It is also not possible to imply or infer a right from the guarantee of free speech which only a few can enjoy.

(c) Broadcasting media is inherently different from Press or other means of communication/information. The analogy of press in misleading and inappropriate. This is also the view expressed by several Constitutional Courts including that of the United States of America.

(d) I must clarify what I say; it is that the right claimed by the petitioners (CAB and BCCI) which in effect is no different in principles from a right to establish and operate a private TV station does not flow from Article 19 (1) (a); that such a right is not implicit in it. The question whether such right should be given to the citizens of this country is a matter of policy for the Parliament. Having regard to the revolution in information technology and the developments all around, Parliament may, or may not, decide to confer such right. If it wishes to confer such a right, it can only be by way of an Act made by Parliament. The Act made should be consistent with the right of free speech of the citizens and must have to contain strict programme and other controls, as has been provided, for example, in the Broadcasting Act, 1991 in the United Kingdom. This is the implicit command of Article 19 (1) (a) and is essential to preserve and promote plurality and diversity of views, news, opinions and ideas.

(e) There is an inseparable inter-connection between freedom of speech and the stability of the society i.e., stability of a nation-State. They contribute to each other. Ours is a nascent republic. We are yet to achieve the goal of a stable society. This country cannot also afford to read into Article 19 (1) (a) an unrestricted right to licensing (right of broadcasting) as claimed by the petitioners herein.

(f) In the case before us both the petitioners have sold their right to telecast the matches to a foreign agency.

They have parted with the right. The right to telecast the matches, including the right to import, install and operate the requisite equipment, is thus really sought by the foreign agencies and not by the petitioners. Hence, the question of violation of their right under Article 19 (1) (a) resulting from refusal of license/ permission to such foreign agencies does not arise.

2. The Government monopoly of broadcasting media in this country is the result of historical and other factors. This is true of every country, to start with. That India was not a free country till 1947 and its citizens did not have constitutionally guaranteed fundamental freedom till 1950 coupled with the fact that our Constitution is just about forty-five years into operation explains the Government monopoly. As pointed out in the body of the judgement, broadcasting media was a monopoly of the Government, to start with in every country except the United States where a conscious decision was taken at the very beginning not to have State monopoly over the medium. Until recently, the broadcasting media has been in the hands of public/statutory corporations in most of the West European countries. Private broadcasting is comparatively a recent phenomenon. The experience in Italy of allowing private broadcasting at local level (while prohibiting it at national level) has left much to be desired. It has given rise to powerful media empires which development is certainly not conductive to free speech right of the citizens.

3 (a) It has been held by this Court—and rightly that broadcasting media is affected by the free speech right of the citizens guaranteed by Article 19 (1) (a). This is also the view expressed by all the Constitutional Courts whose opinions have been referred to in the body of the judgement. Once this is so monopoly of this medium (broadcasting media), whether by Government or by an individual, body or organisation is unacceptable. Clause (2) of Article 19 does not permit a monopoly in the matter of freedom of speech and expression as is permitted by clause (6) of Article 19 vis-a-vis the right guaranteed by

Article 19 (1) (a).

(b) The right of free speech and expression includes the right to receive and impart information. For ensuring the free speech right of the citizens of this country, it is necessary that the citizens have the benefit of plurality of views and a range of opinions on all public issues. A successful democracy posits an 'aware' citizenry. Diversity of opinions, views, ideas and ideologies is essential to enable the citizens to arrive at informed judgement on all issues touching by a monopoly—whether the monopoly is of the State or any other individual, group or organisation. As a matter of fact, private broadcasting stations may perhaps be more prejudicial to free speech right of the citizens than the Government controlled media, as explained in the body of the judgement. The broadcasting media should be under the control of the public as distinct from Government. This is the command implicit in Article 19 (1) (a). It should be operated by a public statutory corporation or corporations, as the case may be, whose Constitution and composition must be such as to ensure its/their impartiality in political, economic and social matters and on all other public issues. It/they must be required by law to present news, views and opinions in a balanced way ensuring pluralism and diversity of opinions and views. It/they must provide equal access to all the citizens and groups to avail of the medium.

4. The Indian Telegraph Act, 1885 is totally inadequate to govern an important medium like the radio and television, i.e., broadcasting media. The Act was intended for an altogether different purpose when it was enacted. This is the result of the law in this country not keeping pace with the technological advances in the field of information and communications. While all the leading democratic countries have enacted laws specifically governing the broadcasting media, the law in this country has stood still, rooted in the Telegraph Act of 1885. Except Section 4 (1) and the definition of telegraph, no other provision of the Act is shown to have

any relevance to broadcasting media. It is therefore, imperative that the Parliament makes a law placing the broadcasting media in the hands of a public/statutory corporate or the corporations, as the case may be. This is necessary to safeguard the interest of public and the interests of law as also to avoid uncërtainty, confusion and consequent litigation.

5. The CAB did not ever apply for a license under the first provision to Section 4 of the Telegraph Act nor did its agents ever make such an application. The permissions, clearances or exemption obtained by it from the several departments (mentioned in judgement) are no substitute for a license under Section 4 (1) provision. In the absence of such a license, the CAB had no right in law to have its matches telecast by an agency of its choice. The legality or validity of the orders passed by Sri. N. Vittal, Secretary to the Government of India Telecommunications Department need not be gone into since it has become academic. In the facts and circumstances of the case, the charge of malafides or of arbitrary and authoritarian conduct attributed to Doordarshan and Ministry of Information and Broadcasting is not acceptable. No opinion need be expressed on the allegations made in the Interlocutory Application filed by BCCI in these matters. Its intervention was confined to legal questions only.

6. Now the question arises, what is the position till the Central Government or the Parliament takes steps as contemplated in Para (4) of the summary, i.e., if any sporting event or other event is to be telecast from the Indian soil ? The obvious answer flowing from the judgement (and Paras (1) and (4) of this summary) is that the nodal Ministry as specified in the decision of the Meeting of the Committee of Secretaries held on November 12, 1993. I have no reason to doubt that such are quest; would be considered by the nodal Ministry and the AIR and Doordarshan on its merits, keeping in view the public interest. In case of any difference of opinion or dispute regarding the monetary

terms on which such telecast is to be made, matter can always be referred to an Arbitrator or a panel of Arbitrators. In case the nodal Ministry or the AIR or Doordarshan find such broadcast/telecast not feasible, then they may consider the grant of permission to the organisers to engage an agency of their own for the purpose. Of course, it would be equally open to the nodal Ministry (Government of India) to permit such foreign agency in addition to AIR/Doordarshan, if they are of the opinion that such a course is called for in the circumstances.

For the above reasons, the appeals, write petition and applications are disposed of in the above terms. No costs.

Appendix IV

FINDINGS OF MULTI-STATE SURVEY

Table 1 INDIVIDUAL LEVEL IMPACT (Percentage of viewers indicating impact)

	Sleeping timing	*Cooking or eating habit*	*Homework/ office work*	*Playing habits*	*Spending habits*	*Dressing habits*	*Speaking style*	*Socialising/ Party habits*	*Health care/ fitness*
ALL VIEWERS									
Cable	54.0	19.7	14.7	11.5	15.0	22.5	18.9	13.7	25.3
DD	44.7	19.4	15.3	13.4	12.7	10.8	14.7	12.0	22.1
SEX									
Male									
Cable	50.4	13.0	13.7	16.5	13.4	19.3	23.5	12.9	25.9
DD	42.2	15.3	13.6	16.0	13.7	16.5	14.3	13.0	21.7
Female									
Cable	57.0	26.6	15.4	11.9	16.4	26.1	19.7	13.6	25.1
DD	47.7	24.5	17.6	10.5	11.7	18.0	15.4	11.0	22.3
AGE GROUPS									
9-15 yrs									
Cable	57.8	23.2	32.7	41.3	19.8	29.3	26.7	17.2	23.3
DD	42.9	14.7	31.2	31.2	8.5	27.2	17.9	10.3	12.1
16-24 yrs									
Cable	61.4	23.7	17.1	17.4	19.6	33.2	28.2	18.9	27.9
DD	58.3	26.5	16.6	20.3	19.8	25.6	24.0	17.2	29.2
25 yrs +									
Cable	48.8	16.4	9.8	7.4	11.4	15.3	12.0	10.3	24.1
DD	37.7	16.9	10.4	4.9	10.4	9.5	9.2	10.0	21.0

Table 1 INDIVIDUAL LEVEL IMPACT (Contd.)

	Sleeping timing	*Cooking or eating habit*	*Homework/ office work*	*Playing habits*	*Spending habits*	*Dressing habits*	*Speaking style*	*Socialising/ Party habits*	*Health care/ fitness*
OCCUPATION									
Student									
Cable	58.7	23.5	24.0	26.4	20.5	34.3	28.7	17.9	20.7
DD	55.0	22.9	25.8	28.3	18.5	29.2	24.1	15.9	24.6
Housewife									
Cable	60.2	29.1	12.1	6.3	11.2	14.6	11.2	8.7	23.8
DD	39.4	23.0	11.5	3.0	7.9	9.4	11.2	6.1	21.5
Employee									
Cable	48.3	10.6	7.7	7.7	11.6	12.6	12.1	10.1	27.0
DD	43.3	17.0	11.3	8.5	12.0	12.0	10.2	16.3	21.6
Business/self-employed									
Cable	43.7	15.6	10.4	9.6	12.6	18.5	15.6	11.9	16.3
DD	41.2	10.7	9.9	8.4	9.9	9.9	9.2	8.4	19.8
Unemployed/ Retired									
Cable	47.9	9.9	8.5	8.5	12.7	19.7	18.3	18.3	31.0
DD	50.0	22.6	10.7	10.7	25.0	21.4	13.1	19.0	33.3
Farmer									
Cable	—	—	—	—	—	—	—	—	—
DD	20.0	8.8	7.2	4.8	8.8	5.6	4.0	3.2	13.6
Agri labour									
Cable	—	—	—	—	—	—	—	—	—
DD	30.0	10.0	—	10.0	—	—	—	—	—
Others									
Cable	—	—	—	—	—	—	—	—	—
DD	53.6	21.4	10.7	7.1	14.3	3.6	14.3	3.6	14.3

Table 1
INDIVIDUAL LEVEL IMPACT (Contd.)

	Sleeping timing	*Cooking or eating habit*	*Homework/ office work*	*Playing habits*	*Spending habits*	*Dressing habits*	*Speaking style*	*Socialising/ Party habits*	*Health care/ fitness*	*Imitate styles/ Mannerisms*
TOWN CLASS										
Metro										
Cable	53.3	21.1	13.6	15.6	15.0	20.6	19.7	14.0	28.9	9.4
DD	47.0	19.4	14.5	11.0	14.3	15.0	14.7	15.2	26.5	10.0
Urban										
Cable	56.2	18.0	17.7	12.4	15.5	27.0	19.3	13.4	17.7	14.0
DD	46.9	21.1	85.1	18.1	14.7	21.0	17.7	14.4	19.2	13.4
Rural										
Cable	—	—	—	—	—	—	—	—	—	—
DD	39.4	18.3	10.9	12.8	9.2	16.0	12.6	6.0	18.6	12.8
TV VIEWING										
Moderate										
Cable	38.8	15.6	10.4	10.4	9.5	17.6	14.7	10.0	22.8	8.8
DD	29.4	17.3	11.4	9.3	8.9	14.2	11.4	9.8	19.7	10.0
Heavy										
Cable	61.6	22.2	17.3	15.7	17.3	24.8	21.2	14.9	26.5	12.3
DD	55.5	22.7	17.3	16.8	16.6	20.0	18.0	14.9	23.4	12.3
TV Addicts										
Cable	60.4	25.0	16.7	18.7	14.6	27.1	22.9	18.7	10.5	10.5
DD	74.4	16.3	6.9	2.3	2.5	18.6	23.3	9.3	37.2	7.0

Table 2 MEDIA HABITS

(Percentage of viewers)

	Frequency of going to cinema halls	*Reading daily Newspaper*	*Reading Magazines*	*Listening to Radio*	*Reading books and novels*	*Video viewing*
ALL VIEWERS						
Cable	69.5	30.1	36.7	55.3	41.5	49.8
DD	61.8	34.8	38.9	36.6	41.5	38.8
SEX						
Male						
Cable	65.6	26.5	31.5	53.2	39.1	46.0
DD	62.6	34.1	38.8	57.5	43.8	40.8
Female						
Cable	79.0	33.0	41.5	56.6	43.9	52.9
DD	60.6	36.1	39.1	55.5	39.0	36.7
AGE GROUP						
9-15 yrs						
Cable	65.5	37.9	38.8	51.8	44.9	50.0
DD	68.3	45.1	85.2	52.7	48.2	47.8
16-24 yrs						
Cable	75.3	35.4	40.8	55.7	44.6	57.6
DD	68.2	36.4	41.0	61.0	45.8	43.7
25 yrs +						
Cable	66.3	25.0	33.6	55.4	38.6	44.8
DD	56.8	31.1	35.7	55.5	37.6	34.1

Table 2 MEDIA HABITS (Contd.)

	Frequency of going to cinema halls	*Reading daily Newspaper*	*Reading Magazines*	*Listening to Radio*	*Reading books and novels*	*Video viewing*
OCCUPATION						
Student						
Cable	70.1	36.3	40.5	54.6	44.3	54.5
DD	66.8	38.1	40.4	56.7	43.2	42.9
Housewife						
Cable	72.8	32.5	41.3	55.4	41.3	44.2
DD	57.3	33.9	37.0	55.1	36.4	34.8
Employee						
Cable	68.6	25.6	29.5	53.4	41.1	49.8
DD	53.2	24.8	34.0	50.0	34.1	25.9
Business/self-employed						
Cable	63.7	23.0	36.3	53.3	34.8	40.8
DD	54.2	27.5	26.7	47.3	33.6	28.2
Unemployed/Retired						
Cable	67.6	18.3	22.5	56.3	38.0	56.3
DD	70.2	21.5	34.6	61.9	46.5	44.0
Farmer						
Cable	—	—	—	—	—	—
DD	80.0	64.8	67.2	75.2	70.2	63.4
Agri labour						
Cable	—	—	—	—	—	—
DD	20.0	20.0	20.0	50.0	20.0	10.0
Others						
Cable	—	—	—	—	—	—
DD	82.1	42.8	67.9	71.5	71.4	60.7

Table 2 MEDIA HABITS (Contd.)

	Frequency of going to cinema halls	*Reading daily Newspaper*	*Reading Magazines*	*Listening to Radio*	*Reading books and novels*	*Video viewing*
TOWN CLASS						
Metro						
Cable	30.9	31.9	36.4	51.5	33.9	48.9
DD	57.0	30.6	32.8	55.1	39.5	29.5
Urban						
Cable	76.7	28.6	38.8	55.6	44.0	53.1
DD	69.0	28.0	34.1	56.6	46.3	43.2
Rural						
Cable						
DD	62.1	45.6	51.0	63.3	49.9	48.0
TV VIEWING						
Moderate						
Cable	60.0	26.7	31.6	50.5	40.1	45.3
DD	58.2	38.7	42.5	60.8	44.2	40.7
Heavy						
Cable	73.0	29.6	37.9	55.9	42.0	50.5
DD	63.2	30.1	35.3	52.7	37.5	37.0
TV Addicts						
Cable	77.1	31.3	35.5	62.6	33.3	56.2
DD	74.4	27.9	16.3	44.2	37.2	30.3

Table 3 FAMILY IMPACT

(Percentage of viewers)

	Time spent with your family members	*Communication with other members of your family*	*Frequency of visiting your friends*	*Attention given to children in your family*	*Care of old people in your family*
ALL VIEWERS					
Cable	30.1	28.2	27.4	13.5	8.0
Only DD	27.4	22.8	24.3	15.8	10.3
SEX					
Male					
Cable	27.5	23.9	22.9	12.0	7.6
DD	28.6	21.8	24.3	16.1	11.8
Female					
Cable	31.9	32.4	31.3	15.1	8.2
DD	26.2	24.5	24.5	15.3	8.5
AGE GROUP					
9-15 yrs					
Cable	39.7	39.7	41.4	15.5	13.0
DD	34.8	26.8	32.1	14.3	12.9
16-24 yrs					
Cable	38.0	34.8	33.2	12.3	7.6
DD	35.0	27.2	34.1	17.9	13.8
25 yrs +					
Cable	23.4	22.3	21.2	13.8	7.0
DD	21.3	19.2	17.2	14.9	7.7

Table 3 FAMILY IMPACT (Contd.)

	Time spent with your family members	*Communication with other members of your family*	*Frequency of visiting your friends*	*Attention given to children in your family*	*Care of old people in your family*
TOWN CLASS					
Metro					
Cable	29.6	28.0	28.1	12.7	7.1
DD	20.2	23.0	25.5	16.6	9.7
Urban					
Cable	33.2	30.8	26.1	15.5	9.6
DD	27.7	21.6	24.0	12.0	9.3
Rural					
Cable	—	—	—	—	—
DD	24.7	23.9	22.8	17.5	11.7
TV VIEWING					
Moderate					
Cable	23.8	21.5	21.5	14.0	7.2
DD	22.4	19.9	18.5	14.2	7.4
Heavy					
Cable	31.2	29.8	29.4	13.9	9.0
DD	30.5	25.0	28.5	17.4	12.1
TV Addicts					
Cable	37.5	31.1	35.5	12.5	6.3
DD	34.9	23.3	18.6	16.3	16.0

Table 4 SOCIETAL IMPACT

(Percentage of viewers)

	Vulgarity in Public life	Violence in society	Eve teasing/ harassment of women	Crime and aggressive behaviour in people	Promotes economic growth	Brings the world closer	Promoting healthy competition in consumer market	Increases consumer awareness
ALL VIEWERS								
Cable	66.1	65.4	56.5	56.3	67.4	88.5	70.5	75.0
DD	69.2	66.3	56.0	57.6	60.8	85.4	65.4	69.7
SEX								
Male								
Cable	67.0	66.5	53.4	56.6	69.9	88.5	72.3	75.7
DD	67.9	64.2	52.7	55.8	66.0	87.7	68.3	71.0
Female								
Cable	65.7	64.6	59.7	59.7	65.1	88.4	68.9	62.6
DD	71.7	69.5	60.6	60.6	55.4	82.7	74.3	68.2
AGE GROUP								
9-15 yrs								
Cable	47.4	50.0	36.2	41.4	43.1	76.7	50.9	56.0
DD	41.1	41.1	32.1	33.9	43.3	74.1	44.7	54.5
16-24 yrs								
Cable	56.0	58.5	52.2	47.5	71.2	91.1	75.3	77.2
DD	67.5	64.1	52.7	54.8	67.7	90.8	71.9	74.4
25 yrs +								
Cable	75.5	72.2	62.5	64.0	70.2	89.5	71.6	77.5
DD	77.6	74.3	64.1	65.3	62.3	85.5	67.9	71.6

Table 4 SOCIETAL IMPACT (Contd.)

	Vulgarity in Public life	*Violence in society*	*Eve teasing/ harassment of women*	*Crime and aggressive behaviour in people*	*Promotes economic growth*	*Brings the world closer*	*Promoting healthy competition in consumer market*	*Increases consumer awareness*
OCCUPATION								
Student								
Cable	53.1	56.9	46.9	43.7	62.5	86.8	66.9	71.0
DD	55.0	52.8	42.1	45.0	57.3	83.7	63.8	69.6
Housewife								
Cable	72.3	67.0	66.5	69.7	65.1	85.9	66.5	71.4
DD	79.7	77.3	70.6	67.5	51.8	80.9	61.2	64.0
Employee								
Cable	73.4	71.0	58.0	65.2	74.4	90.8	79.4	78.3
DD	72.0	68.1	55.3	59.3	67.7	89.4	70.2	72.7
Business/ self-employed								
Cable	70.4	65.9	57.1	60.0	70.3	92.6	78.5	86.0
DD	71.0	52.6	51.9	50.3	65.6	90.9	71.0	77.8
Unemployed/ Retired								
Cable	74.6	53.6	64.8	69.0	70.4	91.5	73.3	73.2
DD	69.1	57.1	53.5	60.7	63.1	86.9	65.5	64.3
Farmer								
Cable	—	—	—	—	—	—	—	—
DD	86.4	88.0	82.4	82.4	74.4	88.8	67.2	74.4
Agri labour								
Cable	—	—	—	—	—	—	—	—
DD	50.0	60.0	40.0	60.0	40.0	70.0	40.0	60.0
Others								
Cable	—	—	—	—	—	—	—	—
DD	75.0	67.9	53.6	60.7	67.9	92.9	64.3	71.5

Table 4 SOCIETAL IMPACT (Contd.)

	Vulgarity in Public life	*Violence in society*	*Eve teasing/ harassment of women*	*Crime and aggressive behaviour in people*	*Promotes economic growth*	*Brings the world closer*	*Promoting healthy competition in consumer market*	*Increases consumer awareness*
TOWN CLASS								
Metro								
Cable	70.2	69.5	62.6	63.7	63.4	86.8	72.5	76.4
DD	75.0	70.1	59.3	63.1	59.5	86.1	69.5	71.5
Urban								
Cable	58.4	57.7	48.2	44.7	73.0	91.6	65.8	72.7
DD	56.0	55.2	44.0	42.9	57.9	89.3	61.1	64.8
Rural								
Cable	—	—	—	—	—	—	—	—
DD	72.1	69.9	61.0	61.9	65.0	81.2	63.3	71.2
TV VIEWING								
Moderate								
Cable	75.8	69.4	60.9	61.9	67.1	89.0	72.0	76.2
DD	73.5	68.0	63.0	62.5	58.1	87.4	66.6	73.4
Heavy								
Cable	67.6	75.4	55.5	53.4	68.2	88.2	70.0	74.8
DD	67.3	64.6	48.0	52.7	63.2	84.6	65.9	67.2
TV Addicts								
Cable	56.2	64.6	47.9	54.1	64.6	31.2	72.7	68.8
DD	62.8	72.1	53.5	53.5	72.1	46.5	68.4	55.8

Table 5 DEVELOPMENT AWARENESS/CONSCIOUSNESS

	Social issues/evils	*Political events/ Personalities*	*Govt's developmental Programmes*	*Public rights and duties*	*Sanitation and hygiene*	*Areas of career Opportunities*
ALL VIEWERS						
Cable	72.1	69.0	53.3	49.1	53.4	38.1
DD	69.8	64.2	50.1	45.9	50.8	34.1
SEX						
Male						
Cable	71.3	71.7	54.2	50.8	51.6	35.6
DD	71.6	69.8	55.9	50.6	52.9	36.1
Female						
Cable	72.8	66.1	52.9	48.0	56.2	40.8
DD	67.4	57.5	42.6	39.7	48.3	31.4
AGE GROUP						
9-15 yrs						
Cable	56.0	55.2	38.8	33.7	43.1	33.6
DD	51.3	47.8	36.2	33.5	39.3	27.7
16-24 yrs						
Cable	75.6	72.2	55.1	52.5	56.7	49.1
DD	73.9	70.0	55.5	52.8	54.1	56.9
25 yrs +						
Cable	73.5	70.2	55.6	50.2	53.4	32.7
DD	72.4	65.3	50.8	54.5	52.0	30.6

Table 5 DEVELOPMENT AWARENESS/CONSCIOUSNESS (contd.)

	Social issues/evils	*Political events/ Personalities*	*Govt's developmental Programmes*	*Public rights and duties*	*Sanitation and hygiene*	*Areas of career Opportunities*
OCCUPATION						
Student						
Cable	70.0	66.3	47.2	45.1	51.3	43.4
DD	67.1	61.4	44.8	46.8	51.0	39.3
Housewife						
Cable	71.4	63.1	53.9	46.6	55.3	35.5
DD	64.2	52.4	38.8	34.9	47.6	23.7
Employee						
Cable	76.3	74.4	61.8	54.1	54.6	39.2
DD	74.1	67.4	57.1	50.3	52.4	37.3
Business/self-employed						
Cable	71.9	75.6	75.8	50.4	50.4	31.9
DD	80.2	80.9	53.3	51.1	47.3	25.2
Unemployed/Retired						
Cable	73.2	71.8	49.3	60.6	59.2	35.2
DD	73.8	69.0	56.0	48.8	53.6	33.3
Farmer						
Cable	—	—	—	—	—	—
DD	71.2	78.4	61.6	57.6	56.8	44.8
Agri labour						
Cable	—	—	—	—	—	—
DD	80.0	60.0	60.0	20.0	50.0	10.0
Others						
Cable	—	—	—	—	—	—
DD	60.7	57.1	39.3	32.1	53.6	35.7

Table 5 DEVELOPMENT AWARENESS/CONSCIOUSNESS (contd.)

	Social issues/evils	*Political events/ Personalities*	*Govt's developmental Programmes*	*Public rights and duties*	*Sanitation and hygiene*	*Areas of career Opportunities*
TOWN CLASS						
Metro						
Cable	68.4	63.6	43.1	44.4	50.4	36.3
DD	67.4	57.0	41.5	42.6	48.8	30.6
Urban						
Cable	78.3	78.0	70.8	56.9	56.5	40.7
DD	76.0	72.3	61.9	48.8	47.7	37.3
Rural						
Cable	—	—	—	—	—	—
DD	68.0	67.6	52.5	48.2	55.9	36.2
TV VIEWING						
Moderate						
Cable	71.4	71.9	55.7	46.9	48.8	40.4
DD	66.2	64.1	45.3	43.4	49.1	36.7
Heavy						
Cable	73.1	67.6	52.5	50.8	55.6	36.5
DD	48.2	65.3	55.7	50.5	54.9	32.3
TV Addicts						
Cable	75.0	70.8	64.6	58.3	58.3	41.7
DD	76.8	69.8	62.8	60.5	51.2	37.2

Table 6 DD's PERCEIVED ACHIEVEMENTS (contd.)

	TV programmes cultural heritage inform about our	*Inform about our history*	*Awareness of different places, people, traditions of our country*	*Imparting new farming skills and techniques*	*Creatinga sense of pride in being an Indian*	*Guiding household management*	*Increasing consumer awareness*	*Promoting folk traditions*
ALL VIEWERS								
Cable	91.5	92.7	92.7	66.5	68.8	63.8	79.3	80.2
DD	91.0	92.9	91.9	97.0	70.6	64.8	78.0	79.5
SEX								
Male								
Cable	90.5	91.5	92.0	64.0	67.7	57.3	78.3	77.1
DD	90.4	91.8	90.4	73.2	71.4	59.4	78.7	78.5
Female								
Cable	92.9	95.1	93.8	68.1	70.0	71.0	79.7	83.4
DD	92.0	94.8	93.5	73.1	70.2	71.9	76.8	81.4
AGE GROUP								
9-15 yrs								
Cable	93.1	95.7	89.6	63.8	61.2	54.3	66.4	72.4
DD	93.3	96.4	92.8	67.8	74.1	60.3	70.5	78.1
16-24 yrs								
Cable	93.1	94.3	94.0	66.4	67.0	62.7	80.1	81.0
DD	94.3	95.2	93.5	76.3	75.4	68.0	83.2	81.5
25 yrs +								
Cable	90.3	91.3	92.6	66.7	70.1	65.9	81.5	81.2
DD	88.4	90.7	90.6	72.9	67.2	64.1	77.2	78.6

Table 6 DD's PERCEIVED ACHIEVEMENTS (contd.)

TV programmes	*Inform cultural heritage inform about our*	*Awareness of about our history*	*Imparting new different places, people, traditions of our country*	*Creatinga farming skills and techniques*	*Guiding sense of pride in being an Indian*	*Increasing household management*	*Promoting consumer awareness*	*folk traditions*
OCCUPATION								
Student								
Cable	93.9	94.4	92.4	63.0	65.1	58.4	75.4	80.3
DD	93.2	96.5	92.8	70.4	75.2	63.4	78.6	81.3
Housewife								
Cable	90.3	93.7	94.6	67.0	70.9	75.3	78.7	78.7
DD	90.0	92.4	90.4	74.5	70.0	71.2	73.1	78.2
Employee								
Cable	89.3	90.9	90.4	66.7	70.1	62.8	83.1	80.2
DD	89.4	89.7	92.2	70.2	69.5	63.1	81.9	77.6
Business/ self-employed								
Cable	90.4	92.6	94.0	70.4	68.1	63.0	82.9	83.0
DD	88.5	90.1	89.3	67.2	63.4	92.4	74.8	71.0
Unemployed/ Retired								
Cable	90.2	90.1	91.5	69.0	73.2	60.6	80.3	78.9
DD	90.5	90.4	92.8	77.4	—	58.4	82.2	82.1
Farmer								
Cable	—	—	—	—	—	—	—	—
DD	88.8	91.2	91.2	91.2	72.0	74.4	81.6	86.4
Agri labour								
Cable	—	—	—	—	—	—	—	—
DD	90.0	100.0	100.0	90.0	50.0	30.0	50.0	70.0
Others								
Cable	—	—	—	—	—	—	—	—
DD	100.0	96.4	92.9	71.4	67.9	67.9	78.6	89.3

Table 6 DD's PERCEIVED ACHIEVEMENTS

TV programmes	*Inform cultural heritage inform about our*	*Awareness of about our history*	*Imparting new different places, people, traditions of our country*	*Creatinga farming skills and techniques*	*Guiding sense of pride in being an Indian*	*Increasing household management*	*Promoting consumer awareness*	*folk traditions*
TOWN CLASS								
Metro								
Cable	89.6	91.7	91.0	68.1	67.1	65.2	81.1	81.6
DD	99.2	90.7	90.7	71.1	69.4	61.0	80.7	78.9
Urban								
Cable	95.7	95.4	95.7	60.9	72.0	59.3	75.5	76.1
DD	94.1	95.2	94.4	61.3	68.3	62.6	74.6	76.0
Rural								
Cable	—	—	—	—	—	—	—	—
DD	93.2	94.1	91.3	85.5	74.2	71.5	77.2	83.2
TV VIEWING								
Moderate								
Cable	88.6	89.0	91.9	66.1	64.2	58.4	76.9	77.5
DD	88.4	91.2	90.0	76.0	64.9	64.6	79.6	80.1
Heavy								
Cable	92.8	94.8	93.9	66.9	71.5	65.8	79.8	81.8
DD	92.5	94.0	93.3	71.4	75.0	65.0	77.2	78.9
TV Addicts								
Cable	85.5	89.6	87.5	70.9	70.8	68.8	87.5	75.1
DD	95.4	93.0	90.7	76.7	93.0	67.5	69.8	65.2

Appendix V

PROGRAMME AND ADVERTISEMENT CODES

Reproduced below are Rules 6 and 7 made by the Central Government under the powers conferred by the Cable Television Networks (Regulation) Act, 1995, setting out respectively the Programme Code and the Advertising Code.

6. Programme code—(1) No programme should be carried in the cable service which :

(a) Offends against good taste or decency;

(b) Contains criticism of friendly countries;

(c) Contains attack on religions or communities or visuals or words contemptuous of religious groups or which promote communal attitudes;

(d) Contains anything obscene, defamatory, deliberate, false and suggestive innuendos and half truths;

(e) Is likely to encourage or incite violence or contains anything against maintenance of law and order or which promote anti-national attitudes;

(f) Contains anything amounting to contempt of court;

(g) Contains aspersions against the integrity of the President and Judiciary;

(h) Contains anything affecting the integrity of the Nation;

(i) Criticizes, maligns or slanders any individual in person or certain groups, segments of social, public and moral life of the country;

(j) Encourages superstition or blind belief;

(k) Denigrates women through the depiction in any manner of the figure of a woman, her form or body or any part thereof in such a way as to have the effect of being indecent, or derogatory to women, or is likely to deprave, corrupt or injure the public morality or morals;

(l) Denigrates children;

(m) Contains visuals or words which reflect a slandering, ironical and snobbish attitude in the portrayal of certain ethnic, linguistic and regional groups;

(n) Contravenes the provisions of the Cinematograph Act, 1952.

(2) The cable operator should strive to carry programmes in his cable service which project women in a positive, leadership role of sobriety, moral and character building qualities.

(3) Programmes meant for adults should normally be carried in the cable service after 11 p.m. and before 6 a.m.

(4) Care should be taken to ensure that programmes meant for children do not contain any bad language or explicit scenes of violence.

(5) Programmes unsuitable for children must not be carried in the cable service at times when the largest numbers of children are viewing.

7. Advertising Code—(1) Advertising carried in the cable service shall be so designed as to conform to the laws of the country and should not offend morality, decency and religious susceptibilities of the subscribers.

(2) No advertisement shall be permitted which :

(i) derides any race, caste, colour, creed and nationality;

(ii) is against any provision of the Constitution of India;

(iii) tends to incite people to crime, cause disorder or violence or breach of law or glorifies violence or obscenity in any way;

(iv) presents criminality as desirable;

(v) exploits the national emblem, or any part of the Constitution or the person or personality of a national leader or a State dignitary;

(vi) in its depiction of women violates the Constitutional guarantees to all citizens. In particular, no advertisement shall be permitted which projects a derogatory image of women. Women must not be portrayed in a manner that emphasises possessive, submissive qualities and encourages them to play a subordinate, secondary role in the family and society. The cable operator shall ensure that the portrayal of the female form, in the programmes carried in his cable service is tasteful and aesthetic, and is within the well established norms of good taste and decency;

(vii) Exploits social evils like dowry, child marriage.

(3) No advertisement shall be permitted the objects whereof are wholly or mainly of a religious or political nature; advertisements must not be directed towards any religious or political end.

(4) The goods or services advertised shall not suffer from any defect or deficiency as mentioned in Consumer Protection Act, 1986.

(5) No advertisement shall contain references which are likely to lead the public to infer that the product advertised or any of its ingredients has some special or miraculous or super natural property or quality which is difficult of being proved.

(6) The picture and the audible matter of the advertisement shall not be excessively 'loud'.

(7) No advertisement which endangers the safety of children or creates in them any interest in unhealthy practices or shows them begging or in an undignified or indecent manner shall not be carried in the cable service.

(8) Indecent, vulgar, suggestive repulsive or offensive themes or treatment shall be avoided in all advertisements.

(9) No advertisement which violates the standards of

practice for advertising agencies as approved by the Advertising Agencies Association of India, Bombay, from time to time shall be carried in the cable service.

(10) All advertisement should be clearly distinguishable from the programme and should not in any manner interfere with the programme, viz., use of lower part of screen to carry captions, static or moving alongside the programme.

Appendix VI

MEDIA ADVISORY COMMITTEE'S VIEWS ON JOSHI WORKING GROUP'S REPORT ON SOFTWARE FOR DOORDARSHAN

The Media Advisory Committee considered the report of the Working Group on Software for Doordarshan at three meetings and studied the recommendations carefully.

The Joshi Group's Report is to be welcomed for the earnestness and clarity of its emphasis on the values which Indian television should promote. It repeatedly stresses the importance of the role of television in development, social and economic as well as cultural. It points out the dangers of an organisation giving undue importance to the income from commercial broadcasts. The history of sound broadcasting and television is full of examples of well-meaning commercial systems which aimed at raising adequate funds for the creation of better programmes and have invariably ended up as the tools of commercialism. The Joshi Report has drawn attention to this experience and calls upon Doordarshan to be aware of the pitfalls.

There are other important points raised in the report. It has underlined the importance of community receivers in every village of India, which alone will take Doordarshan to the common people, and of providing programmes of local interest and relevance besides those which promote national integration and widen the mental horizons of viewers. The Joshi Report has pointed to the need for a total re-orientation in the broadcasting of news. It has recommended a restructuring of Doordarshan so as to give the professional staff more freedom to produce creative programmes without interference from non-professionals at the Ministry. It has stressed the need and importance of training.

Many of these suggestions have been made before. But there is no harm in repeating things which can never be over-emphasised, such as the concepts which should govern public service broadcasting. It is now for the authorities to bridge the gap between sound recommendations by professionals and their implementation. An example of the gap pertains to the Media Advisory Committee itself and to the guidelines prepared by us on News Policy for the Broadcast Media. This document has been endorsed by the Government in the Ministry of Information and Broadcasting and circulated by it to Akashvani and Doordarshan; it has been placed before Parliament; and has been widely welcomed by professionals connected with public affairs communication, or journalism in the broad sense, but implementation has been slow and hesitant.

The Media Advisory Committee agrees with the Working Group's statement that Doordarshan should have an Indian personality; also that the medium should be concerned with social change without uprooting itself from India's rich culture and civilisation. The Committee feels that this projection should be informed by a scientific outlook and humanistic values which are of universal applicability. The scientific temper and outlook should be deliberately cultivated. The visual medium of television is particularly suitable for bringing about this change among the people.

Television in India should be a major vehicle for all-round national development. This should be the guiding principle in the planning of software, including the programmes prepared by outside agencies and by those who produce programmes for sponsorship. Television is an expensive medium and in a country like India advertising on television and sponsored programmes cannot be totally dispensed with, but advertising and sponsored programmes should neither dilute the social objectives of television nor be so presented as to project consumerism with all its social consequences. Advertising should not add to frustrations and social tensions. Sponsored programmes should provide healthy entertainment as well as promote positive values. The Media Advisory Committee is, therefore, of the opinion that the code for commercials on television should be carefully revised in view of the experience gained so far. Advertisements should not appear to be a part of a programme, nor should programmes be interrupted by advertisements. In fact it may be useful to consider whether all advertising on television should not be grouped together at a given time so that while viewers interested in such information would get it, others need not and, even more important, that the intended effect of a programme is not lost.

We would like to emphasize in this context that Doordarshan should not fall into the popularity trap and the tyranny of ratings which govern so much of commercial TV. Improving public taste and appreciation is a part of Doordarshan's role, along with informing and educating, which should be constantly kept in mind.

Television as a powerful visual medium should reflect the society as a whole and not a particular class of the people. Even if the present composition of viewers is somewhat limited due to lack of purchasing power of a large section of the community, the projection of the life of various sections and social groups among the people is important for a national medium. Such projection should not foster bigotry, superstition or fatalism. It should aim at preserving the richness of our culture with a forward-looking and rational approach to life as a whole.

The Media Advisory Committee agrees with the Software Working Group that access to television should be considerably widened through a large number of community TV receivers. In fact, if we are serious about television reaching every nook and corner of the country, we should aim at installing a set in every one of our nearly 600,000 villages. This would appear, on the face of it, an expensive operation. The cost of the sets alone may come to some 250 crore of rupees. But with the experience we are gaining in manufacturing quality sets in large numbers, an order of such magnitude could bring the price down. In addition to this, there will be the problems and the expenses involved in providing power sources—whether battery packs or solar cells or any other—in non-electrified villages, and the maintenance of the 600,000 sets. To set up a few thousand sets in some selected villages will be a step in the right direction but steps in the right direction alone are not what we are looking for. What is needed is a nation-wide service which can change the face of television in India and thereby help to change the face of India.

Community receivers will be required to be installed not only in the rural areas but also in some depressed urban areas. There is need to work out in detail the scheme for the purchase, installation and maintenance of community sets. State governments and local authorities including panchayats in the villages, should be fully involved in the community viewing scheme. Unless the access to television viewing is widened, the claim of 70 per cent coverage of the population will remain, as it is now, purely notional. There is also the danger of the affluent section of the people continuing to influence largely the software contents of television.

The Media Advisory Committee is in full agreement with the Working Group that the news room of Doordarshan should be manned by competent journalists who understand the medium. They should not belong to the Central Information Service where due to frequent transfers from one medium to another within the Ministry of I & B, specialisation and acquisition of skills are not possible. The point to be noted is that television news is the product of an entire team consisting of producer, editor, reporter, cameraman, sound recordist and editor of film or video. They all need to have a clear perception of what makes news and the process of news-gathering, selection and presentation. The news-reader is part of this chain. He or she should have a sound understanding of news values and should be actively associated with the preparation of the bulletins. In most countries, news-readers are chosen for the authority and conviction they carry and convey as broadcasters rather than for their appearance. This should be our approach as well.

The news department of Doordarshan should develop greater specialisation. It needs to be given the freedom of fast operation, and the financial powers necessary for prompt and adequate coverage of news and of economic and social development issues.

The Media Advisory Committee agrees that programme-making facilities should be available at all relay centres in order that a substantial part of the transmission should be area-specific and in the language and dialect of the people served by the transmitter.

The emphasis laid by the Working Group on the role of TV in formal and non-formal education is timely. The impression is that the educational role of television has been given scanty importance hitherto, whether in the allocation of time or in promoting innovative programme-making. The potential of television to educate people and provide vocational guidance to a large number of viewers is enormous. Doordarshan should make a closer-study of educational and public interest programmes put out by major TV organisations elsewhere, both in socialist and capitalist countries. It should also develop a good cultural exchange policy covering not only programmes but also the deputing of personnel for observation and training in the area of public service broadcasting.

Above all, television can play a significant role in promoting adult literacy as the experience of some countries has shown. Carefully planned and concentrated efforts through television to teach adults to read and write should be an essential part of our adult literacy campaign.

The Working Group on Software draws attention to a number of useful adjuncts to the organisation such as Advisory Committees on programmes for special audiences, educational broadcasts, etc. Many of these are already built into the structure of All India Radio and Television. What is needed is earnest and imaginative use of these institutions.

The Media Advisory Committee also endorses the Working Group's suggestion that Doordarshan could make conscious efforts to promote folk art forms. For this purpose it should establish close liaison with official and non-official organisations working in this field. Though the preservation of folk art forms is not really Doordarshan's responsibility, the preservation of the tapes of all programmes dealing with the Performing Arts could provide excellent material for study and dissemination. In fact, the role of the mass media in the preservation and development of the Arts could be a subject for special study.

There is need to revamp and expand training facilities for Doordarshan production staff. It has been the view of the Media Advisory Committee that the existing facilities for training are inadequate and are not geared to meet the increasing requirements of the medium. The philosophy of training itself needs to be carefully reviewed. As the Joshi Report says, the training should not be confined to improvement of skills but should also promote awareness of the social responsibility of the medium and help the personnel to explore the potentialities of the medium and to utilise it creatively for conveying messages.

Doordarshan, like A.I.R., has an in-house research unit. Its scope should be broadened so as to elicit audience reactions not only regarding the intelligibility and appeal of a programme but its desirability or otherwise in the context of home viewing, the effect on the reading habits of students in the home and the use of leisure time by other members, etc. Audience research should acquire these dimensions if it is to assist a public service broadcasting organisation in fulfilling its proper role.

The Working Group has recommended the creation of an Advisory Council for Doordarshan. The Media Advisory Committee agrees with this suggestion and feels that it would be appropriate to have a Council with a distinguished public figure as its Chairman. The members of the Committee should include professional communicators with a serious interest in the media. They should be persons of integrity and stature who will command respect. They should be able to strengthen the functional and professional freedom of the organisation. The Advisory Council should be compact and should meet at least six times in a year. An unwieldy body holding a meeting once or twice a year would be a mere ritual.

This leads us on to consider the changes in the structure of Doordarshan (DD) and Akashvani (AKV), and of the Ministry itself, which the Joshi Group has suggested as being necessary, in its view, for providing functional and professional freedom. Whereas, in the foregoing paragraphs, we have endorsed, with some modifications or amplification, almost all the important recommendations of the Joshi Group which pertain directly to software, in respect of structural change we would suggest an alternative approach which is set out in the paragraphs that follow.

At present, Doordarshan (DD) and Akashvani (AKV) are both Directorates of the Ministry of Information and Broadcasting (I & B). According to prevailing government norms and practices, this makes DD and AKV 'attached offices' of the Ministry. The present set-up imposes serious limitations on speed and flexibility in administrative, financial and personnel management terms. For example, all recruitments are through the UPSC; many purchases are through DGS & D; construction is done by a Civil Construction wing, staffed heavily with general purpose civil engineering personnel on deputation from CPWD. The administrative and financial powers of the Directorates are also limited even in regard to such operational matters as travel in general, and the movement of video and audio programme production teams to and in the field, the hiring of private services, etc., however urgent and immediate the needs be. This lack of operational freedom, combined with the fact that both DD and AKV are currently headed by IAS officers, has resulted in DD and AKV having to make references to the Ministry on numerous operational matters not entailing policy.

The important thing is to make a clear demarcation between the roles of the Ministry of I & B on the one hand and of Doordarshan and Akashvani on the other. Basically this should mean that the Ministry should be responsible for policy planning and formulation. DD and AKV should be clear about their goals, plans and programmes, and have full functional and professional freedom (administrative, personnel and financial) to implement those plans.

To be able to do so, DD and AKV should be converted from Directorates to full-fledged Departments of government, with Boards of Management having adequate financial powers. Government has done precisely this in March 1985 in regard to the former Telecommunication and Postal 'Wings' of the P & T Department, viz., set up a Department of Telecommunications with a Telecommunication Board and a Postal Department with a Postal Board. Specifically, therefore, we propose that a Doordarshan Department and an Akashvani Department be set up in the Ministry of I & B. There should be a Doordarshan Board with the following composition :

DG Doordarshan	Chairman
DDG (Software)	Member
Engineer-in-Chief (Doordarshan)	Member
F.A. of Doordarshan working for and under DGD	Member
DDG (Administration) of Doordarshan	Member
Secretary to the DD Board	Secretary

There should be an identical structure for the Akashvani Department and Board. The DG, DD and the DG, AKV should not be less in rank than Additional Secretaries to Government, and the individuals selected should be professionals in the respective area of communication and not civil service officers.

As in the case of the recently formed Telecom and Postal Boards, the DD and AKV Boards should exercise all the powers of the Ministry of I & B in so far as DD/AKV matters are concerned. In financial matters, the two Boards should exercise all the powers of the Ministry of I & B, plus the enhanced powers that will need to be delegated to the

Board concerned by the Finance Ministry for the effective and speedy functioning of the Department.

A key aspect of this relates to all aspects of personnel policies and practices right from selection. Government must face the hard reality that continuance of the present policy and practice whereby all inductions into DD/AKV—both hardware-related and software-related—are done through the UPSC is fundamentally inconsistent with the professionalisation and specialisation of DD/AKV.

Today television and radio broadcasting have become high technology fields. As such, they call for specialisation and flexibility of personnel management broadly comparable to what government have accepted for over 15 years now for fields like Atomic Energy, Space and Electronics, and in the last few years in regard to Defence Research. A critical dependence on (or maximum exploitation of) satellite communication technology has been accepted as government (indeed *national*) policy since the INSAT decision in 1976-77. It is surprising that despite this, it has not been appreciated that, as the operational user agency, DD needs at least as modern a personnel system as the agency (DOS) which is responsible for the space segment. To even consider going in for new communication services like Teletext, let alone planning, preparing for and inducting Digital TV at the appropriate time, is meaningless without such a modern personnel policy and practices, appropriate to the highly specialised tasks involved. Government should therefore take an early decision that within a defined time frame, say, 5 years, both DD and AKV will undertake their own recruitment and career advancement, in much the same way as those specialised scientific departments do.

To ensure integrated and coherent policy planning, policy making and overall coordination, both between the Ministry on the one hand and DD and AKV on the other, as also for coordination between DD and AKV, there should be a Broadcasting Policy Committee. This should be chaired by Minister of I & B, and have a core membership comprising the Secretary, I & B, the two DGs as well as representatives of the Communication Ministry, Electronics Commission,

Department of Space and the Media Advisory Committee.

It is our considered view that the structure proposed above, with appropriate conventions, would ensure functional freedom and thereby the effectiveness of the medium. Needless to say, the professionals at Doordarshan should assert their professional competence and integrity, and the government should respect it.

There has been a growing interest in television among the public and an awareness on the part of the government of the need to expand its coverage and serve national purposes. There has been noticeable improvement in the choice of themes and their treatment. Also, there has been a rejection of some of the banal programmes, which is welcome. An effort is also being made to encourage public participation and lively debate. Some well-known directors and artistes are coming forward to produce serious programmes of quality. These are encouraging signs, but a great deal more remains to be done. The value of the Joshi Committee's report lies in its stress on the fundamental objectives of Doordarshan and the tasks that lie ahead.

Appendix VII

COMPETITION IN BROADCASTING : THE OPTIONS

Following are extracts from the report given in October 1991 by an inter-departmental committee on 'Introducing competition in the Electronic Media', constituted by the Ministry of Information & Broadcasting.

APPROACHES TO A NEW BROADCASTING SYSTEM

The following approaches can be adopted :

(1) Lease out a particular chunk of time from an existing TV/Radio channel.

(2) Lease out one of the radio/TV channels in the same station to a licencee.

(3) Permit an agency or a consortium of agencies to set up and operate a series of additional TV/Radio transmitters in different programmes over regional transmitters and network them at some specified time of the day for national broadcast.

(4) Permit a licencee to set up TV/Radio transmitters in a particular station for local transmission. A series of such licencees can be permitted to set up transmitters in different stations in the country. They can come together for networking for specific national broadcast. In particular, FM Radio stations and low power TV transmitters can be set up in cities and small towns to serve as local stations.

(5) All transmitting infrastructure—existing and planned can be vested in a central authority which will be responsible for its management. This authority will lease out transmitting infrastructure to various licencees. The agency can either depend on government for funds or be enabled to operate in such a manner that they generate surpluses for investments in new infrastructure.

(6) Leasing of a transponder on a satellite suitably positioned in order that a satellite-derived direct broadcast (DBS) could be provided all over the country.

Leasing out time chunks

2.6 A suggestion has been made that in the existing channel, a specific time chunk can be given to the licencee who would be responsible for the content of the telecast over the transmitters during the allotted time chunk. The licencee would also be responsible for collecting advertisements and managing the programme. While this system has the advantage of appearing to immediately implement the policy to provide an alternate channel, in reality it would hardly be an improvement over the existing system. Such time sharing may not only prove cumbersome in practice but the listeners or the viewers may also remain unconvinced that he has got an additional choice. It would also lead to a certain clash of objectives when both the public service function and the licencee's objectives are performed using the same channel.

Leasing out an existing channel

2.7 Another suggestion is to retain the primary channel of AIR and Doordarshan and lease out only the second channel wherever it exists, so that the public broadcasting functions can continue to be carried out on the primary channel. While leasing out one of the existing channels will obviate some of the difficulties stated in sub-para 2.6 above, it is to be noted that in most places the channels play complementary roles.

Programme formats and programme planning will have to second channel of Doordarshan a limited coverage in terms of area, the competition will perforce be limited to a small geographical area. Nevertheless, this option has the advantage of being implemented in a very short period after a decision is taken. The option of permitting the nation-wide alternative channel may be financially attractive to advertisers because of a larger audience for such a channel. It would also have to be considered if it is desirable to handover the entire alternate channel to one agency or consortium and whether the regional aspiration would find full expression in such an arrangement.

Operation of transmitters on a regional basis

2.8 Yet another route can be to give the licence to an agency or a consortium of agencies to set up and operate a series of additional TV/Radio transmitters in different regions of the country under which they can transmit different programmes over regional transmitters and network them at some specified time of the day for national broadcast. The option of regional franchise to one agency or consortium provides a plurality of choice. This would meet the growing aspirations for reflecting the cultures of different parts of the country through the electronic media. This system has worked efficiently in many other countries notably in the United Kingdom.

Licensing TV/Radio Transmitters for local transmission

2.9 Under this system, licence can be given to set up TV/Radio transmitters in a particular station for local transmission in different stations of the country. Such licencees can of course come together for networking for specific national broadcast. It would, thus combine the need for reflecting the local aspirations with the broader purpose of a common programme for a region or the country as a whole. In particular FM radio stations and Low Power TV Transmitters can be set up in cities and small towns to serve as local stations.

Centralisation and leasing of transmitting infrastructure

2.10 In the course of the discussions and study of broadcasting systems in different countries of the world, the committee came across a very important suggestion. Instead of giving a licence to an agency to set up and run a channel, one could conceive of a model in which all transmitting infrastructure existing and planned can be vested in a central authority who will be responsible for its management. This authority will lease out transmitting infrastructure to various licencees. This option of one central authority holding all the hardware will enable Prasar Bharati to be rid of a heavy overhead and allow its programme personnel to devote their entire energies to software production. This is the system that operates, for example, in France. This arrangement would, however imply an important departure from the provisions of the Prasar Bharati Act.

Leasing of a transponder

2.11 This option of hiring a transponder for satellite based broadcasts is dependent upon the availability of additional S-band transponders in 1992-93 in INSAT. However, possibility exists of leasing transponders on other geo-stationary satellites like ASLASAT. The Committee understands that in the globally agreed Plan (1977) for Broadcasting Satellite Service under the aegis of International Telecommunication Union (ITU), India has got allocation for 48 DBS channels in KU band, which have great potential for exploitation for broadcasting purposes. This would provide an efficient programme distribution system covering very large areas and may suit, in particular, the large variety of programme needs of the country.

Viability

2.12 Before spelling out our preference to the approaches to the new broadcasting system, the Committee would wish to emphasise that no system can survive unless it is financially viable. At the same time, the Committee has recommended that certain requirements regarding quality, content of programmes, etc., may be imposed. The way the advertisement market would behave when these new channels operate is perhaps somewhat difficult to forecast. It is therefore, very important that a potential licencee makes a second judgement about the viability of his proposal before offering to set up a channel. Almost all parties have made the claim that their different proposals would be financially viable. One of the parties which met the Committee has categorically stated that the cost of production of good TV programmes being high, no new channel can operate viably unless it taps, at the same time, all the major cities and towns in the country almost on the lines of the national channel of Doordarshan. There has been no objective basis on which the correctness of these claims can be judged. Further in the absence of any clear data, the committee would not venture to pass any judgement on the relative merits of these claims.

2.13 The Committee has also considered the views expressed by some individuals that since the proposed competition is only for the Prasar Bharati, the new system should come up only after Prasar Bharati starts functioning and stabilities itself. The Committee notes that the Government has declared on the floor of the Parliament that it was committed to bringing in Prasar Bharati as well as offering broadcasting right to public corporation. The Committee has recommended in Chapters III and IV the need for comprehensive legislation and monitoring systems to lay own guidelines for the new channels. All this preliminary process is bound to take time. The Committee, therefore recommends that the preliminary work relating to setting up of new channels should proceed, pari passu, with the work of establishing Prasar Bharati Recommended Approach.

2.14 The Committee has already listed out the various approaches available to setting up the new broadcasting system as well as the pros and cons of these approaches. The committee, after careful deliberation, hereby recommends the following :

(i) Subject to viability of operations, preference should be given to setting up new TV/Radio channels in different parts of the country for regional broadcasts. These transmitters can, over a period or time, link up suitably either by forming a consortium or by entering into suitable arrangement amongst themselves. Such a link-up would provide inter-regional network.

(ii) (a) Simultaneously, the second Doordarshan channels in the four metropolitan cities can be leased out to suitable licencees.

(b) Also simultaneously, additional radio channels including FM stations, wherever available, may also be similarly leased out.

These actions under this option should be taken only after suitable legislation is passed.

(iii) The option to permit one agency or consortium to set up a series of transmitters in the country (option No. 3 of para 2.5) will, be in the opinion of the Committee, rank only next to the option of permitting a number of licencees to set up different TV/Radio transmitters in the country (option No. 4 of para 2).

(iv) The Committee does not recommend leasing out a particular chunk of time from an existing TV/Radio channels.

(v) The option of a licencee leasing a transponder on a satellite for satellite-derived direct broadcast would perhaps be appropriate for developmental or educational telecast. The Committee notes that as of now there is no such spare space segment available. As and when one becomes available, the Government can take an appropriate decision.

Management of transmitting infrastructure

2.15 A Central authority to own the transmitting infrastructure for leasing out to various licencees, including Prasar Bharati, was conceived in the context of the Planned development of hardware for broadcasting purpose. After considerable deliberation, the Committee felt that fragmentation of transmitting infrastructure and programme transmission may create problems of management and it would be preferable to have an integrated management either in Prasar Bharati or with the licencees. The Committee, however feels that in order to mitigate the initial handicap of the licences in setting up the transmitting infrastructure and the need to bring in Programme variety, it would be appropriate if only the transmitting infrastructure of Doordarshan's 2nd channel and an extra channel of AIR are divested for leasing to potential licencees. Future investments in transmitting infrastructure would be done by both Prasar Bharati and the licencees from their own resources and there is no need to establish any control authority for owning and leasing transmitting infrastructure.

THE NEW BROADCASTING SYSTEM

3.1 The various options available to the government in regard to licensing or leasing new channel and the stages in which it can be done have been dealt with in the previous chapter. Whatever may be the ultimate choice, there are certain essential elements of this process which have to be defined. These are proposed to be dealt with in some detail in this chapter.

Selection Process

3.2 After the government decides on the approach as recommended in Chapter II, detailed guidelines regarding eligibility of an applicant and the procedure of selection have to be formulated.

3.3 One view that has been held is that the grant of such licence is the prerogative of the Government and should appropriately vest in it as is the case with other licences. Certain views have also been expressed to this Committee that in view of the revenue and power that a broadcasting channel implies, the process of selecting the licencee should be done with deliberate openness and objectivity. This Committee, after careful consideration recommends that the selection should be done by an independent authority of stature and that the process of selection should be fully transparent. The most suitable arrangement would be to set up a public body under the Law to dispense such licences. This authority could be called the Broadcasting Council of India (BCI). The Chairman and the members of the BCI should be eminent public men with unimpeachable probity. In particular, the Chairman of the BCI should be a person who has the qualifications required for appointment as a judge in the Supreme Court of India. The eligibility criteria in respect of the applicants for a licence should include the following conditions :

(i) The applicant company must be a 'Public Limited Company' whose shares are listed in the stock market.

(ii) All the directors of the company should be citizens of India and should be drawn from major interest groups in broadcasting as may be prescribed.

(iii) The Company as an entity and the directors individually should not have been declared as insolvent or convicted in a criminal prosecution.

(iv) The financial condition of the Company should be adjudged by the competent authority to be sound enough to support the proposed broadcasting enterprise.

(v) The applicant company should declare, in writing, its willingness to abide by guidelines regarding programmes to be spelt out under the law (dealt with in Chapter IV) and to conform to the frequency and other technical.

(vi) A company applying for broadcasting licence for a region must be subjected to cross-media restrictions as may be specified.

(vii) The applicant company should not have any affiliation with any political party or religious or communal body.

(viii) The applicant company should undertake to conform to any other condition that may be stipulated under the law for this purpose.

3.4 It has been ably argued before the Committee that broadcasting rights should be given to public bodies such as universities, well managed cooperative institutions, Trust, etc., whose primary objective is in the area of education, culture or communication. The Committee recommends that such organisations may also be licensed to broadcast. The Committee further recommends that in the regions where such organisations apply for licences, they may be given preference over other applicants provided they meet all the eligibility criteria.

Guidelines for Programmes

3.5 In most countries of the world, it is quite a normal feature of the radio broadcast systems to have an exclusive music channel. Lovers of music of different forms such as classical music, semi classical, light devotional Western music, etc., may like to have access to music at any time in the day or till late at night. Such an exclusive music channel will be a great boon for such music lovers. Indeed, in a country like ours with a rich and varied musical tradition an exclusive channel can provide a veritable feast of music on a sustained basis. In the circumstances the committee is inclined to recommend that, while offering broadcasting rights, the need for such a facility may also be kept in view.

3.6 As pointed out earlier, it is inevitable, in the Indian context, that when broadcasting rights are given to an agency such rights will have to be governed by some broad guidelines regarding the programme content of their broadcasts. The Committee, after careful study of various broadcasting systems in the world, and also based on its discussions with many specialists in the field recommend the following set of guidelines :

(i) The licencee will fully conform to what are now applicable to All India Radio and Doordarshan and to future modifications therein.

(ii) News, current affairs and other programmes on their channels will not be such as to offend the religious sentiments of any group.

(iii) The programmes, including news and current affairs should not in any way be prejudicial to the sovereignty and integrity of India; security of the State; friendly relations with foreign States, public order; decency or morality or of such nature as will be likely to involve defamation or contempt of court or incite the commission of any offence.

(iv) The programmes shall conform to the same principles in relation to programme content as may be specified by Central Government from time to time, in exercise of powers under the provisions of sub-section (2) of Section 5B of the Cinematograph Act, 1952.

(v) The programmes should not infringe the provisions of the Copyright Act.

(vi) The programmes should endeavour to use the talent available in the area of broadcast to the extent possible. At any rate, not more than ten per cent in terms of time of the programmes broadcast in this channel can be imported from abroad.

(vii) The channel must carry at least for twenty per cent of its broadcasting time, programmes considered by the Broadcasting Council (see para 3.3) to be socially relevant and necessary for developmental purpose.

(viii) The channel shall carry such programmes of importance to the Nation as may be directed by the Government from time to time. This would include Addresses to the Nation by the President and the Prime Minister.

(ix) The programmes broadcast by the channel should not be the means for furtherance of the interests of any political party.

(x) During election time, in respect of broadcast by or about political parties, the channel shall conform to the guidelines issued by the Election Commission.

(xi) While dealing with any matter of controversy the programmes shall present all points of view in a fair and impartial manner.

3.7 It is obvious that there has to be an arrangement under which the programmes put out by the licencees are continuously monitored to ensure that they do not violate these guidelines. Suggestions regarding such an arrangement will be dealt with later in this chapter (see para 3.12).

Quality Rating

3.8 Since one of the primary objectives of providing competition in broadcasting is to bring about a general improvement in the quality of programmes, the Committee considers it necessary that there should be an arrangement by which credible and autonomous body assesses continuously the quality of the programmes put out by the existing and the new channels. Periodical publication of the results of such assessment can itself be expected to have a wholesome influence on these channels. In addition, the Committee recommends that whenever the quality goes below a certain threshold as decided by this authority, the concerned channel should be warned about it for necessary corrective action. When the time comes for renewal of licence the track record in terms of quality would certainly be one of the criteria for appropriate decisions.

System of Redressal

3.9 The Prasar Bharati Act, 1990 contains a provision (sections 14 & 15) regarding the setting up and functioning of the Broadcasting Council. The Council shall consider complaints against any particular programmes broadcast by the Prasar Bharati Corporation and gives its recommendations. The Prasar Bharati Board is to consider these recommendation and take appropriate action. The Prasar Bharati can also be directed by the Broadcasting Council to broadcast its recommendations with respect to a complaint. These provisions are intended to ensure that a forum for redressal is available to an individual or institution as may be approved by any programme broadcast by the Prasar Bharati. This Committee considers that it is appropriate that such redress is also available to any individual or institution in respect of programmes broadcast by the new channels which we are discussing. We recommend, therefore, that the provisions regarding the Broadcasting Council are appropriately taken out of the Prasar Bharati Act and placed as part of the legislation—dealt with in Chapter IV for the purpose of the new broadcasting system.

Agencies for Implementing the New Broadcasting System

3.10 In this Chapter we have dealt with a number of aspects in new broadcasting system which would require appropriate agencies for their implementation. We propose to consider and make some recommendations here regarding these agencies and their functions. We recommend that there may be a single statutory/autonomous body known as the Broadcasting Council of India to perform the functions listed hereafter in respect of the management of the new broadcasting system. This body will also perform prescribed functions in respect of Prasar Bharati as provided in the Act. Hence this suggestion does not amount to creating a new statutory body apart from what will be otherwise created under the Prasar Bharati

Act.

(a) Licensing

3.11 We have, as against the option of government issuing licences for a new channel, already recommended that a body known as the Broadcasting Council of India should be vested under the law with the powers to do so. (see para 3.3)

(b) Monitoring of Programmes

3.12 We have recommended that the new channels shall be governed by certain guidelines regarding their programmes. We have also suggested that there should be an arrangement for monitoring the programmes to ensure that they conform to guidelines. We recommend that the Broadcasting Council of India dealt with in para 3.10 can be that agency. They can work out appropriate modalities for monitoring the programmes and sending warnings to erring channels whenever the guidelines are violated. We also recommend that when such violation recur frequently and the Broadcasting Council of India for reasons to be recorded in writing considers such violation wilful and avoidable may then cancel the licence. The Committee notes that there are provisions in the Prasar Bharati Act for a Parliamentary Committee to ensure that the Prasar Bharati carries out its functions in accordance with the provisions of the Act to submit a report thereon to the Parliament. The Government for certain specific defaults of the Prasar Bharati can also submit a report to the Parliament. The Parliament can recommend appropriate action against the Board including supercession. The Committee feels that these provisions should be adequate to ensure that there is equity as between Prasar Bharati and the new channels in respect of penal action for lapses.

(c) Quality Rating

3.13 We have already recommended (see para 3.8) that in order to bring about healthy competition between the channels, an Authority with credibility can monitor the programmes and evaluate their quality. We recommend that the Broadcasting Council can do this function. Such evaluation will include both the existing media (and the Prasar Bharati when formed) and the new channels to be set up. The findings of this Authority may be published periodically.

The legal Framework

4.1 Sub-section 1 of Section 4 of the Indian Telegraph Act 1885 empower the Government to license any person for operating a telegraph. This provision has been interpreted to mean that government can give new broadcasting licences. However in practice, this provision has been rarely invoked. Since for the first time, governmental agencies also operate broadcasting system since this new policy would require a comprehensive legal frame for proper implementation, we recommend that a new legislation be enacted to govern the setting up and operation of broadcast channels in India.

4.2 The new council and the rules framed thereunder may provide for the following matters :

(i) Setting up of the Broadcasting Council of India and prescribing the qualifications, conditions of services, etc., of Chairman and Members thereof (para 3.3).

(ii) Specifying the functions of the Broadcasting Council.

(iii) Laying down the eligibility criteria for applicants for broadcasting licences (para 3.3).

(iv) Laying down the guidelines that would govern the programmes put out by the new channels (para 3.6).

(v) The Broadcasting Council monitoring programmes and sending out warning, etc.

(vi) Punitive action in case of persistent violation of guidelines, (para 3.12).

(vii) The Broadcasting Council evaluating the quality of programmes put out by the existing and new channels on the basis of criteria to be specified (para 3.13).

(viii) Periodical publication of the results of the evaluation of programmes quality (para 3.13).

(ix) Renewal of licences, etc., based Open the performances of the channels including the quality ratings.

(x) Allocation of frequencies to the existing and new channels by the appropriate authorities in the government and adherence to stipulated technical parameters for ensuring national radio frequency management.

(xi) Control and/or management of all broadcasting by the government in the event of war or natural calamities.

(xii) Consequential amendments in the Prasar Bharati Act, the Indian Telegraph Act or any other Act as may be necessary.

□□

Index